English Grammar
FOR
DUMMIES®
2ND EDITION

by Geraldine Woods

WILEY

Wiley Publishing, Inc.

English Grammar For Dummies,® 2nd Edition

Published by
Wiley Publishing, Inc.
111 River St.
Hoboken, NJ 07030-5774
www.wiley.com

WILEY

About the Author

Geraldine Woods began her education when teachers still supplied ink wells to their students. She credits her 35-year career as an English teacher to a set of ultra-strict nuns armed with thick grammar books. She lives in New York City, where with great difficulty she refrains from correcting signs containing messages such as "Bagel's for sale." She is the author of more than 40 books, including *English Grammar Workbook For Dummies, Research Papers For Dummies, College Admission Essays For Dummies,* and *The SAT 1 Reasoning Test For Dummies.*

Dedication

I dedicated the first edition of *English Grammar For Dummies* to my husband and son, who were then — and remain — the hearts of my life. Since the first edition was published, I've acquired two new hearts: my daughter-in-law and granddaughter. This book is dedicated with great love to all of them.

Author's Acknowledgments

I owe thanks to my colleagues in the English Department of the Horace Mann School, who are always willing to discuss the finer points of grammar with me. Keeping me up to date on technology and language were Gresa Matoshi, Eliza Montgomery, Sam Schalman-Bergen, and. I appreciate the work of Susan Hobbs and Martha Payne, editors whose attention and intelligence guided my writing. Any errors that remain are mine alone. I also appreciate the efforts of Lisa Queen, my agent, and of Stacy Kennedy, Wiley acquisitions editor.

Publisher's Acknowledgments

We're proud of this book; please send us your comments at http://dummies.custhelp.com. For other comments, please contact our Customer Care Department within the U.S. at 877-762-2974, outside the U.S. at 317-572-3993, or fax 317-572-4002.

Some of the people who helped bring this book to market include the following:

Acquisitions, Editorial, and Media Development

Project Editor: Susan Hobbs

Acquisitions Editor: Stacy Kennedy

Copy Editor: Susan Hobbs

Assistant Editor: Erin Calligan Mooney

Editorial Program Coordinator: Joe Niesen

Technical Editor: Martha Payne

Editorial Manager: Jennifer Ehrlich

Editorial Supervisor and Reprint Editor: Carmen Krikorian

Editorial Assistant: David Lutton, Jennette ElNaggar

Art Coordinator: Alicia B. South

Cover Photos:

Cartoons: Rich Tennant (www.the5thwave.com)

Composition Services

Project Coordinator: Sheree Montgomery

Layout and Graphics: Ashley Chamberlain, Joyce Haughey, Erin Zeltner

Proofreader: Nancy L. Reinhardt

Indexer: Potomac Indexing, LLC

Publishing and Editorial for Consumer Dummies

Diane Graves Steele, Vice President and Publisher, Consumer Dummies

Kristin Ferguson-Wagstaffe, Product Development Director, Consumer Dummies

Ensley Eikenburg, Associate Publisher, Travel

Kelly Regan, Editorial Director, Travel

Publishing for Technology Dummies

Andy Cummings, Vice President and Publisher, Dummies Technology/General User

Composition Services

Debbie Stailey, Director of Composition Services

Contents at a Glance

Table of Contents

Introduction

When you're a grammarian, people react to you in interesting — and sometimes downright strange — ways. When the first edition of *English Grammar For Dummies* came out in 2001, an elderly man asked me about something that had puzzled him for eight decades: Why did his church, St. Paul's, include an apostrophe in its name? (For the answer, turn to Chapter 11.) My nephew called to inquire whether his company's sign in Times Square should include a semicolon. I said no, though the notion of a two-story-tall neon semicolon *was* tempting. Lots of people became tongue-tied, sure that I was judging their choice of *who* or *whom*. They worried needlessly, because I consider myself off-duty when I'm not teaching or writing.

In this second edition of *English Grammar For Dummies*, I explain modern, up-to-the-minute usage. Grammar *does* change, though usually an elderly snail moves faster than a grammarian pondering whether to drop a comma. As the world is now texting, tweeting, and PowerPointing all over the place, this edition of *English Grammar For Dummies* shows you how to handle all sorts of electronic communications, with special attention to business situations. In the current fragile economy, you need every possible edge, and proper grammar is always an advantage. Besides, you don't want to sit around deciding how to create a grammatically correct bullet point when you could be lobbying the boss for a raise.

If you're at a desk and *not* getting paid, you still need good grammar. No matter what subject you're studying, teachers favor proper English. Also, the SAT — that loveable exam facing college applicants — added a writing section recently. It's heavy on grammar and, ironically, light on writing. This book covers all the material likely to be tested on the SAT and the ACT (another fun hurdle of the college-admissions process) and alerts you to exam favorites with a special new icon. If you're aiming for higher education, *English Grammar For Dummies,* 2nd Edition, will raise your standardized-test scores.

As in the first edition, in this book, I tell you the tricks of the grammar trade, the strategies that help you make the right decision when you're facing such grammatical dilemmas as the choice between *I* and *me, had gone* and *went,* and so forth. I explain *what* you're supposed to do, but I also tell you *why* a particular word is correct or incorrect. You won't have to memorize a list of meaningless rules (well, maybe a couple from the punctuation chapter!) because when you understand the reason for a particular choice, you'll pick the correct word automatically.

About This Book

In *English Grammar For Dummies*, 2nd Edition, I concentrate on what English teachers call the common errors. You don't have to read this book in order, though you can, and you don't have to read the whole thing. Just browse through the table of contents and look for things that you often get wrong. Or, turn to Chapter 1 where you'll find a list of the usage issues voted "most likely to succeed" — in giving you a headache.

How to Use This Book

Each chapter introduces some basic ideas and then shows you how to choose the correct sentence when faced with two or three alternatives. If I define a term — linking verbs, for example — I show you a practical situation in which identifying a linking verb matters — in choosing the right pronoun, perhaps. I center the examples in the text so that you can find them easily. One good way to determine whether or not you've mastered a particular section is to try the pop quizzes sprinkled around every chapter. If you get the right answer, move on. If you're puzzled, however, backtrack through the relevant section. Also, watch for Demon icons. They identify the little things — the difference between two similar words, commonly misused words, and so on — that may sabotage your writing.

What You Are Not to Read

I tried to resist, but here and there throughout this book I threw in some advanced grammatical terminology. No human being in the history of the world has ever needed to know those terms for any purpose connected with speaking and writing correct English. In fact, I recommend that you skip them and go skateboarding instead. For those of you who actually enjoy obscure terminology for the purpose of, say, clearing a room within ten seconds, feel free to revel in such exciting grammatical terms as *subjective complement* and *participial phrase*. Everyone else, fear not: These terms are clearly labeled and completely skippable.

Foolish Assumptions

I wrote the second edition of *English Grammar For Dummies* with a specific person in mind. I assume that you, the reader, already speak English to some extent and that you want to speak it better. I also assume that you're a busy person with better things to do than worry about pronouns. You want to speak and write well, but you don't want to get a doctorate in English Grammar. (Smart move. Doctorates in English probably move you up on the salary scale less than any other advanced degree, except maybe Doctorates in Philosophy.)

This book is for you if you want

- ✔ Better grades
- ✔ Skill in communicating exactly what you mean
- ✔ A higher-paying or higher-status job
- ✔ Speech and writing that presents you as an educated, intelligent person
- ✔ A good score on the SAT I Writing or the ACT exam
- ✔ Polished skills in English as a second language

How This Book Is Organized

The first two parts of this book cover the basics, the minimum for reasonably correct English. Part III addresses what English teachers call *mechanics* — not the people in overalls who aim grease guns at your car, but the nuts and bolts of writing: punctuation and capital letters. A number of punctuation and capitalization rules have changed in recent year, but rest assured. *English Grammar For Dummies,* 2nd Edition contains all the new-and-improved standards. Parts IV and V — considerably longer in the second edition than the first — hit the points of grammar that separate regular people from Official Grammarians. In those parts, you find the stuff that appears in a starring role on standardized tests or in executive memos. If you understand the information in Parts IV and V, you'll have a fine time finding mistakes in the daily paper, score big on the SAT and ACT, and impress the authority figures in your life — your boss, English teacher, badminton coach, whatever.

Here's a more specific guide to navigating *English Grammar For Dummies.*

Part 1: Getting Down to Basics: The Parts of the Sentence

This part explains how to distinguish between the three Englishes — the breezy slang of friend-to-friend chat, the slightly more proper conversational language, and the I'm-on-my-best-behavior English. I pay special attention to the intersection between these "languages" and the technology transmitting them — texting, for example. I explain the building blocks of a sentence, subjects and verbs, and show you how to put them together properly. In this part, I also provide a guide to the complete sentence, telling you what's grammatically legal and what's not (a favorite topic on standardized tests). I also define objects and linking-verb complements and show you how to use each effectively.

Part II: Avoiding Common Errors

In this part, I describe other members of Team Grammar — the two types of descriptive words (adjectives and adverbs) and prepositions — the bane of many speakers of English as a second language. Of course, I give tips for correct usage and explain how to avoid tiny missteps that wreck your writing. In this part I tell you how to avoid mismatches between singular and plural words, by far the most common mistake in ordinary speech and writing. Part II also contains an explanation of pronoun gender. Reading this section will help you avoid sexist pronoun usage.

Part III: No Garage, but Plenty of Mechanics

If you've ever asked yourself whether you need a capital letter or if you've sometimes gotten lost in quotation marks and semicolons, Part III is for you. I explain all the rules that govern the use of the worst invention in the history of human communication: the apostrophe. I also show you how to quote speech or written material and where to place the most common (and the most commonly misused) punctuation mark, the comma. I outline the ins and outs of capital letters: when you need them, when you don't, and when they're optional. I also devote an entire section to the newest punctuation mark — the bullet point — and show you how to create proper presentation slides. Lastly, I tackle texting and e-mail, especially as they're used in the business world.

Part IV: Polishing Without Wax — The Finer Points of Grammar

Part IV inches up on the pickiness scale — not all the way to Grammar Heaven, but at least as far as the gate. In this part, I tell you the difference between subject and object pronouns and pronouns of possession. (You need an exorcist.) I also go into detail on verb tenses, explaining which words to use for all sorts of situations. I show you how to distinguish between active and passive verbs and how to use each type properly. I illustrate some common errors of sentence structure and tackle comparisons — both how to form them and how to ensure that your comparisons are logical and complete. Finally, I explain parallelism, an English teacher's term for balance and order in the sentence.

Part V: Rules Even Your Great-Aunt's Grammar Teacher Didn't Know

Anyone who masters the material in Part V has the right to wear a bun and tsk-tsk a lot. This part covers the moods of verbs (ranging from grouchy to just plain irritable) and explains how to avoid double-negative errors. Part V also gives you the last word on pronouns, those little parts of speech that make everyone's life miserable. The dreaded *who/whom* section is in this part, as well as the explanation for all sorts of errors of pronoun reference. I explain subordinate clauses and verbals, which aren't exactly a hot stock tip, but a way to bring more variety and interest to your writing. (The SAT and ACT are big fans of these topics.) I also give you some other pointers on writing with style, even in a 140-character tweet.

Part VI: The Part of Tens

Part VI is the Part of Tens, which offers some quick tips for better grammar. Here I show you ten methods for fine-tuning your proofreading skills. I also suggest ways (apart from *English Grammar For Dummies*) to improve your ear for proper English.

Icons Used in This Book

Wherever you see this icon, you'll find helpful strategies for understanding the structure of the sentence or for choosing the correct word form.

Not every grammar trick has a built-in trap, but some do. This icon tells you how to avoid common mistakes as you construct a sentence.

Think you know how to find the subject in a sentence or choose the correct verb tense? Take the pop quizzes located throughout this book to find out what you know and what you may want to learn.

Keep your eye out for these little devils; they point out the difference between easily confused words and show you how to make your sentence say what you want it to say.

Are you hoping to spend some time behind ivy-covered walls? To put it another way: Are you aiming for college? Then you should pay special attention to the information next to this icon because college-admissions testers *love* this material.

Where to Go from Here

Now that you know what's what and where it is, get started. Before you do, however, one last word. Actually, two last words: *Trust yourself.* You already know a lot. If you're a native speaker, you've communicated in English all of your life, including the years before you set foot in school and saw your first textbook. If English is an acquired language for you, you've probably already learned a fair amount of vocabulary and grammar, even if you don't know the technical terms. For example, you already understand the difference between

> The dog bit Agnes.
>
> and
>
> Agnes bit the dog.

You don't need me to tell you which sentence puts the dog in the doghouse and which sentence puts Agnes in a padded room. So take heart. Browse the table of contents, check out Chapter 1, and dip a toe into the Sea of Grammar. The water is fine.

Part I

Getting Down to Basics: The Parts of the Sentence

The 5th Wave   By Rich Tennant

In this part . . .

So it's like, communication, y'know?

Can you make a statement like that without bringing the grammar police to your door? Maybe. Read Chapter 1 for a discussion of formal and informal language and a guide to when each is appropriate, whether you're speaking, texting, or writing with a quill pen. The rest of this part explains the building blocks of the sentence. Chapter 2 shows you how to find the verb, and Chapter 3 tells you what to do with it once you've got it. Chapter 4 provides a road map to the subject of the sentence and explains the basics of matching subjects and verbs properly. Chapter 5 is all about completeness — why the sentence needs it and how to make sure that the sentence gets it. In Chapter 6, I explore the last building block of a sentence — the complement.

Chapter 1

I Already Know How to Talk. Why Should I Study Grammar?

In the Middle Ages, *grammar* meant the study of Latin, the language of choice for educated people. In fact, grammar was so closely associated with Latin that the word referred to any kind of learning. This meaning of *grammar* shows up when people of grandparent-age and older talk about their *grammar school,* not their elementary school. The term *grammar school* is a leftover from the old days. The very old days.

These days *grammar* is the study of language, specifically, how words are put together. Because of obsessive English teachers and their rules, grammar also means a set of standards that you have to follow in order to speak and write better. However, the definition of *better* changes according to situation, purpose, and audience. In this chapter, I show you the difference between formal and informal English and explain when each is called for. I also tell you what your computer can and can't do to help you write proper English and give you some pointers about appropriate language for texting, tweeting, instant messaging, and similar technology.

Deciding Which Grammar to Learn

I can hear the groan already. *Which* grammar? You mean there's more than one? Yes, there are actually several different types of grammar, including *historical* (how language has changed through the centuries) and *comparative* (how languages differ from or resemble each other). Don't despair; in *English Grammar For Dummies,* I deal with only two — the two you have to know in order to improve your speech and writing.

Descriptive grammar gives names to things — the parts of speech and parts of a sentence. When you learn descriptive grammar, you understand what every word is (its part of speech) and what every word does (its function in the sentence). If you're not careful, a study of descriptive grammar can go overboard fast, and you end up saying things like *"balloon" is the object of the gerund, in a gerund phrase that is acting as the predicate nominative of the linking verb "appear."* Never fear: I wouldn't dream of inflicting that level of terminology on you. However, there is one important reason to learn some grammar terms — to understand *why* a particular word or phrase is correct or incorrect.

Functional grammar makes up the bulk of *English Grammar For Dummies.* Functional grammar tells you how words behave when they are doing their jobs properly. Functional grammar guides you to the right expression — the one that fits what you're trying to say — by ensuring that the sentence is put together correctly. When you're agonizing over whether to say *I* or *me,* you're actually solving a problem of functional grammar.

So here's the formula for success: A little descriptive grammar plus a lot of functional grammar equals better grammar overall.

Distinguishing between the Three Englishes

Good grammar sounds like a great idea, but *good* is tough to pin down. Why? Because the language of choice depends on your situation. Here's what I mean. Imagine that you're hungry. What do you say?

Wanna get something to eat?

Do you feel like getting a sandwich?

Will you accompany me to the dining room?

These three statements illustrate the three Englishes of everyday life. I call them friendspeak, conversational English, and formal English.

Before you choose, you need to know where you are and what's going on. Most important, you need to know your audience.

Phat grammar

Psst! Want to be in the in-crowd? Easy. Just create an out-crowd and you're all set. How do you create an out-crowd? Manufacture a special language (slang) with your friends that no one else understands, at least until the media picks it up. It's the ultimate friendspeak. You and your pals are on the inside, talking about a *sketchy neighborhood* (*sketchy* means "dangerous"). Everyone else is on the outside, wondering how to get the *411* (information). Should you use slang in your writing? Probably not, unless you're dealing with a good friend. The goal of writing and speaking is communication, and slang may be a mystery to your intended audience. Also, because slang changes so quickly, even a short time after you've written something, the meaning may be obscure. Instead of cutting-edge, you sound dated.

When you talk or write in slang, you also risk sounding uneducated. In fact, sometimes breaking the usual rules is the point of slang. In general, you should make sure that your readers know that you understand the rules before you start breaking them (the rules, not the readers) safely.

Wanna get something to eat? Friendspeak

Friendspeak is informal and filled with slang. Its sentence structure breaks all the rules that English teachers love. It's the language of *I know you and you know me and we can relax together.* In friendspeak the speakers are on the same level. They have nothing to prove to each other, and they're comfortable with each other's mistakes. In fact, they make some mistakes on purpose, just to distinguish their personal conversation from what they say on other occasions. Here's a conversation in friendspeak:

> Me and him are going to the gym. Wanna come?

> He's like, I did 60 push-ups, and I'm like, no way.

I doubt that the preceding conversation makes perfect sense to many people, but the participants understand it quite well. Because they both know the whole situation (the guy they're talking about gets muscle cramps after 4 seconds of exercise), they can talk in shorthand.

I don't deal with friendspeak in this book. You already know it. In fact, you've probably created a version of it with your best buds.

Do you feel like getting a sandwich? Conversational English

A step up from friendspeak is *conversational English.* Although not quite friendspeak, conversational English includes some friendliness. Conversational English doesn't stray too far from your English class rules, but it does break some. You can relax, but not completely. It's the tone of most everyday speech, especially between equals. Conversational English is — no shock here — usually for conversations, not for writing. Specifically, conversational English is appropriate in these situations:

- Chats with family members, neighbors, acquaintances
- Informal conversations with teachers and co-workers
- Friendly conversations (if there are any) with supervisors
- Notes, e-mails, instant messages, and texts to friends
- Comments in Internet chat rooms, bulletin boards, and so on
- Friendly letters to relatives

Conversational English has a breezy sound. Letters are dropped in contractions (*don't, I'll, would've,* and so forth). You may also skip words (*Got a minute? Be there soon!* and similar expressions), especially if you're writing in electronic media with a tight space requirement. (For more on electronic communication, see "Thumbing Your Way to Better Grammar" later in this chapter.) In written form, conversational English relaxes the punctuation rules, too. Sentences run together, dashes connect all sorts of things, and half sentences pop up regularly. I'm using conversational English to write this book because I'm pretending that I'm chatting with you, the reader, not teaching grammar in a classroom situation.

Will you accompany me to the dining room? Formal English

You're now at the pickiest end of the language spectrum: formal, grammatically correct speech and writing. Formal English displays the fact that you have an advanced vocabulary, a knowledge of etiquette, and command of standard rules of English usage. You may use formal English when you have less power, importance, and/or status than the other person in the conversation. Formal English shows that you've trotted out your best behavior in his or her honor. You may also speak or write in formal English when you have *more* power, importance, and/or status than the other person. The goal of using formal English is to impress, to create a tone of dignity, or to provide a suitable role model for someone who is still learning. Situations that call for formal English include:

✔ Business letters or e-mails (from or between businesses as well as from individuals to businesses)

✔ Letters or e-mails to government officials

✔ Office memos or e-mails

✔ Reports

✔ Homework

✔ Communications to teachers

✔ Speeches, presentations, oral reports

✔ Important conversations (for example, job interviews, college interviews, parole hearings, congressional inquiries, inquisitions, sessions with the principal in which you explain that unfortunate incident with the stapler, and so on)

Think of formal English as a business suit. If you're in a situation where you want to look your best, you're also in a situation where your words matter. In business, homework, or any situation in which you're being judged, use formal English.

Using the Right English at the Right Time

Which type of English do you speak? Friendspeak, conversational English, or formal English? Probably all of them. (See preceding section for more information.) If you're like most people, you switch from one to another without thinking, dozens of times each day. Chances are, the third type of English — formal English — is the one that gives you the most trouble. In fact, it's probably why you bought this book. (Okay, there is one more possibility that I haven't mentioned yet. Maybe your nerdy uncle, the one with ink stains on his nose, gave *English Grammar For Dummies* to you for Arbor Day and you're stuck with it. But you're not playing paintball or listening to your favorite indie band right now, so you must be reading the book. Therefore, you've at least acknowledged that you have something to think about, and I'm betting that it's formal English.) All the grammar lessons in this book deal with formal English because that's where the problems are fiercest and the rewards for knowledge are greatest.

Which is correct?

A. Hi, Ms. Sharkface! What's up? Here's the 411. I didn't do no homework last night — too much going on. Ttyl. Love, Ralph

B. Dear Ms. Sharkface,

Just a note to let you know that I've got no homework today. Had a lot to do last night! I'll explain later!

Your friend,

Ralph

C. Dear Ms. Sharkface:

I was not able to do my homework last night because of other pressing duties. I will speak with you about this matter later.

Sincerely,

Ralph

Answer: The correct answer depends upon a few factors. How willing are you to be stuck in the corner of the classroom for the rest of the year? If your answer is "very willing," send note A, which is written in friendspeak. (By the way, "ttyl" means "talk to you later.") Does your teacher come to school in jeans and sneakers? If so, note B is acceptable. Note B is written in conversational English. Is your teacher prim and proper, expecting you to follow the Rules? If so, note C, which is written in formal English, is your best bet.

Thumbing Your Way to Better Grammar

I live in New York City, and I seldom see thumbs that aren't glued to very small keyboards — texting (sending written notes over the phone), IMing (instant messaging), twittering (sending 140-character notes), or simply jotting down ideas and reminders. I can't help wondering what sort of grammar will evolve from these new forms of communication. Perhaps the ninth edition of *English Grammar For Dummies* will be only ten pages long, with "sentences" like *u ok?* and g2g — bbl. (Translation for the techno-challenged: "Are you okay?" and "I have got to go. I'll be back later.") If it's up to me, however, English will evolve this way "omdb" ("over my dead body").

At present, however, match the level of formality in electronic communication to your situation, message, and audience. If you're dealing with a friend, feel free to abbreviate and shorten anything you like. If you're communicating with a co-worker or an acquaintance, conversational English is probably fine, though the more power the recipient has, the more careful you should be. (For more information on conversational English, check out "Distinguishing between the Three Englishes" earlier in this chapter.) When you're unsure of your audience or writing to a stranger or a superior, play it safe and opt for formal English. Proper grammar is, well, proper for all media.

Relying on Computer Grammar Checkers Is Not Enough

Your best friend — the one who's greasing the steps to the cafeteria while you're reading *English Grammar For Dummies* — may tell you that learning correct grammar in the third millennium is irrelevant because computer grammar checkers make human knowledge obsolete. Your friend is wrong about the grammar programs, and the grease is a very bad idea also.

It is comforting to think that a little green or red line will tell you when you've made an error and that a quick mouse-click will show you the path to perfection. Comforting, but unreal. English has a half million words, and you can arrange those words a couple of gazillion ways. No program can catch all of your mistakes, and most programs identify errors that aren't actually wrong.

Spelling is also a problem. Every time I type *verbal,* the computer squawks. But *verbal* — a grammar term meaning a word that comes from a verb but does not function as a verb — is a real word. Nor can the computer tell the difference between *homonyms* — words that sound alike but have different meanings and spelling. For example, if I type

Eye through the bawl at hymn, but it went threw the window pain instead.

the computer underlines nothing. However, I was actually trying to say

I threw the ball at him, but it went through the window pane instead.

In short, the computer knows some grammar and spelling, but you have to know the rest.

What's Your Problem? Solutions to Your Grammar Gremlins

I love to stroll around my neighborhood pondering prepositions. (Okay, I'm lying. Most of the time I'm actually thinking about my favorite television shows or Yankee relief pitching.) With my head in the clouds, I sometimes stub my toe on a sidewalk crack. Once I know where the cracks are, however, I can avoid them. If you can figure out where the cracks are in your *grammatical neighborhood* — the gremlins likely to catch your toes — your sentences will roll along without risk of falling flat. Table 1.1 shows common usage problems and the location of their solutions. Skim the first column until you recognize something that stumps you. Then turn to the chapter listed in the second column.

Table 1-1	Problems and Solutions

Problem	Solution Chapter
The winner is he? him?	2
Taxes go? are going? never ever go? down.	3
The IRS apologized? had apologized? in your dreams apologizes?	3
She done? did? can't be convicted for doing? the crime.	3
Mary, as well as Alice, is? are? feeding her little lamb.	4
There was? were? some doughnuts on the table, until Mary's lamb gobbled them down.	4
Three deers? deer? Two dogcatchers-in-chief? dogcatcher-in-chiefs?	4
You used too much chocolate sauce, nevertheless, you can have a cherry. Correct? Incorrect?	5
The superhero is. Complete? Incomplete?	5
She told me? I? an incredibly ridiculous story.	6
Jonas feels bad? badly? about the doughnut shortage.	7
Granny only bought? bought only? one cheap souvenir.	7
Keep this secret between you and I? me? the tabloids?	8
Everyone needs their? his? your? this? grammar book.	9
Each of the grammar books is? are? on the bestseller list.	10
Either the grammarians or Lester has? have? too many verbs.	10
Bagels' ? Bagels are on sale.	11
Bo declared that he was "tired." Correct? Incorrect?	12
Say it isn't so Bo. Comma needed?	13
Grammatically correct sentence? Grammatically-correct sentence?	14
The pigeon flew East? east?	15
Are you and the boss bff? or best friends forever?	16
My mother doesn't like me? my? surfing.	17
The window was broken by me. Correct? Incorrect?	18
Being fifteen, the video game is great. Correct? Incorrect?	19
While combing my hair, the game ended. Correct? Incorrect?	19
The emperor is more powerful than any? any other? ruler.	20
I like grammar, ice cream, and to be on vacation? vacations?	21
If I was? were? would have been? a grammarian.	22
This book is for whoever? whomever? needs grammar help.	23
The books everyone thinks will make the bestseller list is? are? Dummies titles.	24

Chapter 2

Verbs: The Heart of the Sentence

Think about a sentence this way: A sentence is a flatbed truck. You pile all your ideas on the truck, and the truck takes the meaning to your audience (your reader or your listener). The verb of the sentence is a set of tires. Without the verb, you may get your point across, but you're going to have a bumpy ride.

Every sentence needs a verb, so you start with the verb when you want to do anything to your sentence — including correct it. Verbs come in all shapes and sizes. In this chapter, I explain how to distinguish between linking and action verbs and to sort helping verbs from main verbs. Then I show you how to choose the correct verb for each sentence. Finally, I explain which pronouns you need for sentences with linking verbs.

Linking Verbs: The Giant Equal Sign

Linking verbs are also called *being verbs* because they express states of being — what is, will be, or was. Here's where math intersects with English. Linking verbs are like giant equal signs plopped into the middle of your sentence. For example, you can think of the sentence

> Ralph's uncle *is* a cannibal with a taste for finger food.

as

> Ralph's uncle = a cannibal with a taste for finger food.

Or, in shortened form,

> Ralph's uncle = a cannibal

Just as in an algebra equation, the word *is* links two ideas and says that they are the same. Thus, *is* is a linking verb. Here are more linking verbs:

> Lulu *will be* angry when she hears about the missing bronze tooth.
>
> Lulu = angry (*will be* is a linking verb)

> Stan *was* the last surfer to leave the water when the tidal wave approached.
>
> *Stan* = last surfer (*was* is a linking verb)

> Edgar *has been* depressed ever since the fall of the House of Usher.
>
> Edgar = depressed (*has been* is a linking verb)

Being or linking — what's in a name?

In the preceding section, you may have noticed that all the linking verbs in the sample sentences are forms of the verb *to be,* which is (surprise, surprise) how they got the name *being verbs.* When I was a kid (sometime before they invented the steam engine), these verbs were called *copulative,* from a root word meaning "join." However, copulative is out of style with English teachers these days (perhaps because you can also use the root for words referring to sex). I prefer the term *linking* because some equal-sign verbs are not forms of the verb *to be.* Check out these examples:

> With his foot-long fingernails and sly smile, Big Foot *seemed* threatening.
>
> Big Foot = threatening (*seemed* is a linking verb)

> A jail sentence for the unauthorized use of a comma *appears* harsh.
>
> jail sentence = harsh (*appears* is a linking verb in this sentence)

> The penalty for making a grammar error *remains* severe.
>
> penalty = severe (*remains* is a linking verb in this sentence)

> Lochness *stays* silent whenever monsters are mentioned.
>
> Lochness = silent (*stays* is a linking verb in this sentence)

Seemed, appears, remains, and *stays* are similar to forms of the verb *to be* in that they express states of being. They simply add shades of meaning to the basic concept. You may, for example, say that

With his foot-long fingernails and sly smile, Big Foot *was* threatening.

but now the statement is more definite. *Seemed* leaves room for doubt. Similarly, *remains* (in the third sample sentence) adds a time dimension to the basic expression of being. The sentence implies that the penalty was and still is severe.

No matter how you name it, any verb that places an equal sign in the sentence is a *being, linking,* or *copulative verb.*

Savoring sensory verbs

Sensory verbs — verbs that express information you receive through the senses of sight, hearing, smell, taste, and so forth — may also be linking verbs:

Two minutes after shaving, Ralph's double chin *feels* scratchy.

Ralph's double chin = scratchy (*feel* is a linking verb)

The ten-year-old lasagna in your refrigerator *smells* disgusting.

lasagna = disgusting (*smells* is a linking verb)

The ten-year-old lasagna in your refrigerator also *looks* disgusting.

lasagna = disgusting (*looks* is a linking verb)

Needless to say, the ten-year-old lasagna in your refrigerator *tastes* great!

lasagna = great (*tastes* is a linking verb)

Verbs that refer to the five senses are linking verbs only if they act as an equal sign in the sentence. If they aren't equating two ideas, they aren't linking verbs. In the preceding example sentence about Ralph's double chin, *feel* is a linking verb. Here's a different sentence with the same verb:

With their delicate fingers, Lulu and Stan *feel* Ralph's chin.

In this sentence, *feel* is not a linking verb because you're not saying that

> Lulu and Stan = chin.

Instead, you're saying that Lulu and Stan don't believe that Ralph shaved, so they went stubble hunting.

Which sentence has a linking verb?

A. That annoying new clock sounds the hour with a recorded cannon shot.

B. That annoying new clock sounds extremely loud at four o'clock in the morning.

Answer: Sentence B has the linking verb. In sentence B, clock = extremely loud. In sentence A, the clock is doing something — sounding the hour — not being. (It's also waking up the whole neighborhood, but that idea isn't in the sentence.)

Try another. In which sentence is "stay" a linking verb?

A. Larry stays single only for very short periods of time.

B. Stay in the yard, Fido, or I cut your dog-biscuit ration in half!

Answer: Sentence A has the linking verb. In sentence A, Larry = single (at least for the moment). In sentence B, Fido is being told to do something — to stay in the backyard — clearly an action.

If you're dying to learn more grammar terminology, read on. Linking verbs connect the subject and the subject complement, also known as the *predicate nominative* and *predicate adjective.* For more on complements, read Chapter 6.

Here is a list of the most common linking verbs:

✔ Forms of *to be:* am, are, is, was, were, will be, shall be, has been, have been, had been, could be, should be, would be, might have been, could have been, should have been, shall have been, will have been, must have been, must be

✔ Sensory verbs: look, sound, taste, smell, feel

✔ Words that express shades of meaning in reference to a state of being: appear, seem, grow, remain, stay

Due to a grammar error

The picnic has been cancelled *due to? because of?* the arrival of killer sparrows from their Southern nesting grounds.

Okay, which one is correct — *due to* or *because of?* The answer is *because of.* According to a rule that people ignore more and more every day:

✔ *Due to* describes nouns or pronouns. It may follow a linking verb if it gives information about the subject. (See "Linking Verbs: The Giant Equal Sign," earlier in the chapter, for more information.)

✔ *Because of* is a description of an action. (See "Lights! Camera! Action Verb!" later in this chapter for information on action verbs.)

The semi-logical reasoning that underlies this rule draws you deep into grammatical trivia, so keep reading only if you're daring (or bored). *Due to,* by definition, means "owing to." *Owing* is in the adjective family, whose members may only describe nouns and pronouns. In a linking verb sentence, the subject (always a noun or pronoun) may be linked to a description following the verb. An example:

Lola's mania for fashion is *due to* her deprived upbringing in an all-polyester household.

Due to her deprived upbringing in an all-polyester household describes *mania.*

Because of and *on account of* describe an action, usually answering the question why. An example:

The bubble-gum gun that George fired is no longer being manufactured *because of* protests from the dental association.

Why is the gun no longer being manufactured? Because of protests from the dental association.

In real life (that is to say, in everyday conversational English), *due to* and *because of* are interchangeable. When you need your most formal, most correct language, be careful with this pair! One easy solution (easier than remembering which phrase is which) is to avoid them entirely and simply add *because* with a subject–verb pair.

Completing Linking Verb Sentences Correctly

A linking verb begins a thought, but it needs another word to complete the thought. Unless your listener is a mind reader, you can't walk around saying things like "the president is" or "the best day for the party will be" and expect people to know what you mean.

You have three possible completions for a linking verb: a descriptive word, a noun, or a pronoun (a word that subs for a noun). Take a look at some descriptions that complete the linking-verb equation:

> After running 15 miles in high heels, Renee's thigh muscles are *tired*.

> thigh muscles = *tired* (tired is a description, an adjective in grammatical terms)

> Renee's high heels are *stunning*, especially when they land on your foot.

> high heels = *stunning* (*stunning* is a description, also called an adjective)

> Oscar's foot, wounded by Renee's heels, seems particularly *painful*.

> foot = *painful* (*painful* is a description, an adjective)

> Lola's solution, to staple Oscar's toes together, is not very *helpful*.

> solution = *helpful* (*helpful* is a description, an adjective. The other descriptive words, *not* and *very,* describe *helpful,* not *solution.*)

You may also complete a linking verb equation with a person, place, or thing — a noun, in grammatical terms. Here are some examples:

> The most important part of a balanced diet is *popcorn*.

> part of a balanced diet = *popcorn* (*popcorn* is a thing, and therefore a noun)

> Lulu's nutritional consultant has always been a complete *fraud*.

> Lulu's nutritional consultant = *fraud* (*fraud* is a noun)

Sometimes you complete a linking verb sentence with a *pronoun,* a word that substitutes for the name of a person, place, or thing. For example:

> The winner of the all-state spitball contest is *you!*

> winner = *you* (*you* is a substitute for the name of the winner, and therefore a pronoun)

> Whoever put glue in the teapot is *someone* with a very bad sense of humor.

> Whoever put glue in the teapot = *someone* (*someone* is a substitute for the name of the unknown prankster and therefore a pronoun)

You can't do much wrong when you complete linking verb sentences with descriptions or with nouns. However, you can do a lot wrong when you complete a linking verb sentence with a pronoun — a fact that has come to the attention of standardized test-makers, who love to stump you with this sort of sentence. Never fear: in the next section, I show you how to avoid common linking verb–pronoun errors.

Placing the Proper Pronoun in the Proper Place

How do you choose the correct pronoun for a sentence with a linking verb? Think of a linking-verb sentence as reversible. That is, the pronoun you put after a linking verb should be the same kind of pronoun that you put before a linking verb. First, however, I give you an example with a noun, where you can't make a mistake. Read these sentence pairs:

> *Ruggles* is a *resident* of Red Gap.
>
> A *resident* of Red Gap is *Ruggles.*

> Lulu was a resident of Beige Gap.
>
> A resident of Beige Gap was Lulu.

Both sentences in each pair mean the same thing, and both are correct. Now look at pronouns:

> The winner of the election is *him!*
>
> *Him* is the winner of the election!

Uh oh. Something's wrong. You don't say *him is.* You say *he is.* Because you have a linking verb (*is*), you must put the same word after the linking verb that you would put before the linking verb. Try it again:

> The winner of the election is *he!*
>
> *He* is the winner of the election!

Now you've got the correct ending for your sentence.

If you pay attention to linking verbs, you'll choose the right pronouns for your sentence. Subject pronouns are *I, you, he, she, it, we, they, who,* and *whoever.* Pronouns that are not allowed to be subjects include *me, him, her, us, them, whom,* and *whomever.* (In case you're curious, these pronouns act as objects. More on objects in Chapter 6.)

Remember that in the previous examples, I discuss formal English, not conversational English. In conversational English, the following exchange is okay:

> Who's there?
>
> It is me. OR It's me.

In formal English, the exchange goes like this:

Who is there?

It is I.

Because of the linking verb *is,* you want the same kind of pronoun before and after the linking verb. You can't start a sentence with *me,* but you can start a sentence with *I.*

Now you've probably, with your sharp eyes, found a flaw here. You can't reverse the last reply and say

I is it.

I takes a different verb — *am.* Both *is* and *am* are forms of the verb *to be* — one of the most peculiar creations in the entire language. So yes, you sometimes have to adjust the verb when you reverse a sentence with a form of *to be* in it. But the idea is the same; *I* can be a subject. *Me* can't.

You don't need to know this information, but in case you're having a slow day: grammarians divide pronouns into groups called *cases.* One group, the *nominative* or *subject case,* includes all the pronouns that may be subjects. The pronoun that follows the linking verb should also be in nominative, or subject, case. Another group of pronouns, those in *objective case,* acts as objects. Avoid object pronouns after linking verbs. (For more information on pronoun case, see Chapter 17.)

Lights! Camera! Action Verb!

Linking verbs are important, but unless you're in some sort of hippie commune left over from the sixties, you just can't sit around being all the time. You have to do something. Here's where action verbs come into the picture. Everything that is not *being* is *action,* at least in the verb world. Unlike the giant equal sign associated with linking verbs (see "Linking Verbs: The Giant Equal Sign," earlier in the chapter), something *happens* with an action verb:

Drew *slapped* the offending pig right on the snout. (*Slapped* is an action verb.)

Fred *will steal* third base as soon as his sneezing fit *ends.* (*Will steal* and *ends* are action verbs.)

According to the teacher, Roger *has shot* at least 16 spitballs in the last ten minutes. (*Has shot* is an action verb.)

Don't let the name *action* fool you. Some action verbs aren't particularly ener-getic: *think, sit, stay, have, sleep, dream,* and so forth. Besides describing my ideal vacation, these words are also action verbs! Think of the definition this way: if the verb is *not* a giant equal sign (a linking verb), it's an action verb.

Getting by with a Little Help from My Verbs

You've probably noticed that some of the verbs I've identified throughout this chapter are single words and others are made up of several words. The extra words are called *helping verbs.* They don't carry out the trash or dust the living room, but they do help the main verb express meaning, usually changing the time, or *tense,* of the action. (For more on tense, see Chapter 3.)

Here are some sentences with helping verbs:

> Alice *will have sung* five arias from that opera by the time her recorder *runs* out of tape and her listeners *run* out of patience.

> (In *will have sung, sung* is the main verb; *will* and *have* are helping verbs; *runs* and *run* are both main verbs without helping verbs.)

> Larry *should have refused* to play the part of the villain, but his ego simply *would* not *be denied.*

> (In *should have refused, refused* is the main verb; *should* and *have* are helping verbs; in *would be denied, denied* is the main verb; *would* and *be* are helping verbs.)

Distinguishing between helping verbs and main verbs isn't particularly impor-tant, as long as you get the whole thing when you're identifying the verb in a sentence. If you find only part of the verb, you may confuse action verbs with linking verbs. You want to keep these two types of verbs straight when you choose an ending for your sentence, as I explain in "Placing the Proper Pronoun in the Proper Place," earlier in the chapter.

To decide whether you have an action verb or a linking verb, look at the main verb, not at the helping verbs. If the main verb expresses action, the whole verb is action, even if one of the helpers is a form of *to be.* For example:

> is going

> has been painted

> should be strangled

are all action verbs, not linking verbs, because *going, painted,* and *strangled* express action.

Pop the Question: Locating the Verb

A scientific study by a blue-ribbon panel of experts found that 90 percent of all the errors in a sentence occurred because the verb was misidentified. Okay, there was no study. I made it up! But it is true that when you try to crack a sentence, you should always start by identifying the verb. To find the verb, read the sentence and ask two questions:

- ✔ What's happening?
- ✔ What is? (or, What word is a "giant equal sign"?)

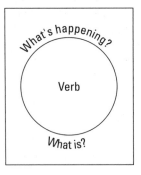

If you get an answer to the first question, you have an action verb. If you get an answer to the second question, you have a linking verb.

For example, in the sentence

Archie flew around the room and then swooped into his cage for a bird-seed snack.

you ask "What's happening?" and your answer is *flew* and *swooped. Flew* and *swooped* are action verbs.

If you ask, "What is?" you get no answer, because there's no linking verb in the sentence.

Try another:

Lola's new tattoo will be larger than her previous fifteen tattoos.

What's happening? Nothing. You have no action verb. What is? *Will be. Will be* is a linking verb.

The way it's suppose to be?

Do these sentences look familiar?

Lola *was suppose* to take out the garbage, but she refused to do so, saying that garbage removal was not part of her creative development.

Ralph *use* to take out the trash, but after that unfortunate encounter with a raccoon and an empty potato chip bag, he is reluctant to venture near the cans.

George *is suppose* to do all kinds of things, but of course he never does anything he *is suppose* to do.

If these sentences look familiar, look again. Each one is wrong. Check out the italicized verbs: *was suppose, use,* and *is suppose.* All represent what people hear but not what the speaker is actually trying to say. The correct words to use in these instances are *supposed* and *used* — past tense forms.

Pop the question and find the verbs in the following sentences. For extra credit, identify the verbs as action or linking.

A. Michelle scratched the cat almost as hard as the cat had scratched her.

B. After months of up-and-down motion, Lester is taking the elevator sideways, just for a change of pace.

C. The twisted frown on Larry's face seems strange because of the joyful background music.

Answers: A. *scratched* is an action verb, *had scratched* is an action verb. B. *is taking* is an action verb. C. *seems* is a linking verb.

Forget To Be or Not To Be: Infinitives Aren't Verbs

You may hear English teachers say, "the verb *to sweep*" or some such expression. In fact, in this chapter I refer to "all forms of the verb *to be.*" But *to be* is not actually a verb. It's an infinitive. An *infinitive* is to + a verb (yet another mixing of math and English). Examples or infinitives include *to laugh, to sing, to burp, to write,* and *to be.*

The most important thing to know about infinitives is this: When you pop the question to find the verb, don't choose an infinitive as your answer. If you do, you'll miss the real verb or verbs in the sentence. Other than that, forget about infinitives!

Okay, you can't forget about infinitives completely. Here's something else you should know about infinitives in formal English: Don't split them in half. For example, you commonly see sentences like the following:

> Matt vowed to really study if he ever got the chance to take the flight instructor exam again.

This example is common, but incorrect. Grammatically, *to study* is a unit — one infinitive. You're not supposed to separate its two halves. Now that you know this rule, read the paper. Everybody splits infinitives, even the grayest, dullest papers with no comics whatsoever. So you have two choices. You can split infinitives all you want, or you can follow the rule and feel totally superior to the professional journalists. The choice is yours.

Two not for the price of one

Here's a spelling tip: the following words are often written as one — incorrectly! Always write them as two separate words: *a lot*, *all right*, *each other*.

Example: Ella has *a lot* of trouble distinguishing between the sounds of "l" and "r," so she tries to avoid the expression *"all right"* whenever possible. Ella and Larry (who also has pronunciation trouble), help *each other* prepare state-of-the-union speeches every January.

Here's another tip. You can write the following words as one or two words, but with two different meanings:

Altogether means "extremely, entirely."

All together means "as one."

Example: Daniel was *altogether* disgusted with the way the entire flock of dodo birds sang *all together*.

Another pair of tricky words:

Sometime means "at a certain point in time."

Some time means "a period of time."

Example: Lex said that he would visit Lulu *sometime*, but not now because he has to spend *some time* in jail for murdering the English language.

Still more:

Someplace means "an unspecified place" and describes an action.

Some place means "a place" and refers to a physical space.

Example: Lex screamed, "I have to go *someplace* now!" Lulu thinks he headed for *some place* near the railroad station where the pizza is hot and no one asks any questions.

And another pair:

Everyday means "ordinary, common."

Every day means "occurring daily."

Larry loves *everyday* activities such as cooking, cleaning, and sewing. He has the palace staff perform all of those duties *every day*.

Last set, I promise:

Anyway means "in any event."

Any way means "a way, some sort of way."

Example: *"Anyway,"* added Roy, "I don't think there is *any way* to avoid jail for tax evasion."

Chapter 3

Relax! Understanding Verb Tense

In This Chapter

▶ Expressing time with verbs

▶ Understanding the meanings of verb tenses

▶ Applying the correct verb tenses

▶ Dealing with irregular verb forms

*Y*ou can tell time lots of ways: look at a clock, pull out your phone, or check the verb. Surprised you with that last one, didn't I? Besides showing the action or state of being in the sentence, the verb also indicates the time the action or "being" took place. (For more information on finding the verb in a sentence, see Chapter 2.)

In some lucky languages — Thai, for example — the verb has basically one form. Whether the sentence is about the past, the present, or the future, the verb is the same. Extra words — yesterday, tomorrow, now, and so forth — indicate the time. Not so in English (sigh). In English, six different tenses of verbs express time. In other words, each tense places the action or the state of being discussed in the sentence at a point in time.

Three of the six English tenses are called *simple.* In this chapter, I explain the simple tenses in some detail, such as the difference between *I go* and *I am going.* The other three tenses are called *perfect.* (Trust me, the perfect tenses are far from it.) I touch upon the basics of the perfect tenses: present perfect, past perfect, and future perfect in this chapter. Then I dig a little more deeply into present perfect tense. The other two perfect tenses — past and future — are real headaches and far less common than present perfect, so I save them for later. For an in-depth explanation of the past perfect and future perfect tenses, see Chapter 18.

Simplifying Matters: The Simple Tenses

The three simple tenses are present, past, and future. Each of the simple tenses (just to make things even *more* fun) has two forms. One is the unadorned, no-frills, plain tense. This form doesn't have a special name; it is just called *present, past,* or *future.* It shows actions or states of being at a point in time, but it doesn't always pin down a specific moment. The other form is called *progressive.* It shows actions or a state of being *in progress.*

Present tense

Present tense tells you what is going on right now. As mentioned in the previous section, this simple tense has two forms — one is called *present,* and the other is *progressive.* The present form shows action or a state of being that is occurring now, that is generally true, or that is always happening. The present *progressive* form is similar, but it often implies a process. (The difference between the two is subtle. I go into more details about using these forms below.) For now, take a look at a couple of sentences in the no-frills present tense:

> Reggie *rolls* his tongue around the pastry. (*rolls* is in present tense)

> George *plans* nothing for New Year's Eve because he never *has* a date. (*plans, has* are in present tense)

Now here are two sentences in the present progressive form:

> Alexei *is axing* the proposal to cut down the national forest. (*is axing* is in present progressive form)

> Michael and Lulu *are skiing* far too fast toward that cliff. (*are skiing* is in present progressive form)

Past tense

Past tense tells you what happened before the present time. This simple tense also has two forms — plain and chocolate-sprinkled. Sorry, I mean plain, which is called *past,* and *past progressive.* Consider these two past-tense sentences:

> When the elastic in Ms. Belli's girdle *snapped,* we all *woke* up. (*snapped* and *woke* are in past tense)

> Despite the strong plastic ribbon, the package *became* unglued and *spilled* onto the conveyor belt. (*became* and *spilled* are in past tense)

Here are two more examples, this time in the past progressive form:

> While Buzz *was sleeping,* his cat, Catnip, *was* completely *destroying* the sofa. (*was sleeping* and *was destroying* are in the progressive form of the past tense)

> Lola's friends *were passing* tissues to Lulu at a rate of five per minute. (*were passing* is in the progressive form of the past tense)

You can't go wrong with the past tense, except for the irregular verbs, which I address later in this chapter. But one very common mistake is to mix past and present tenses in the same story. Here's an example:

> So I go to the restaurant looking for Cindy because I want to tell her about Grady's date with Eleanor. I walk in and I see Brad Pitt! So I went up to him and said, "How are the kids?"

The speaker started in present tense — no problem. Even though an event is clearly over, present tense is okay if you want to make a story more dramatic. (See the sidebar "The historical present," later in this chapter.) But the last sentence switches gears — suddenly we're in past tense. Problem! Don't change tenses in the middle of a story. And don't bother celebrities either.

Future tense

Future tense talks about what has not happened yet. This simple tense is the only one that always needs helping verbs to express meaning, even for the plain, no-frills version.

Helping verbs (see Chapter 2) such as *will, shall, have, has, should,* and so forth change the meaning of the main verb.

Future tenses — this will shock you — come in two forms. I'm not talking about alternate universes here; this book is about grammar, not sci-fi adventures! One form of the future tense is called *future,* and the other is *future progressive.* The unadorned form of the future tense goes like this:

> Nancy *will position* the wig in the exact center of her head. (*will position* is in future tense)

> Lisa and I *will* never *part,* thanks to that bottle of glue! (*will part* is in future tense)

A couple of examples of the future progressive:

> During the post-election period, George *will be pondering* his options. (*will be pondering* is in the progressive form of the future tense)

> Lola *will be sprinkling* the flowers with fertilizer in a vain attempt to keep them fresh. (*will be sprinkling* is in the progressive form of the future tense)

Find the verbs and sort them into present, past, and future tenses.

A. When the tornado whirls overhead, we run for the camera and the phone number of the television station.

B. Shall I compare you to a winter's day?

> C. When you were three, you blew out all the candles on your birthday cake.

Answers: In sentence A, the present tense verbs are *whirls* and *run*. In sentence B, the future tense verb is *shall compare*. In sentence C, the past tense verbs are *were* and *blew*.

Now find the verbs and sort them into present progressive, past progressive, and future progressive forms.

> A. Exactly 5,000 years ago, a dinosaur was living in that mud puddle.

> B. Zeus and Apollo are establishing a union of mythological characters.

> C. The pilot will be joining us as soon as the aircraft clears the Alps.

Answers: In sentence A, the past progressive verb is *was living*. In sentence B, the present progressive verb is *are enrolling*. In sentence C, the future progressive verb is *will be joining*.

Using the Tenses Correctly

What's the difference between each pair of simple tense forms? Not a whole lot. People often interchange these forms without creating any problems. But shades of difference in meaning do exist.

Present and present progressive

The single-word form of the present tense may be used for things that are generally true at the present time but not necessarily happening right now. For example:

> Ollie *attends* wrestling matches every Sunday.

If you call Ollie on Sunday, you'll get this annoying message he recorded on his answering machine because he's at the arena (*attends* is in present tense). You may also get this message on a Thursday (or on another day) and it is still correct, even though on Thursdays Ollie stays home to play chess. Now read this sentence:

> Ollie *is playing* hide-and-seek with his dog Spot.

This sentence means that right now (*is playing* is in the progressive form of the present tense), as you write or say this sentence, Ollie is running around the living room looking for Spot, who is easy to find because he ran through that tray of fluorescent paint.

Past and past progressive

The difference between the plain past tense and the past progressive tense is pretty much the same as in the present tense. The single-word form often shows what happened in the past more generally. The progressive form may pinpoint action or a state of being at a specific time or occurring in the past on a regular basis.

Gulliver *went* to the store and *bought* clothes for all his little friends.

This sentence means that at some point in the past Gulliver whipped out his charge card and finished off his Christmas list (*went* and *bought* are in past tense).

While Gulliver *was shopping,* his friends *were planning* their revenge.

This sentence means that Gulliver shouldn't have bothered because at the exact moment he was spending his allowance, his friends were deciding what time to pour ink into his lunchbox (*was shopping* and *were planning* are in the progressive form of the past tense).

Gulliver *was shopping* until he *was dropping,* despite his mother's strict credit limit.

This sentence refers to one of Gulliver's bad habits, his tendency to go shopping every spare moment (*was shopping* and *was dropping* are in the progressive form of the past tense). The shopping was repeated on a daily basis, over and over again. (Hence, Gulliver's mom imposed the strict credit limit.)

Future and future progressive

You won't find much difference between these two. The progressive gives you slightly more of a sense of being in the middle of things. For example:

The actor *will be playing* Hamlet with a great deal of shouting.

The actor's actions in the sentence above may be a little more immediate than

The actor *will play* Hamlet with a great deal of shouting.

In the first example, *will be playing* is in the progressive form of the future tense. In the second example, *will play* is in future tense.

The historical present

Not surprisingly, you use present tense for actions that are currently happening. But (Surprise!) you may also use present tense for some actions that happened a long time ago and for some actions that never happened at all. The historical present is a way to write about history or literature:

> On December 7, 1941, President Franklin Delano Roosevelt *tells* the nation about the attack on Pearl Harbor. The nation immediately *declares* war.

> Harry Potter *faces* three tests when he *represents* Hogwarts in the tournament.

In the first sentence, *tells* and *declares* are in present tense, even though the sentence concerns events that occurred decades ago. Here the historical present makes the history more dramatic. (Non-historians often tell a story in present tense also, just to make the account more vivid.) In the second sentence, *faces* and *represents* are in present tense. The idea is that for each reader who opens the book, the story begins anew. With the logic that we have come to know and love in English grammar, the events are always happening, even though Harry Potter is a fictional character and the events never happened.

Understanding the difference between the two forms of the simple tenses entitles you to wear an Official Grammarian hat. But if you don't catch on to the distinction, don't lose sleep over the issue. If you can't discern the subtle differences in casual conversation, your listeners probably won't either. In choosing between the two forms, you're dealing with shades of meaning, not Grand-Canyon-sized discrepancies.

Perfecting Verbs: The Perfect Tenses

Now for the hard stuff. These three tenses — present perfect, past perfect, and future perfect — may give you gray hair, even if you are only twelve. And they have progressive forms too! As with the simple tenses, each tense has a no-frills version called by the name of the tense: present perfect, past perfect, and future perfect. The progressive form adds an "ing" to the mix. The progressive is a little more immediate than the other form, expressing an action or state of being in progress.

In this section, I state the basics and provide examples. For a complete explanation of present perfect and present perfect progressive tense, see "Using Present Perfect Tense Correctly" later in this chapter. For a full discussion of the correct sequence with past and future perfect tenses, see Chapter 18.

Present perfect and present perfect progressive

The two present perfect forms show actions or states of being that began in the past but are still going on in the present. These forms are used whenever any action or state of being spans two time zones — past and present.

First, check out examples with present perfect tense:

Roger and his friends *have spent* almost every penny of the inheritance. (*have spent* is in present perfect tense)

Lulu's mortal enemy, Roger, *has pleaded* with her to become a professional tattooist. (*has pleaded* is in present perfect tense)

Now peruse these progressive examples:

Roger *has been studying* marble shooting for fifteen years without learning any worthwhile techniques. (*has been studying* is in the progressive form of the present perfect tense)

Lulu and her mentor Lola *have been counting sheep* all night. (*have been counting* is in the progressive form of the present perfect tense)

Past perfect and past perfect progressive

Briefly, each of these forms places an action in the past in relation to another action in the past. In other words, a timeline is set. The timeline begins some time ago and ends at some point before NOW. At least two events are on the timeline. (For more information about how to use the past perfect, see Chapter 18.) Here are a couple of examples of the past perfect tense:

After she *had sewn* up the wound, the doctor realized that her watch was missing! (*had sewn* is in past perfect tense)

The watch *had ticked* for ten minutes before the nurse discovered its whereabouts. (*had ticked* is in past perfect tense)

Compare the preceding sentences with examples of the past perfect progressive (try saying *that* three times fast without spraying your listener!):

The patient *had been considering* a lawsuit but changed his mind. (*had been considering* is in the progressive form of the past perfect tense)

The doctor *had been worrying* about a pending lawsuit, but her patient dropped his case. (*had been worrying* is in the progressive form of the past perfect tense)

Future perfect and future perfect progressive

These two forms talk about events or states of being that have not happened yet in relation to another event even further in the future. In other words, these forms create another timeline, with at least two events or states of being on it. (For a complete explanation of how to use the future perfect tense, see Chapter 18.)

First, take a look at the plain version of the future perfect:

> Appleby *will have eaten* the entire piece of fruit by the time the bell rings at the end of recess. (*will have eaten* is in future perfect tense)

> When Appleby finally arrives at grammar class, the teacher *will have* already *outlined* at least 504 grammar rules. (*will have outlined* is in future perfect tense)

Now take a look at the progressive form of the future perfect tense:

> When the clocks strikes four, Appleby *will have been chewing* for 29 straight minutes without swallowing even one bite. (*will have been chewing* is in the progressive form of the future perfect tense)

> By the time he swallows, Appleby's teacher *will have been explaining* the virtues of digestion to her class for a very long time. (*will have been explaining* is in the progressive form of the future perfect tense)

Using Present Perfect Tense Correctly

This mixture of present *(has, have)* and past is a clue to its use: present perfect tense ties the past to the present. When you use it, you're expressing an idea that includes an element of the past and an element of the present.

> I *have gone* to the school cafeteria every day for six years, and I *have* not yet *found* one edible item.

This sentence means that at present I am still in school, still trying to find something to eat, and for the past six years I was in school also, trudging to the cafeteria each day, searching for a sandwich without mystery meat in it.

> Bertha *has* frequently *called* Charles, but Charles *has* not *called* Bertha back.

This sentence means that in the present Bertha hasn't given up yet; she's still trying to reach Charles from time to time. In the past Bertha also phoned Charles. In the present and in the past, Charles hasn't bothered to check his voice mail, which now has 604 messages.

Some tense pairs

Helping verbs, as well as main verbs, have tenses. Some of the most common pairs are *can/could* and *may/might.* The first verb in each pair is in present tense; the second is in past tense. If you *can* imagine, you are speaking about the present. If you *could* imagine, you are speaking about the past. More and more people interchange these helping verbs at random, but technically, the verbs do express time. So remember:

Now you *may* talk about how much you hate writing school reports.

Yesterday you *might* have gone to the store if the sky hadn't dumped a foot of snow on your head.

After six years of lessons, you *can* finally dance a mean tango.

No one ever danced as well as Fred Astaire *could* in those old movie musicals.

As with the simple present tense, the present perfect tense takes two forms. One is called *present perfect,* and the other *present perfect progressive.* Shades of difference in meaning exist between the two — the progressive is a little more immediate — but nothing you need to worry about.

Which one is correct?

   A. Bertha moved into that building in 1973 and lived there ever since.

   B. Bertha has moved into that building in 1973 and lived there ever since.

   C. Bertha moved into that building in 1973 and has lived there ever since.

Answer: Sentence C is correct. You cannot use the simple past, as in sentence A, because a connection to the present exists (the fact that Bertha still lives in that building). Sentence B is wrong because the moving isn't connected to the present; it's over and done with. So you can't use present perfect for the move. Sentence C has the right combination — the move, now over, should be expressed in simple past. The event that began in the past and is still going on (Bertha's living in the building) needs present perfect tense.

Forming Present and Past Participles of Regular Verbs

I used to tell my classes that my gray hair came from my struggles with *participles,* but I was just trying to scare them into doing their grammar homework. Participles are not very mysterious; as you may guess from the spelling, a *participle* is simply a *part* of the verb. Each verb has two participles — a present participle and a past participle. You may have noticed the *present participle* in the present progressive tenses. The present participle is the *ing* form of the verb. The past participle helps form the present perfect tense because this tense spans both the past and present. Regular past participles are formed by adding *ed* to the verb. Table 3-1 shows a selection of regular participles.

Table 3-1	Examples of Regular Participles	
Verb	*Present Participle*	*Past Participle*
ask	asking	asked
beg	begging	begged
call	calling	called
dally	dallying	dallied
empty	emptying	emptied
fill	filling	filled
grease	greasing	greased

Just to Make Things More Difficult: Irregular Verbs

When you're out bargain hunting, irregulars look good, because a tiny variation from "regular" merchandise lowers the price considerably. Unfortunately, an irregular is not a bargain in the grammar market. In this section, I break down the irregulars into two parts. The first part is the mother of all irregular verbs, *to be.* Second is a list of irregular past-tense forms and past participles.

"To be or not to be" is a complete pain

Possibly the weirdest verb in the English language, the verb *to be,* changes more frequently than any other. Here it is, tense by tense.

Present Tense

Singular	**Plural**
I am	we are
you are	you are
he, she, it is	they are

Note that the singular forms are in the first column and plural forms are in the second column. Singulars are for one person or thing and plurals for more than one. "You" is listed twice because it may refer to one person or to a group. (Just one more bit of illogic in the language.)

Past Tense

Singular	**Plural**
I was	we were
you were	you were
he, she, it was	they were

Future Tense

Singular	**Plural**
I will be	we will be
you will be	you will be
he, she, it will be	they will be

Present Perfect

Singular	**Plural**
I have been	we have been
you have been	you have been
he, she, it has been	they have been

Past Perfect

Singular	**Plural**
I had been	we had been
you had been	you had been
he, she, it had been	they had been

Future Perfect

Singular	**Plural**
I will have been	we will have been
you will have been	you will have been
he, she, it will have been	they will have been

Irregular past and past participles

Are you having fun yet? Now the true joy begins. Dozens and dozens of English verbs have irregular past tense forms, as well as irregular past participles. (The present participles, except for the occasional change from the letter *y* to the letter *i*, are fairly straightforward. Just add *ing*.) I won't list all the irregular verbs here, just a few you may find useful in everyday writing. If you have questions about a particular verb, check your dictionary. In Table 3-2, the first column is the infinitive form of the verb. (The infinitive is the "to + verb" form — to laugh, to cry, to learn grammar, and so on.) The second column is the simple past tense. The third column is the past participle, which is combined with *has* (singular) or *have* (plural) to form the present perfect tense. The past participle is also used with *had* to form the past perfect tense.

Table 3-2	Forms of Irregular Participles	
Verb	*Past*	*Past Participle*
bear	bore	borne
become	became	become
begin	began	begun
bite	bit	bitten
break	broke	broken
bring	brought	brought
catch	caught	caught
choose	chose	chosen
come	came	come
do	did	done
drink	drank	drunk
drive	drove	driven
eat	ate	eaten
fall	fell	fallen
feel	felt	felt
fly	flew	flown
freeze	froze	frozen
get	got	got or gotten
go	went	gone
know	knew	known
lay	laid	laid
lead	led	led

Verb	Past	Past Participle
lend	lent	lent
lie	lay	lain
lose	lost	lost
ride	rode	ridden
ring	rang	rung
rise	rose	risen
run	ran	run
say	said	said
see	saw	seen
set	set	set
shake	shook	shaken
sing	sang	sung
sink	sank or sunk	sunk
sit	sat	sat
sleep	slept	slept
speak	spoke	spoken
steal	stole	stolen
swim	swam	swum
take	took	taken
throw	threw	thrown
wear	wore	worn
win	won	won
write	wrote	written

Setting Up Correct Verbs

To sit and *to set* are perfectly fine verbs, but they're not interchangeable. *Sit* is what you do when you stop standing and make a lap. *Set* is what you do to something else — to place an object somewhere or to adjust or regulate something. Check out these examples:

Anna sits in front of the television, even when it's broken. (Anna's on the couch, staring at a blank screen.)

Arthur set the raygun to "stun" and then set it carefully on the shelf. (Arthur's turned the dial on his weapon and then placed it out of harm's way.)

In some parts of the world, "to set a spell" means to rest. That expression is perfectly fine when informality is acceptable, but in formal English, be sure you *sit*, not *set* on your chair.

Chapter 4

Who's Doing What? How to Find the Subject

*I*n Chapter 2, I describe the sentence as a flatbed truck carrying your meaning to the reader or listener. Verbs are the wheels of the truck, and subjects are the drivers. Why do you need a subject? Can you imagine a truck speeding down the road without a driver? Not a pleasant thought!

Who's Driving the Truck? Why the Subject Is Important

All sentences contain verbs — words that express action or state of being. (For more information on verbs, see Chapter 2.) But you can't have an action in a vacuum. You can't have a naked, solitary state of being either. Someone or something must also be present in the sentence — the *who* or *what* you're talking about in relation to the action or state of being expressed by the verb. The "someone" or "something" doing the action or being talked about is the subject.

A "someone" must be a person and a "something" must be a thing, place, or idea. So guess what? The subject is usually a noun because a noun is a person, place, thing, or idea. I say *usually* because sometimes the subject is a pronoun — a word that substitutes for a noun — *he, they, it*, and so forth. (For more on pronouns, see Chapter 9.)

Teaming up: Subject and verb pairs

Another way to think about the subject is to say that the subject is the "who" or "what" part of the subject–verb pair. The subject–verb pair is the main idea of the sentence, stripped to essentials. A few sentences:

> *Jasper gasped* at the mummy's sudden movement.

In this sentence, *Jasper gasped* is the main idea; it's also the subject–verb pair.

> *Justin will judge* the beauty contest only if *his ex-girlfriend competes*.

You should spot two subject–verb pairs in this sentence: *Justin will judge* and *ex-girlfriend competes*.

Now try a sentence without action. This one describes a state of being, so it uses a linking verb:

> *Jackhammer has* always *been* an extremely noisy worker.

The subject–verb pair is *Jackhammer has been*. Did you notice that *Jackhammer has been* sounds incomplete? *Has been* is a linking verb, and linking verbs always need something after the verb to complete the idea. I give you more links in the verb chain in Chapter 2; now back to the *subject* at hand. (Uh, sorry about that one.) The subject–verb pair in action-verb sentences may usually stand alone, but the subject–verb pair in linking verb sentences may not.

Compound subjects and verbs: Two for the price of one

Subjects and verbs pair off, but sometimes you get two (or more) for the price of one. You can have two subjects (or more) and one verb. The multiple subjects are called *compound subjects*. Here's an example:

> *Dorothy* and *Justin* went home in defeat.

Here you notice one action *(went)* and two people *(Dorothy, Justin)* doing the action. So the verb *went* has two subjects.

Now take a look at some additional examples:

> *Lola* and *Lulu* ganged up on George yesterday to his dismay and defeat. (*Lola, Lulu* = subjects)

> The *omelet* and *fries* revolted Eggworthy. (*omelet, fries* = subjects)

Snort and *Squirm* were the only two dwarves expelled from Snow White's band. *(Snort, Squirm* = subjects)

Another variation is one subject paired with two (or more) verbs. For example:

Justin's ex-girlfriend *burped* and *cried* after the contest.

You've got two actions *(burped, cried)* and one person doing both *(ex-girlfriend)*. *Ex-girlfriend* is the subject of both *burped* and *cried*.

Some additional samples of double verbs, which in grammatical terms are called *compound verbs:*

George *snatched* the atomic secret and quickly *stashed* it in his navel. *(snatched, stashed* = verbs)

Ella *ranted* for hours about Larry's refusal to hold an engagement party and then *crept* home. *(ranted, crept* = verbs)

Eggworthy *came* out of his shell last winter but *didn't stay* there. *(came, did stay* = verbs)

Pop the Question: Locating the Subject–Verb Pairs

Allow me to let you in on a little trick for pinpointing the subject–verb pair of a sentence: Pop the question! (No, I'm not asking you to propose.) Pop the question tells you what to ask in order to find out what you want to know. The correct question is all important in the search for information, as all parents realize.

WRONG QUESTION FROM PARENT: What did you do last night?

TEENAGER'S ANSWER: Nothing.

RIGHT QUESTION FROM PARENT: When you came in at 2 a.m., were you hoping that I'd ignore the fact that you went to the China Club?

TEENAGER'S ANSWER: I didn't go to the China Club! I went to Moomba.

PARENT: Aha! You went to a club on a school night. You're grounded.

In Chapter 2, I explain that the first question to ask is not "Is this going to be on the test?" but "What's the verb?" (To find the verb, ask *what's happening?* or *what is?*) After you uncover the verb, put "who" or "what" in front of it to form a question. The answer is the subject.

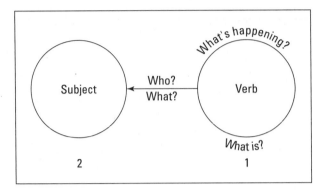

Try one:

Jackknife sharpens his dives during hours of practice.

1. Pop the question: What's happening? Answer: *sharpens. Sharpens* is the verb.

2. Pop the question: Who or what *sharpens?* Answer: *Jackknife sharpens. Jackknife* is the subject.

A pop quiz on popping the question. What are the subject and verb in the following sentence?

Jolly Roger will soon be smiling because of all the treasure in his ship.

Answer: The verb is *will be smiling* and the subject is *Jolly Roger.* Try one more. Identify the subject and verb.

No matter what the weather, Roger never even considers wearing a hat.

Answer: The verb is *considers* and the subject is *Roger.*

What's a Nice Subject Like You Doing in a Place Like This? Unusual Word Order

Most of the sentences you encounter are in the normal subject–verb order, which is (gasp) subject–verb. In other words, the subject usually comes before the verb. Not every sentence follows that order, though most do. Sometimes a subject hides out at the end of the sentence or in some other weird place. (Hey, even a subject needs a change of scenery sometime.)

Me, myself, and I

You can use *I* as a subject, but not *me* or *myself*.

Wrong: Bill and me are going to rob that bank. Bill and myself will soon be in jail.

Right: Bill and I are going to rob that bank. Bill and I will soon be in jail.

Me doesn't perform actions; it receives actions. To put this rule another way: *me* is an object of some action or form of attention: He gave the check to *me*.

Myself is appropriate only for actions that double back on the person performing the action: I told *myself* not to be such a nerd! *Myself* may also be used for emphasis (though some grammarians object to the repetition), along with the word *I*: *I myself* will disclose the secret to the tabloid offering the most bucks.

If you pop the question and answer it according to the meaning of the sentence — not according to the word order — you'll be fine. The key is to put the subject questions (who? what?) in front of the verb. Then think about what the sentence is actually saying and answer the questions. And voilà! Your subject will appear.

Try this one:

> Up the avenue and around the park trudged Godzilla on his way to tea with the Loch Ness Monster.

1. Pop the question: What's happening? What is? Answer: *trudged. Trudged* is the verb.

2. Pop the question: Who *trudged?* What *trudged?* Answer: *Godzilla. Godzilla* is the subject. (I'll let you decide whether Godzilla is a who or a what.)

If you were answering by word order, you'd say *park*. But the *park* did not *trudge, Godzilla trudged*. Pay attention to meaning, not to placement in the sentence, and you can't go wrong.

What are the subjects and verbs in the following sentences?

A. Alas, what a woefully inadequate grammarian am I.

B. Across the river and through the woods to the grammarian's house go Ella and Larry.

Answers: In sentence A, *am* is the verb and *I* is the subject. In sentence B, the verb is *go* and the subjects are *Ella* and *Larry.*

Always find the verb first. Then look for the subject.

Find That Subject! Detecting You-Understood

"Cross on the green, not in between."

"Eat your vegetables."

"Don't leave your chewing gum on the bedpost overnight."

What do these sentences have in common? Yes, they're all nagging comments you've heard all your life. More importantly, they're all commands. The verbs give orders: *cross, eat, don't leave.* So where's the subject in these sentences?

If you pop the question, here's what happens:

1. Pop the question: What's happening? What is? Answer: *cross, eat, don't leave.*

2. Pop the question: Who *cross, eat, don't leave?* Answer: Uh . . .

The second question appears to have no answer, but appearances can be deceiving. The answer is *you. You* cross at the green, not in between. *You* eat your vegetables. *You* don't leave your chewing gum on the bedpost overnight. What's that you say? *You* is not in the sentence? True. *You* is not written, but it's implied. And when your mom says, "Eat your vegetables," you understand that she means *you.* So grammarians say that the subject is *you-understood.* The subject is *you,* even though *you* isn't in the sentence and even though *you* don't intend to eat any taste-free lima beans.

Pop the questions and find the subject–verb pairs in these three sentences.

A. Ella, dancing the cha-cha, forgot to watch her feet.

B. Stop, Ella!

C. Over the bandleader and across five violin stands fell Ella, heavily.

Answers: In sentence A, *forgot* is the verb and *Ella* is the subject. *Dancing* is a fake verb. (I discuss finding fake verbs and subjects later in this chapter.) In sentence B, *stop* is the verb and *you-understood* is the subject. The remark is addressed to *Ella,* but *you-understood* is still the subject. In sentence C, *fell* is the verb and *Ella* is the subject.

Searching for the Subject in Questions

Does everyone love grammar? Don't answer that! I started this section with that sentence not to check attitudes toward grammar (I'd rather not know) but to illustrate the subject's favorite location in a question. Most questions in English are formed by adding a helping verb — *do, does, will, can, should,* and so forth — to a main verb. (For everything you need to know about helping verbs, turn to Chapter 2.) The subject is generally tucked between the helping verb and the main verb, but you don't have to bother remembering that fascinating bit of trivia. To locate the subject in a question, simply "pop the question" the same way you do for any other sentence. Here's how to attack the first sentence of this paragraph:

1. Pop the question: What's happening? What is? Answer: *does love.*

2. Pop the question: Who *does love?* Answer: *everyone.*

When you're "popping the subject question" for a question, the "popped question" may sound a little odd. Why? Because in a question, the subject usually isn't located in front of the verb. But if you ignore the awkwardness of the phrasing and concentrate on meaning, you can easily — and correctly — identify the subject of a question.

Pop the questions and find the subject–verb pairs in these three questions.

A. Will George ever floss his teeth?

B. Could I possibly care less about George's hygiene?

C. Won't George's dentist charge extra?

Answers: In sentence A, *will floss* is the verb and *George* is the subject. In sentence B, *could care* is the verb and the subject is *I.* Sentence C is a bit tricky. The word "won't" is short for "will not." So the verb in C is *will charge,* and the subject is *George's dentist.* You may be wondering what happened to the *not. Not* is an adverb, not that you need to know that fact. It changes the meaning of the verb from positive to negative. (For more on adverbs, turn to Chapter 7.)

Don't Get Faked Out: Avoiding Fake Verbs and Subjects

As I walk through New York City, I often see "genuine" Rolex watches (retail $10,000 or so) for sale from street peddlers for "$15 — special today only!" You need to guard against fakes when you're on the city streets (no surprise there). Also (and this may be a surprise), you need to guard against fakes when you're finding subject–verb pairs.

Finding fake verbs

Verbs in English grammar can be a little sneaky sometimes. You may ask *who?* or *what?* in front of a verb and get no answer or at least no answer that makes sense. When this happens, you may gather that you haven't really found a verb. You've probably stumbled upon a lookalike, or, as I call it, a "fake verb." Here's an example:

> Wiping his tears dramatically, Alex pleaded with the teacher to forgive his lack of homework.

Suppose you pop the verb question *(What's happening? What is?)* and get *wiping* for an answer. A reasonable guess. But now pop the subject question: *Who wiping? What wiping?* The questions don't sound right, and that's your first hint that you haven't found a real verb. But the question is not important. The answer, however, is! And there is no real answer in the sentence. You may try *Alex,* but when you put him with the "verb," it doesn't match: *Alex wiping.* (*Alex is wiping* would be okay, but that's not what the sentence says.) So now you know for sure that your first "verb" isn't really a verb. Put it aside and keep looking. What's the real verb? *Pleaded.*

To sum up: Lots of words in the sentence express action or being, but only some of these words are verbs. (Most are what grammarians call verbals; check out Chapter 24 for more on verbals.) At any rate, if you get no answer to your pop-the-subject question, just ignore the "verb" you think you found and look for the real verb.

Watching out for "here" and "there" and other fake subjects

Someone comes up to you and says, "Here is one million dollars." What's the first question that comes into your mind? I know, good grammarian that you are, that your question is *What's the subject of that sentence?* Well, try to answer your question in the usual way, by popping the question.

> Here is one million dollars.
>
> 1. Pop the question: What's happening? What is? Answer: *is.*
>
> 2. Pop the question: Who *is?* What *is?* Answer: ?

What did you say? *Here is?* Wrong. *Here* can't be a subject. Neither can *there.* Both of these words are fake subjects. (*Here* and *there* are adverbs, not nouns. See Chapter 7 for more on adverbs.) What's the real answer to the question *What is? One million dollars.* Here and there are fill-ins, place markers; they aren't what you're talking about. *One million dollars* — that's what you're talking about!

Choosing the correct verb for "here" and "there" sentences

If you write *here* and *there* sentences, be sure to choose the correct verb. Because *here* and *there* are never subjects, you must always look *after* the verb for the real subject. When you match a subject to a verb (something I discuss in detail in Chapter 10), be sure to use the real subject, not *here* or *there*. Example:

Here are ten anteaters. NOT Here is ten anteaters. (anteaters = subject)

If you want to check your choice of verb, try reversing the sentence. In the sample sentence above, say *ten anteaters is/are*. Chances are your "ear" will tell you that you want *ten anteaters are*, not *ten anteaters is*.

Standardized tests often check whether you can detect the right verb for a "here" or "there" sentence. Test-taker beware!

Which sentence is correct?

A. There are 50 reasons for my complete lack of homework.
B. There's 50 reasons for my complete lack of homework.

Answer: Sentence A is correct. In sentence B, *there's* is short for *there is,* but *reasons,* the plural subject, takes a plural verb.

Subjects Aren't Just a Singular Sensation: Forming the Plural of Nouns

Distinguishing between singular and plural subjects is a really big deal, and I go into it in detail in Chapter 10. But before I go any further, I want to explain how to form the plural of nouns (words that name persons, places, or things) because most subjects are nouns. If you learn how to form plurals, you'll also be able to recognize them.

Regular plurals

Plain old garden-variety nouns form plurals by adding the letter *s*. Check out Table 4-1 for some examples.

Table 4-1	Examples of Regular Plurals
Singular	*Plural*
xylophone	xylophones
quintuplet	quintuplets
worrywart	worrywarts
nerd	nerds
lollipop	lollipops
eyebrow	eyebrows

Singular nouns that end in *s* already, as well as singular nouns ending in *sh, ch,* and *x* form plurals by adding *es.* Some examples are shown in Table 4-2.

Table 4-2	Examples of Regular Plurals Ending in -s and -ch
Singular	*Plural*
grinch	grinches
box	boxes
kiss	kisses
George Bush	both George Bushes
mess	messes
catch	catches

The -IES and -YS have it

If a noun ends in the letter *y,* and the letter before the *y* is a vowel (a, e, i, o, u), just add *s.* For examples, see Table 4-3.

Table 4-3	Examples of Regular Plurals Ending in a Vowel Plus y
Singular	*Plural*
monkey	monkeys
turkey	turkeys
day	days
boy	boys
honey	honeys
bay	bays

If the noun ends in *y* but the letter before the -*y* is not a vowel, form the plural by changing the *y* to *i* and adding *es*. For examples, see Table 4-4.

Table 4-4	Examples of Regular Plurals Ending in a Consonant Plus -y
Singular	*Plural*
sob story	sob stories
unsolvable mystery	unsolvable mysteries
a cute little ditty (it means *song*)	cute little ditties
pinky	pinkies
bat-filled belfry	bat-filled belfries
tabby	tabbies

Never change the spelling of a name when you make it plural. The plural of *Sammy* is S*ammys,* not *Sammies.*

No knifes here: Irregular plurals

This topic wouldn't be any fun without irregulars, now would it? Okay, you're right. Irregulars are always a pain. However, they're also always around. Table 4-5 gives you examples of irregular plurals.

Table 4-5	Examples of Irregular Plurals
Singular	*Plural*
knife	knives
sheep	sheep
man	men
woman	women
child	children
deer	deer

Listing all the irregular plurals is an impossible task. Check the dictionary for any noun plural that puzzles you.

Are you affected? Or effected?

Has the study of grammar affected or effected your brain? Should you set or sit on the porch to think about this sentence? These two pairs of words are a complete annoyance, but once you learn them, you're all set. (And I do mean set.) Here are the definitions:

Affect versus effect: Affect is a verb. It means to influence. Effect is a noun meaning result. Hence

Sunlight affects Ludwig's appetite; he never eats during the day.

Ludmilla thinks that her vegetarian pizza will affect Ludwig's dietary regimen, but I think the effect will be disastrous.

Special note: Affect may also be a noun meaning "the way one relates to and shows emotions." Effect may act as a verb meaning "to cause a complete change." However, you rarely need these secondary meanings.

Sit versus set: Sit is a verb meaning "to plop yourself down on a chair, to take a load off your feet." Set means "to put something else down, to place something in a particular spot." Thus

Ratrug seldom sits for more than two minutes.

I'd like to sit down while I speak, but only if you promise not to set that plate of pickled fish eyeballs in front of me.

The brother-in-law rule: Hyphenated plurals

If you intend to insult your relatives, you may as well do so with the correct plural form. Remember: Form the plural of hyphenated nouns by adding *s* or *es* to the important word, not to the add-ons. These words are all plurals:

- mothers-in-law
- brothers-in-law
- vice-presidents
- secretaries-general
- dogcatchers-in-chief

You may hear references to "attorney generals." If you do, call the grammar police. An "attorney general" is a lawyer, not a military officer. Therefore, *attorney* is the important part of this title, and it's a noun. The *general* is a description — a reference to the rank of the *attorney*. To form a plural, you deal with the noun, not with the descriptive word. Therefore, you have one *attorney general* and two or more *attorneys general*.

Chapter 5

Having It All: The Complete Sentence

. . . .

In This Chapter

▶ Identifying the elements of a complete sentence

▶ Uniting two or more complete sentences properly

▶ Joining ideas of unequal importance

▶ Dealing with sentence fragments

▶ Placing periods, questions marks, and exclamation points in the correct spot

. . . .

*E*veryone knows the most important rule of English grammar: All sentences must be complete. But everyone breaks the rule. I just did! *But everyone breaks the rule* is not a complete sentence; it's a sentence *fragment*. At times, fragments are perfectly acceptable, and in this chapter I show you when you can get away with writing one. The other extreme — more than one complete sentence improperly glued together — is a *run-on sentence*. A run-on sentence — and its variation, a *comma splice* — are never okay. In fact, they're grammatical felonies. Never fear: in this chapter I explain how to join ideas without risking a visit from the Grammar Police. I also provide everything you need to know about *endmarks*, the punctuation separating one sentence from another.

Completing Sentences: The Essential Subjects and Verbs

A complete sentence has at least one subject–verb pair. They're a pair because they match. They both enjoy long walks on the beach, singing in the rain, and making fun of American Idol contestants. Just kidding. They match because, well, they work smoothly as a team. One half of the pair (the verb)

expresses action or being, and the other half (the subject) is whatever or whoever does the action or exists in the state of being. (For more information on verbs, see Chapters 2 and 3; for more information on subjects, see Chapter 4.) A few subject–verb pairs that match are

> Eggworthy scrambled
>
> Ms. Drydock has repaired
>
> Eva will be

Just for comparison, here is one mismatch:

> Eggworthy scrambling

When you're texting or IMing (instant messaging), space is tight. Every character counts, including spaces. Therefore, many people opt for "sentences" that contain only verbs, when the meaning is clear. Check out this "text":

> Went home. Fed cow. Cleaned barn.

The missing subject, *I*, is obvious. If you're talking about someone else, however, you need to supply a subject:

> Abner went home. Fed cow. Cleaned barn.

Now the person receiving the message understands that Abner did all the work, not the texter — who, of course, was too busy texting to do chores. By the way, I used capital letters in the preceding examples. Lots of people opt for lowercase only in messages like these. Check out Chapter 15 for a guide to capitalization and electronic media.

You may find some mismatches in your sentences when you go subject–verb hunting. Mismatches are not necessarily wrong; they're simply not subject–verb pairs. Take a look at the preceding mismatch, this time inside its sentence:

> Eggworthy, scrambling for a seat on the plane, knocked over the omelet plate.

When you're checking a sentence for completeness, ignore the mismatches. Keep looking until you find a subject–verb pair that belongs together. If you can't find one, you don't have a complete sentence.

Complete sentences may also include more than one subject–verb pair:

Dorothy fiddled while the orchestra pit burned. (*Dorothy* = subject of the verb *fiddled, orchestra pit* = subject of the verb *burned*)

Because Lester jumped on the trampoline, the earth shook. (*Lester* = subject of the verb *jumped, earth* = subject of the verb *shook*)

Not only did George swim, but he also sipped the pool water. (*George* = subject of the verb *did swim, he* = subject of the verb *sipped*)

Complete sentences may also match one subject with more than one verb, and vice versa:

The lizard with a British accent appeared in three commercials but sang in only two. (*lizard* = subject of verbs *appeared, sang*)

Alice and Archie will fight endlessly over a single birdseed. (*Alice, Archie* = subjects of the verb *will fight*)

Roger and I put crayons on the radiator. (*Roger, I* = subjects of the verb *put*)

Complete sentences that give commands may match an understood subject (you) with the verb:

Give me a coupon. (*you-understood* = subject of the verb *give*)

Visit Grandma, you little creep! (*you-understood* = subject of the verb *visit*)

To find the subject–verb pair, start with the verb. Pop the verb question: *What's happening?* or *What is?* The answer is the verb. Then pop the subject question: Ask *who?* or *what?* in front of the verb. The answer is the subject. (For a more complete explanation, see Chapter 4.)

The sentence below contains one true subject–verb pair and one mismatch. Can you find the subject–verb pair?

The angry ant caught in a blob of glue vowed never to walk near a model airplane again.

Answer: The subject–verb pair is *ant vowed.* The mismatch is *ant caught.* The sentence isn't saying that the *ant caught* something, so *ant caught* is not a match.

In the preceding pop quiz, *to* walk is not the verb. *To walk* is an infinitive, the basic form from which verbs are made. Infinitives never function as verbs in a sentence. (See Chapter 2 for more information on infinitives.)

Complete Thoughts, Complete Sentences

What's an incomplete sentence? It's the moment in the television show just before the last commercial. You know what I mean. *The hero slowly edges the door open a few inches, peeks in, gasps, and . . . FADE TO DANCING DETERGENT BOTTLE.* You were planning to change the channel, but instead you wait to see if the villain's cobra is going to bite the hero's nose. You haven't gotten to the end, and you don't know what's happening. A complete sentence is the opposite of that moment in a television show. You have gotten to the end, and you do know what's happening. In other words, a complete sentence must express a complete thought. (You've probably noticed that grammar terminology is not terribly original; in fact, it's terribly obvious.)

Check out these complete sentences. Notice how they express complete thoughts:

> Despite Eggworthy's fragile appearance, he proved to be a tough opponent.

> Ms. Drydock will sail solo around the world, as soon as her boat stops leaking.

> I can't imagine why anyone would want to ride on top of a Zamboni.

> Did Lola apply for a job as a Zamboni driver?

For comparison, here are a few incomplete thoughts:

> The reason I wanted a divorce was.

> Because I said so.

I can guess what you're thinking. Both of those incomplete thoughts may be part of a longer conversation. Yes, in context those incomplete thoughts may indeed express a complete thought:

> Sydney: So the topic of conversation was the Rangers' season opener?

> Alice: No! "The reason I wanted a divorce" was!

and

> Sydney: Why do I have to do this dumb homework?

> Alice: Because I said so.

Fair enough. You can pull a complete thought out of the examples. However, the context of a conversation is not enough to satisfy the complete thought/complete sentence rule. To be "legal," your sentence must express a complete thought.

Check out these examples:

> The reason I wanted a divorce was what we discussed, even though his real interest was the Rangers' season opener.

> You have to do this dumb homework because I said so.

Final answer: Every complete sentence has at least one subject–verb pair and must express a complete thought.

In deciding whether you have a complete sentence or not, you may be led astray by words that resemble questions. Consider these three words: *who knits well.* A complete thought? Maybe yes, maybe no. Suppose those three words form a question:

> Who knits well?

This question is understandable and its thought is complete. Verdict: legal. Suppose these three words form a statement:

> Who knits well.

Now they don't make sense. This incomplete sentence needs more words to make a complete thought:

> The honor of making Fido's sweater will go to the person who knits well.

The moral of the story? Don't change the meaning of what you're saying when deciding whether a thought is complete. If you're *questioning,* consider your sentence as a *question.* If you're *stating,* consider your sentence as a *statement.*

Occasionally a complete sentence ends with an ellipsis — three spaced dots. Such sentences show up in dramatic works, to add suspense or to indicate hesitation or confusion. These sentences appear incomplete, but because they fulfill the author's purpose, they *are* complete. For more information on ellipses, see "Oh, Mama, Could This Really Be the End?" later in this chapter.

Which sentence is complete?

A. Martin sings.

B. Martin, who hopes to sing professionally some day but can't get beyond the do-re-mi level.

Answer: Even though it is short, sentence A is complete. *Martin sings* is a complete idea and includes the necessary subject–verb pair. In sentence B, one subject is paired with two verbs *(who + hopes, can get),* but no complete thought is stated.

Why clarity is important

One of my favorite moments in teaching came on a snowy January day. A student named Danny ran into the lunchroom, clearly bursting with news. "Guess what?" he shouted triumphantly to his friends. "A kid on my bus's mother had a baby last night!"

This situation wasn't critical. After all, the baby had already been born. But imagine if Danny had been greeting an ambulance with "Quick! Over here! A kid on my bus's mother is having a baby!" I think everyone agrees that the best reaction from an emergency medical technician isn't "Huh?"

Being clear is probably the first rule of English grammar, and that rule wins a fight with any other rule. Faced with a choice between confusion and incomplete sentences, for example,

incomplete sentences win. Here's the news Danny should have spread that cold January day:

> This kid on my bus? His mother had a baby last night.

Of course, he could also have told his story correctly by saying:

> The mother of a kid on my bus had a baby last night.

Either way, everyone would've yawned, eaten another bite of mystery meat, and filed out to math class. Hearing either of these statements, the students would've understood what Danny was trying to say.

So remember: First comes meaning. Second comes everything else.

Combining Sentences

Listen to the nearest toddler and you may hear something like "I played with the clay and I went to the zoo and Mommy said I had to take a nap and . . ." and so forth. Monotonous, yes. But — surprise, surprise — grammatically correct. Take a look at how the information would sound if that one sentence turned into three: *I played with the clay. I went to the zoo. Mommy said I had to take a nap.* The information sounds choppy. When the sentences are combined, the information flows more smoothly. Granted, joining everything with *and* is not a great idea. Read on for better ways of attaching one sentence to another.

Standardized test-makers enjoy plopping run-on sentences and comma splices into paragraphs and checking whether you can identify the run-ons as grammatically incorrect. (A run-on sentence is two or more complete thoughts joined improperly. A comma splice is a run-on in which a comma attempts to unite two complete thoughts.) Teachers who score the writing section of the SAT also frown on run-ons and comma splices. The best way to avoid this type of grammar error is to figure out how to connect sentences legally, as explained in this section.

Connecting with coordinate conjunctions

The words used to join words or longer expressions are called *conjunctions*. You're familiar with these common words: *for, but, yet, so, nor, and,* and *or.* (*And* is the most popular, for those of you keeping track.) These little powerhouses, which are called *coordinate conjunctions,* eat their spinach and lift weights every day. Their healthful habits make them strong enough to join complete sentences. They may also unite all sorts of equal grammatical elements. Here they are in action, joining complete sentences:

> The rain pelted Abner's gray hair, *and* his green velvet shoes were completely ruined.

> The CEO told Tanya to text the address of the restaurant to everyone, *but* Tanya had no idea where the restaurant was.

> You can take a hike, *or* you can jump off a cliff.

> Ben did not know how to shoe a horse, *nor* did he understand equine psychology.

> The townspeople lined the streets, *for* they had heard a rumor about Lady Godiva.

The coordinate conjunctions give equal emphasis to the elements they join. In the preceding sentences, the ideas on one side of the conjunction have no more importance than the ideas on the other side of the conjunction.

When the conjunctions *and*, *but*, *or*, *nor*, and *for* unite two complete sentences, a comma precedes the conjunction. For the lowdown on commas, turn to Chapter 13.

Some words appear to be strong enough to join sentences, but in reality they're just a bunch of 98-pound weaklings. Think of these words as guys who stuff socks in their sleeves, creating biceps without the hassle of going to the gym. These fellows may look good, but the minute you need them to pick up a truck or something, they're history. False joiners include *however, consequently, therefore, moreover, also,* and *furthermore.* Use these words to add meaning to your sentences but not to glue the sentences together. When you see these words on a standardized exam, be careful! A favorite test-maker trick is to plop these words into a run-on. Take a look at these examples:

> RUN-ON: Levon gobbled the birdseed, consequently, Robbie had nothing to eat.

> CORRECTED VERSION #1: Levon gobbled the birdseed; consequently, Robbie had nothing to eat.

> CORRECTED VERSION #2: Levon gobbled the birdseed. Consequently, Robbie had nothing to eat.

Notice the semicolon in the first corrected sentence? Semicolons are equivalent to coordinate conjunctions. According to the Official Grammarian's Rule Book (which doesn't exist), semicolons can join two complete sentences under certain conditions. See the next section for more details.

With your sharp eyes, you probably spotted a comma after *consequently* in each of the preceding examples. Grammarians argue about whether you must place a comma after a false joiner. (For the record, false joiners are *conjunctive adverbs.* No one in the entire universe needs to know that term.) Some grammarians say that the comma is necessary. Others (I'm one) see the comma as optional — a question of personal style. This is the sort of argument that makes grammarians ideal candidates for Nerds Anonymous.

Attaching thoughts: Semicolons

The semicolon is a funny little punctuation mark; it functions as a pit stop between one idea and another. It's not as strong as a period, which in Britain is called a "full stop" because, well, that's what a period does. It stops the reader. A semicolon lets the reader take a rest, but just for a moment. This punctuation mark is strong enough to attach one complete sentence to another.

I've seen writing manuals that proclaim, "Never use semicolons!" with the same intensity of feeling as, say, "Don't blow up the world with that nuclear missile." Other people can't get enough of them, sprinkling them like confetti on New Year's. As far as I'm concerned, use them if you like them. Ignore them if you don't.

If you do put a semicolon in your sentence, be sure to attach related ideas. Here's an example:

> RIGHT: Grover was born in Delaware; he moved to Virginia when he was four.

> WRONG: I put nonfat yogurt into that soup; I like Stephen King's books.

In the first example, both parts of the sentence are about Grover's living arrangements. In the second, those two ideas are, to put it mildly, not in the same universe. (At least not until Stephen King writes a book about a killer container of yogurt. It could happen.)

Punctuate the following, adding or subtracting words as needed:

> Abner will clip the thorns from that rose stem he is afraid of scratching himself.

Answer: Many combinations are possible, including these two:

Abner will clip the thorns from that rose stem. He is afraid of scratching himself.

Abner will clip the thorns from that rose stem; he is afraid of scratching himself.

Boss and Employee: Joining Ideas of Unequal Ranks

In the average company, the boss runs the show. The boss has subordinates who play two important roles. They must do at least some work, and they must make the boss feel like the center of the universe. Leave the boss alone in the office, and everything's fine. Leave the employees alone in the office, and pretty soon someone is swinging from the light fixture.

Some sentences resemble companies. The "boss" part of a sentence is all right by itself; it expresses a complete thought. The "employee" can't stand alone; it's an incomplete thought. (In case you're into grammar lingo: the boss is an *independent clause*, and the employee is a *subordinate clause*. For more information on independent and subordinate clauses, see Chapter 24.) Together, the "boss" and the "employee" create a more powerful sentence. Check out some examples:

BOSS: Jack ate the bagel.

EMPLOYEE: After he had picked out all the raisins.

JOINING 1: Jack ate the bagel after he had picked out all the raisins.

JOINING 2: After he had picked out all the raisins, Jack ate the bagel.

BOSS: George developed the secret microfilm.

EMPLOYEE: Because he felt traitorous.

JOINING 1: George developed the secret microfilm because he felt traitorous.

JOINING 2: Because he felt traitorous, George developed the secret microfilm.

BOSS: The book bag is in the garage.

EMPLOYEE: That Larry lost.

JOINING: The book bag that Larry lost is in the garage.

The joined example sentences are grammatically legal because they contain at least one complete thought, which can stand on its own as a complete sentence.

Whether or if it rains

Whether and *if* both connect one idea to another in a sentence, but each is used in a different situation. Are you choosing between two alternatives? Select *whether,* as in *whether or not.* Look at the following examples:

> George is not sure *whether* he should activate the wind machine. (He has two choices — to activate or not to activate.)

> *Whether* I go or stay is completely irrelevant to me. (Two choices — going and staying.)

If, on the other hand, describes a possibility. Check out these examples:

> Lulu will reach the top of Mount Everest *if* the sunny weather continues. (The sentence talks about the possibility of sunny weather and Lulu's successful climb.)

> *If* I have my way, the Grammarians' Ball will be held at the Participle Club. (The sentence talks about the possibility of my having what I want and the location of the world's most boring event.)

Choosing subordinate conjunctions

The conjunctions in the boss–employee type of sentence I describe in the preceding section do double duty. These conjunctions emphasize that one idea (the "boss," an independent clause, the equivalent of a complete sentence) is more important than the other (the "employee" or subordinate clause). The conjunctions joining boss and employee give some information about the relationship between the two ideas. These conjunctions are called *subordinate conjunctions.* Some common subordinate conjunctions are *while, because, although, though, since, when, where, if, whether, before, until, than, as, as if, in order that, so that, whenever,* and *wherever.* (Whew!)

Check out how conjunctions are used in these examples:

> Sentence 1: Michael was shaving. (not a very important activity)

> Sentence 2: The earthquake destroyed the city. (a rather important event)

If these two sentences are joined as equals with a coordinate conjunction, the writer emphasizes both events:

> Michael was shaving, *and* the earthquake destroyed the city.

Grammatically, the sentence is legal. Morally, this statement poses a problem. Do you really think that Michael's avoidance of five o'clock shadow is equal in importance to an earthquake that measures 7 on the Richter scale? Better to join these clauses as unequals with the help of a subordinate conjunction, making the main idea about the earthquake the boss:

While Michael was shaving, the earthquake destroyed the city.

or

The earthquake destroyed the city *while* Michael was shaving.

The *while* gives you *time* information, attaches the employee sentence to the boss sentence, and shows the greater importance of the earthquake. Not bad for five letters.

Here's another:

Sentence 1: Esther must do her homework now.

Sentence 2: Mom is on the warpath.

In combining these two ideas, you have a few decisions to make. First of all, if you put them together as equals, the reader will wonder why you're mentioning both statements at the same time:

Esther must do her homework now, *but* Mom is on the warpath.

This joining may mean that Mom is running around the house screaming at the top of her lungs. Although Esther has often managed to concentrate on her history homework while blasting heavy metal music at mirror-shattering levels, she finds that concentrating is impossible during Mom's tantrums. Esther won't get anything done until Mom settles down with a cup of tea. That's one possible meaning of this joined sentence. But why leave your reader guessing? Try another joining:

Esther must do her homework now *because* Mom is on the warpath.

This sentence is much clearer: Esther's mother got one of those little pink notes from the teacher *(Number of missing homeworks: 323)*. Esther knows that if she wants to survive through high school graduation, she'd better get to work now. One more joining to check:

Mom is on the warpath *because* Esther must do her homework now.

Okay, in this version Esther's mother has asked her daughter to clean the garage. She's been asking Esther every day for the last two years. Now the health inspector is due and Mom's really worried. But Esther told her that she couldn't clean up now because she had to do her homework. World War III erupted immediately.

Do you see the power of these joining words? These conjunctions strongly influence the meanings of the sentences.

Being that I like grammar

Many people say *being that* to introduce a reason. Unfortunately, *being that* is a grammatical felony in the first degree (if there are degrees of grammatical felonies — I'm a grammarian, not a lawyer). Here's the issue: People use *being that* as a subordinate conjunction, but *being that* is not acceptable, at least in formal English usage. Try *because.* For example:

> WRONG: *Being that* it was Thanksgiving, Mel bought a turkey.

> RIGHT: *Because* it was Thanksgiving, Mel bought a turkey.

> WRONG: The turkey shed a tear or two, *being that* it was Thanksgiving.

> RIGHT: The turkey shed a tear or two, *because* it was Thanksgiving.

You may like the sound of *since* in the sample sentences. Increasingly, *since* is being used as a synonym for *because,* and so far civilization as we know it hasn't crumbled. The grammarians who like to predict the end of the world because of such issues have a problem with the *since/because* connection. They prefer to use *since* for time statements:

> I haven't seen the turkey *since* the ax came out of the box.

> Since you've been gone, I've begun an affair with Bill Bailey.

Another grammatical no-no is *irregardless.* I think *irregardless* is popular because it's a long word that feels good when you say it. Those *r's* just roll right off the tongue. Sadly, *irregardless* is not a conjunction. It's not even a word, according to the rules of formal English. Use *regardless* (not nearly so much fun to pronounce) or *despite the fact that.*

> WRONG: Irregardless, we are going to eat you, you turkey!

> RIGHT: Regardless, we are going to eat you, you turkey!

> ALSO RIGHT: Despite the fact that you are a tough old bird, we are going to eat you, you turkey!

Employing Pronouns to Combine Sentences

A useful trick for combining short sentences legally is "the pronoun connection." (A *pronoun* substitutes for a noun, which is a word for a person, place, thing, or idea. See Chapter 9 for more information.) Check out these combinations:

Sentence 1: Amy read the book.

Sentence 2: The book had a thousand pictures in it.

Joining: Amy read the book *that* had a thousand pictures in it.

Sentence 1: The paper map stuck to Wilbur's shoe.

Sentence 2: We plan to use the map to take over the world.

Joining: The paper map, *which* we plan to use to take over the world, stuck to Wilbur's shoe.

Sentence 1: Margaret wants to hire a carpenter.

Sentence 2: The carpenter will build a new ant farm for her pets.

Joining: Margaret wants to hire a carpenter *who* will build a new ant farm for her pets.

Sentence 1: The tax bill was passed yesterday.

Sentence 2: The tax bill will lower taxes for the top .00009% income bracket.

Joining: The tax bill *that* was passed yesterday will lower taxes for the top .00009% income bracket.

Alternate joining: The tax bill that was passed yesterday will lower taxes for Bill Gates. (Okay, I interpreted a little.)

That, which, and *who* are pronouns. In the combined sentences, each takes the place of a noun. *(That* replaces *book, which* replaces *map, who* replaces *carpenter, that* replaces *tax bill.)* These pronouns serve as thumbtacks, attaching a subordinate or less important idea to the main body of the sentence. For grammar trivia contests: *that, which,* and *who* (as well as *whom* and *whose*) are pronouns that may relate one idea to another. When they do that job, they are called relative pronouns.

Relative pronouns — like real relatives, at least in some families! — can cause lots of problems. Therefore, the SAT and ACT hit this topic hard. Chapter 23 tells you everything you need to know about relative pronouns.

Combine these sentences with a pronoun.

Sentence 1: Charlie slowly tiptoed toward the poisonous snakes.

Sentence 2: The snakes soon bit Charlie right on the tip of his nose.

Answer: Charlie slowly tiptoed toward the poisonous snakes, *which* soon bit Charlie right on the tip of his nose. The pronoun *which* replaces *snakes* in sentence 2.

Steering Clear of Fragments

I use incomplete sentences, or fragments, here and there throughout this book, and (I hope) these incomplete sentences aren't confusing. Especially now in the Electronic Media Age, quick cuts and short comments are the rule. Everyone today, particularly young people, is much more comfortable with fragments than our elderly relatives were. (I have to point out that the entire older generation, no matter how fanatically correct in grammar, loves one incomplete sentence: *Because I said so.*)

The most common type of fragment uses the words *and, or, but,* and *nor.* These words are *conjunctions,* and as I explain in "Combining Sentences Legally" in this chapter, these conjunctions may combine two complete sentences (with two complete thoughts) into one longer sentence:

> Eggworthy went to his doctor for a cholesterol check, *and* then he scrambled home.

Nowadays, more and more writers begin sentences with *and, or, but,* and *nor,* especially in informal writing or for dramatic effect. For example, the previous sentence may be turned into

> Eggworthy went to his doctor for a cholesterol check. And then he scrambled home.

Beginning sentences with *and, but, or,* and *nor* is still not quite acceptable in formal English grammar. If you see a fragment beginning with one of these words in the error-recognition portion of a standardized test, consider it incorrect English. When you're writing an essay, you should also avoid fragments.

Another common error is to write a fragment that lacks a complete thought. This sort of fragment usually begins with a subordinate conjunction. (See "Choosing Subordinate Conjunctions" in this chapter for a complete explanation.) Don't let the number of words in sentence fragments fool you. Not all sentence fragments are short, though some are. Decide by meaning, not by length.

Here are some examples of this type of sentence fragment, so you know what to avoid:

> When it rained pennies from heaven

> As if he were king of the world

> After the ball was over but before it was time to begin the first day of the rest of your life and all those other clichés that you hear every day in the subway on your way to work

Whether Al likes it or not

Because I said so

Whether you like it or not, and despite the fact that you don't like it, although I am really sorry that you are upset

If hell freezes over

and so on.

Which is a sentence fragment? Which is a complete sentence? Which is a comma splice (a run-on)?

A. Cedric sneezed.

B. Because Cedric sneezed in the middle of the opera, just when the main character removed that helmet with the little horns from on top of her head.

C. Cedric sneezed, I pulled out a handkerchief.

Answers: Sentence A is complete. Sentence B is not really a sentence; it's a fragment with no complete idea. Sentence C is a comma splice because it contains two complete thoughts joined only by a comma.

One more round. Combine these sentences in a grammatically correct way:

Sentence 1: George slipped the microfilm into the heel of his shoe.

Sentence 2: The shoe had been shined just yesterday by the superspy.

Sentence 3: The superspy pretends to work at a shoeshine stand.

Sentence 4: The superspy's name is unknown.

Sentence 5: The superspy's code number is –4.

Sentence 6: George is terrified of the superspy.

Answer: Dozens of combinations are possible. Here are two:

George slipped the microfilm into the heel of his shoe, which had been shined just yesterday by the superspy. The superspy, whose name is unknown but whose code number is –4, pretends to work at a shoeshine stand and terrifies George.

or

After the shoe had been shined by the superspy, who pretends to work at a shoeshine stand, George slipped the microfilm into the heel. George is terrified by the superspy, whose name is unknown and whose code number is –4.

Oh, Mama, Could This Really Be the End? Understanding Endmarks

When you speak, your body language, silences, and tone act as punctuation marks. You wriggle your eyebrows, stop at significant moments, and raise your tone when you ask a question.

When you write, you can't raise an eyebrow or stop for a dramatic moment. No one hears your tone of voice. That's why grammar uses endmarks. The endmarks take the place of live communication and tell your reader how to "hear" the words correctly. Plus, you need endmarks to close your sentences legally. Your choices include the period (.), question mark (?), exclamation point (!), or ellipsis (. . .). The following examples show how to use endmarks correctly.

The period is for ordinary statements, declarations, and commands:

> I can't do my homework.
>
> I refuse to do my homework.
>
> I will never do homework again.

The question mark is for questions:

> Why are you torturing me with this homework?
>
> Is there no justice in the world of homework?
>
> Does no one know how much work in listed in my assignment pad?

The exclamation point adds a little drama to sentences that would otherwise end in periods:

> I can't do my homework!
>
> I absolutely positively refuse to do it!
>
> Oh, the agony of homework I've seen!

An ellipsis (three dots) signals that something has been left out of a sentence. When missing words occur at the end of a sentence, use four dots (three for the missing words and one for the end of the sentence):

> Michael choked, "I can't do my. . . ."
>
> Roger complained, "If you don't shut up, I. . . ."

Don't put more than one endmark at the end of a sentence, unless you're trying to create a comic effect:

He said my cooking tasted like what?!?!?!

Don't put any endmarks in the middle of a sentence. You may find a period inside a sentence as part of an abbreviation; in this case, the period is not considered an endmark. If the sentence ends with an abbreviation, let the period after the abbreviation do double duty. Don't add another period:

WRONG: When Ella woke me, it was six a.m..

RIGHT: When Ella woke me, it was six a.m.

Can you punctuate this example correctly?

Who's there Archie I think there is someone at the door Archie it's a murderer Archie he's going to

Answer: Who's there? Archie, I think there is someone at the door. Archie, it's a murderer! (A period is acceptable here also.) Archie, he's going to. . . .

Chapter 6

Handling Complements

· ·

· ·

Speeding down the grammar highway, the sentence is a flatbed truck carrying meaning to the reader. The verbs are the wheels, and the subject is the driver. Complements are the common, not-always-essential parts of the truck — perhaps the odometer or the defroster. These words are a little more important than those fuzzy dice some people hang from their rearview mirrors or bumper stickers declaring *I stop at railroad tracks.* (What do they think the rest of us do? Leap over the train?) You can sometimes create a sentence without complements, but their presence is generally part of the driving — sorry, I mean *communicating* — experience.

Four kinds of complements show up in sentences: direct objects, indirect objects, objective complements, and subject complements — and this chapter explains all of them. The first three types of complements are related to the *object* of a sentence. (Notice that the word *object* is part of the name. The fourth type of complement is related to the *subject* of a sentence. (Thus the word *subject* is part of its name.) Distinguishing between these two groups helps you choose the proper pronoun, when the sentence calls for that part of speech — a favorite question on standardized tests.

Before I go any farther, it's time to straighten out the compliment/complement divide. The one with an "i" is just a word meaning "praise." *Complement* with an "e" is a grammatical term. A complement adds meaning to the idea that the subject and verb express. That is, a complement completes the idea that the subject and verb begin.

Springing into Action Verb Complements

Action verbs express — surprise! — action. No action verb needs a complement to be grammatically legal. But an action-verb sentence without a complement may sound bare. The complements that follow action verbs — the direct object, indirect object, and objective complement — enhance the meaning of the subject-verb pair.

Receiving the action: Direct objects

Imagine that you're holding a baseball, ready to throw it to a buddy in your yard. In your fantasy, you're facing a Hall-of-Fame hitter. You go into your windup and pitch. The ball arcs gracefully against the clear blue sky — and crashes right through the picture window in your living room.

> You broke the picture window!

Before you can retrieve your ball, your cell phone rings. It's your mom, who has radar for situations like this. *What's going on?* she asks. You mutter something containing the word *broke*. (There's the verb.) *Broke? Who broke something?* she demands. You concede that *you* did. (There's the subject.) *What did you break?* You hesitate. You consider a couple of possible answers: *a bad habit, the world's record for the hundred-meter dash.* Finally you confess: *the picture window.* (There's the complement.)

Here's another way to think about the situation (and the sentence). *Broke* is an action verb because it tells you what happened. The action came from the subject *(you)* and went to an object *(the window).* As some grammarians phrase it, *the window* receives the action expressed by the verb *broke.* Conclusion? *Window* is a *direct object* because it receives the action directly from the verb.

Try another.

> With the force of 1,000 hurricanes, you pitch the baseball.

Pitch is an action verb because it expresses what is happening in the sentence. The action goes from the subject *(you,* the pitcher) to the object *(the baseball).* In other words, *baseball* receives the action of *pitching.* Thus, baseball is the *direct object* of the verb *pitch.*

Here are a few examples of sentences with action verbs. The direct objects are italicized.

The defective X-ray machine took strange *pictures* of my toe. (*took* = verb, *X-ray machine* = subject)

George hissed the secret *word* in the middle of the graduation ceremony. (*hissed* = verb, *George* = subject)

Green marking pens draw naturally beautiful *lines*. (*draw* = verb, *pens* = subject)

Leroy's laser printer spurted *ink* all over his favorite shirt. (spurted = *verb,* printer = *subject*)

You may be able to recognize direct objects more easily if you think of them as part of a pattern in the sentence structure: subject (S) – action verb (AV) – direct object (DO). This S–AV–DO pattern is one of the most common in the English language; it may even be the most common. (I don't know if anyone has actually counted all the sentences and figured it out!) At any rate, think of the parts of the sentence in threes, in the S–AV–DO pattern:

machine took pictures

George hissed words

pens draw lines

printer spurted ink

Of course, just to make your life a little bit harder, a sentence can have more than one DO. Check out these examples:

Al autographed *posters* and *books* for his many admirers.

Roger will eat a dozen *doughnuts* and a few *slabs* of cheesecake for breakfast.

The new president of the Heart Society immediately phoned *Eggworthy* and his *brother.*

George sent *spitballs* and old *socks* flying across the room.

Ella bought *orange juice, tuna, aspirin,* and a *coffee table.*

Some sentences have no DO. Take a look at this example:

Throughout the endless afternoon and into the lonely night, Al sighed sadly.

No one or nothing receives the sighs, so the sentence has no direct object. Perhaps that's why Al is lonely.

The grammar point: This sentence doesn't have a direct object, though it is powered by a verb and expresses a complete thought.

Rare, but sometimes there: Indirect objects

Another type of object is *indirect* because the action doesn't flow directly to it. The *indirect object,* affectionately known as the IO, is an intermediate stop along the way between the action verb and the direct object. Read this sentence, in which the indirect object is italicized:

> Knowing that I'm on a diet, my former friend sent *me* six dozen chocolates.

The action is *sent.* My former *friend* performed the action, so *friend* is the subject. What received the action? Six dozen *chocolates. Chocolates* is the direct object. That's what was *sent*, what received the action of the verb directly. But *me* also received the action, indirectly. *Me* received the sending of the boxes of chocolate. *Me* is called the indirect object.

The sentence pattern for indirect objects is subject (S) – action verb (AV) – indirect object (IO) – direct object (DO). Notice that the indirect object always precedes the direct object: S–AV–IO–DO. Here are a few sentences with the indirect objects italicized:

> Gloria will tell *me* the whole story tomorrow. (*will tell* = verb, *Gloria* = subject, *story* = direct object)

> As a grammarian, I should have given *you* better sample sentences. (*should have given* = verb, *I* = subject, *sentences* = direct object)

> Ella sent *Larry* a sharp message. (*sent* = verb, *Ella* = subject, *message* = direct object)

> The crooked politician offered *Agnes* a bribe for dropping out of the senate race. (*offered* = verb, *politician* = subject, *bribe* = direct object)

Similar to clerks in a shoe store, indirect objects don't appear very often. When indirect objects do show up, they're always in partnership with a direct object. You probably don't need to worry about knowing the difference between direct and indirect objects (unless you're an English teacher). As long as you understand that these words are objects, completing the meaning of an action verb, you recognize the basic composition of a sentence.

No bias here: Objective complements

Finally, a grammar rule that's hard to bungle. Here's the deal: sometimes a direct object doesn't get the whole job done. A little more information is needed (or just desired), and the writer doesn't want to bother adding a whole new subject–verb pair. The solution? An *objective complement* — an added fact about the direct object.

The *objective complement* (italicized in the following sentences) may be a person, place, or thing. In other words, the objective complement may be a noun:

Eggworthy named Lester *copy chief* of the Heart Society Bulletin. (*named* = verb, *Eggworthy* = subject, *Lester* = direct object)

Gloria and others with her world view elected Roger *president.* (*elected* = verb, *Gloria and others* = subject, *Roger* = direct object)

Al called his dog *Al-Too.* (*called* = verb, *Al* = subject, *dog* = direct object)

The objective complement may also be a word that describes a noun. (A word that describes a noun is called an *adjective;* see Chapter 7 for more information.) Take a peek at these sample sentences:

Nancy considered her *hazy* at best. (*considered* = verb, *Nancy* = subject, *her* = direct object)

George dubbed Al-Too *ridiculous.* (*dubbed* = verb, *George* = subject, *Al-Too* = direct object)

Roger called George *heartless.* (*called* = verb, *Roger* = subject, *George* = direct object)

As you see, the objective complements in each of the sample sentences give the sentence an extra jolt. You know more with it than you do without it, but the objective complement is not a major player in the sentence.

Finishing the Equation: Subject Complements

Subject complements are major players in sentences. A *linking verb* begins a word equation; it expresses a state of being, linking two ideas. The complement completes the equation. Because a complement following a linking verb expresses something about the *subject* of the sentence, it is called a *subject complement.* In each of the following sentences, the first idea is the subject, and the second idea (italicized) is the complement:

Nerdo is *upset* by the bankruptcy of the pocket-protector manufacturer. *(Nerdo = upset)*

Gloria was a *cheerleader* before the dog bite incident. *(Gloria = cheerleader)*

The little orange book will be *sufficient* for all your firework information needs. *(book = sufficient)*

It is *I,* the master of the universe. *(It = I)*

Subject complements can take several forms. Sometimes the subject complement is a descriptive word (an *adjective,* for those of you who like the correct terminology). Sometimes the subject complement is a *noun* (person, place, thing, or idea) or a *pronoun* (a word that substitutes for a noun). The first sample sentence equates *Nerdo* with a description (the adjective *upset*). The second equates *Gloria* with a position (the noun *cheerleader*). In the third sample sentence, the subject *book* is described by the adjective *sufficient.* The last sentence equates the subject *it* with the pronoun *I.* Don't worry about these distinctions. They don't matter! As long as you can find the subject complement, you're grasping the sentence structure.

The linking verbs that I mentioned in the previous paragraph are forms of the verb "to be." Other verbs that give sensory information (*feel, sound, taste, smell,* and so on) may also be linking verbs. Likewise, *appear* and *seem* are linking verbs. (For more information on linking verbs, see Chapter 2.) Here are a couple of sentences with sensory linking verbs. The complements are italicized:

> Larry sounds *grouchier* than usual today. *(Larry = grouchier)*

> At the end of each algebra proof, Anna feels strangely *depressed*. *(Anna = depressed)*

You can't mix types of subject complements in the same sentence, completing the meaning of the same verb. Use all descriptions (adjectives) or all nouns and pronouns. Take a look at these examples:

> WRONG: Gramps is grouchy and a patron of the arts.

> RIGHT: Gramps is a grouch and a patron of the arts.

> ALSO RIGHT: Gramps is grouchy and arty.

> WRONG: Lester's pet tarantula will be annoying and a real danger.

> RIGHT: Lester's pet tarantula will be an annoyance and a danger.

> ALSO RIGHT: Lester's pet tarantula will be annoying and dangerous.

Pop the Question: Locating the Complement

In Chapter 2, I explain how to locate the verb by asking the right questions. (*What's happening? What is?*) In Chapter 4, I show you how to pop the question for the subject. (*Who? What?* before the verb). Now it's time to pop the question to find the complements. You ask the complement questions after both the verb and subject have been identified. The complement questions are

Who or whom?

What?

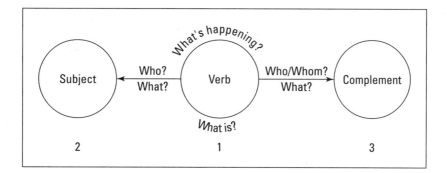

Subject

Who?
What?

What's happening?

Verb

Who/Whom?
What?

Complement

What is?

2   1   3

Try popping the questions in a couple of sentences:

Flossie maintains the cleanest teeth in Texas.

1. Pop the verb question: What's happening? Answer: *maintains. Maintains* is the action verb.

2. Pop the subject question: Who or what *maintains?* Answer: *Flossie maintains. Flossie* is the subject.

3. Pop the complement question: *Flossie maintains* who/whom? No answer. *Flossie maintains* what? Answer: Flossie maintains *the cleanest teeth in Texas* (*teeth* for short). *Teeth* is the direct object.

Remember that objects (direct or indirect) follow action verbs.

Time for you to try another:

The ancient lawn gnome appeared tired and worn.

1. Pop the verb question: What's happening? No answer. What is? Answer: *Appeared. Appeared* is the linking verb.

2. Pop the subject question: Who or what *appeared?* Answer: *Gnome appeared. Gnome* is the subject.

3. Pop the complement question: *Gnome appeared* who? No answer. *Gnome appeared* what? Answer: *Tired* and *worn. Tired* and *worn* are the subject complements.

Remember that subject complements follow linking verbs.

Pop the Question: Finding the Indirect Object

Though indirect objects seldom appear, you can check for them with another "pop the question." After you locate the action verb, the subject, and the direct object, ask

To whom? For whom?

To what? For what?

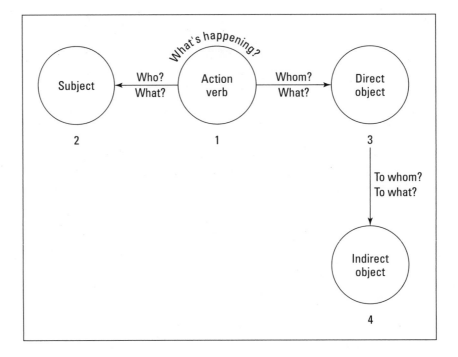

If you get an answer, it should reveal an indirect object. Here's an example:

Mildred will tell me the secret shortly.

1. Pop the verb question: What's happening? Answer: *will tell. Will tell* is an action verb.
2. Pop the subject question: Who will tell? Answer: *Mildred. Mildred* is the subject.

3. Pop the DO question: *Mildred will tell* whom? or what? Answer: *Mildred will tell the secret. Secret* is the direct object.

4. Pop the IO question: *Mildred will tell the secret* to whom? Answer: to *me. Me* is the indirect object.

You may come up with a different answer when you pop the DO question in number 3 (*Mildred will tell* whom? or what?). You can answer *Mildred will tell me*. True. The only problem is that the sentence then has *secret* flapping around with no label. Your attempt to determine the sentence structure has reached a dead end. Luckily for you, all you need to know is that both are objects. Only I-have-no-life grammarians worry about which one is direct and which one is indirect.

Object or subject complement? Identify the italicized words.

Sal seemed *soggy* after his semi-final swim, so we gave *him* a *towel.*

Answer: *Soggy* is the subject complement. (*Seemed* is a linking verb.) *Him* is the indirect object. *Towel* is the direct object. (*Gave* is an action verb.)

Pronouns as Objects and Subject Complements

He told I? He told me? Me, of course. Your ear usually tells you which pronouns to use as objects (both direct and indirect) because the wrong pronouns sound funny. The object pronouns include *me, you, him, her, it, us, them, whom,* and *whomever.* Check them out in context:

Rickie splashed *her* with icy water.

The anaconda hissed *them* a warning.

The babbling burglar told *her* everything.

Your ear may not tell you the correct pronoun to use after a linking verb. That's where you want a *subject* pronoun, not an *object* pronoun. (Just for the record, the subject pronouns include *I, you, he, she, it, we, they, who,* and *whoever.*) Why do you need a subject pronoun after a linking verb? Remember the equation: What's before the verb should be equal to what's after the verb (S = SC). You put subject pronouns before the verb as subjects, so you put subject pronouns after the verb, as subject complements. (For more information, see Chapter 2.)

You gotta problem with grammar?

Do you possess an "ear" for grammar? Do you recognize proper English, distinguishing it from the way everyone else around you speaks? If so, you probably don't say *gotta, gonna, gotcha,* or *hisself.* You never use *done* all by itself as the verb in the sentence. These expressions come from various regional accents and customs (similar to the one that makes New Yorkers shop at a store on *Toidy-toid and Toid* — Thirty-third and Third, for those of you from other parts of the world). Although saying *gotta* when you're chatting with a friend is perfectly okay, it isn't okay when you're speaking to a teacher, a boss, a television interviewer, the supreme ruler of the universe, and anyone else in authority. Thus,

> WRONG: You *gonna* wait for Cedric? He bought *hisself* a new car, and he might give us a ride.

RIGHT: *Are* you *going* to wait for Cedric? He bought a new car for himself, and he might give us a ride.

WRONG: No, I *gotta* go.

RIGHT: No, I *have to* go.

WRONG: We *done* nothing today! I'm not coming anymore. All we do is talk.

RIGHT: We *have done* nothing today! (or, We haven't done anything today!) I'm not coming anymore. All we do is talk.

WRONG: *Gotcha.* Next week we'll go bowling.

RIGHT: *I understand.* Next week we'll go bowling.

I'd add another sample conversation, but it's almost time for lunch. I gotta go.

Which sentence is correct?

A. According to the witness, the burglar is her, the one with the bright orange eyes!

B. According to the witness, the burglar is she, the one with the bright orange eyes!

Answer: Sentence B is correct if you're writing formally. *Is* is a linking verb and must be followed by a subject pronoun, *she.* Sentence A is acceptable in conversation.

Part II
Avoiding Common Errors

The 5th Wave   By Rich Tennant

"Your buddy says the two of you were peripheral
to the incident in question. You just said you were
superficial to the incident. Now which is it,
peripheral or superficial?!"

In this part . . .

Want to build a castle? You can build one using only chunky squares, but how much more interesting it is to throw in cones, arches, and a banner or two! Communication is the same way. To express yourself with any flair, you want to add descriptions to your sentences. In this part, I explain the parts of speech involved in creating descriptions — adjectives and adverbs. I also tackle prepositions, mostly short words that are long on trouble. This part also contains a field guide to the pronoun, a useful little part of speech that resembles a World War II minefield when it comes to error possibilities. Finally, I delve a little further into the complexities of subject–verb agreement, also a trouble magnet. Never fear: I provide a flak jacket's worth of tricks for understanding these grammar rules.

Chapter 7

Do You Feel Bad or Badly? The Lowdown on Adjectives and Adverbs

- -

In This Chapter

▶ Identifying adjectives and adverbs

▶ Deciding whether an adjective or an adverb is appropriate

▶ Placing descriptive words so that the sentence means what you intend

- -

*W*ith the right nouns (names of persons, places, things, or ideas) and verbs (action or being words) you can build a pretty solid foundation in a sentence. The key to expressing your precise thoughts is to build on that foundation by adding descriptive words to your sentence. In this chapter I explain the two basic types of descriptive words of the English language — the parts of speech known as *adjectives* and *adverbs.* I also show you how to use each properly.

Clarifying Meaning with Descriptions

In case you doubt the significance of descriptive words, take a look at this sentence:

> Gloria sauntered past Lord and Taylor's when the sight of a Ferragamo Paradiso Pump paralyzed her.

What must the reader know in order to understand this sentence fully? Here's a list:

✔ The reader should know that Lord and Taylor's is a department store.

✔ The reader should be able to identify Ferragamo as an upscale shoe label.

> ✔ The reader should be familiar with a Paradiso Pump (a shoe style I made up).
>
> ✔ The reader should know that a pump is a type of shoe.
>
> ✔ A good vocabulary — one that includes *saunter* and *paralyze* — is helpful.

If all of those pieces are in place, or if the reader has a good imagination and the ability to use context clues in reading comprehension, your message will get through. But sometimes you can't trust the reader to understand the specifics of what you're trying to say. In that case, descriptions are quite useful. Here's Gloria, version 2:

> Gloria walked *slowly* past the *stately* Lord and Taylor's *department* store when the sight of a *fashionable, green, low-heeled dress* shoe with the *ultra-chic Ferragamo* label paralyzed her.

Okay, I overdid it a bit, but you get the point. The descriptive words clarify the meaning of the sentence, particularly for the fashion-challenged. As you see, adjectives and adverbs are useful, and you should know how to tuck them into your sentences.

Both adjectives and adverbs enhance the meaning of your sentences, but these parts of speech aren't interchangeable. Standardized tests capitalize on that fact by asking questions that require you to spot adjectives and adverbs used incorrectly. For example, you may see a sentence containing "real pretty." You need to know that *real* should be *really.* Not to worry: after you've read this chapter, you'll ace this sort of question.

Adding Adjectives

An *adjective* is a descriptive word that changes the meaning of a noun or a pronoun. An adjective adds information on number, color, type, and other qualities to your sentence.

Where do you find adjectives? In the adjective aisle of the supermarket. Okay, you don't. Most of the time you find them in front of the word they're describing. Keep in mind, however, that adjectives can also roam around a bit. Here's an example:

> George, *sore* and *tired,* pleaded with Lulu to release him from the headlock she had placed on him when he called her *"fragile."*

Sore and *tired* tells you about *George. Fragile* tells you about *her.* (Well, *fragile* tells you what George thinks of *her.* Lulu actually works out with free weights every day and is anything but fragile.) As you can see, these descriptions come after the words they describe, not before.

Adjectives describing nouns

The most common job for an adjective is describing a noun. Consider the adjectives *poisonous, angry,* and *rubber* in these sentences. Then decide which sentence you would like to hear as you walk through the jungle.

> There is a *poisonous* snake on your shoulder.
>
> There is an *angry, poisonous* snake on your shoulder.
>
> There is a *rubber* snake on your shoulder.

The last one, right? In these three sentences, those little descriptive words certainly make a difference. *Angry, poisonous,* and *rubber* all describe *snake,* and all of these descriptions give you information that you would really like to have. See how diverse and powerful adjectives can be?

Find the adjectives in this sentence.

> With a sharp ax, the faithful watchman parted the greasy hair of the seven ugly burglars.

Answer: *sharp* (describing *ax*), *faithful* (describing *watchman*), *greasy* (describing *hair*), *seven* and *ugly* (describing *burglars*).

Adjectives describing pronouns

Adjectives can also describe *pronouns* (words that substitute for nouns). When they're giving you information about pronouns, adjectives usually appear after the pronoun they're describing:

> There's something *strange* on your shoulder. (The adjective *strange* describes the pronoun *something.*)
>
> Everyone *conscious* at the end of Ronald's play made a quick exit. (The adjective *conscious* describes the pronoun *everyone.*)
>
> Anyone *free* should report to the meeting room immediately! (The adjective *free* describes the pronoun *anyone.*)

Attaching adjectives to linking verbs

Adjectives may also follow linking verbs, in which case they describe the subject of the sentence. To find an adjective after a linking verb, ask the question *what.* (See Chapter 6 for more information.)

Just to review for a moment: *Linking verbs* join two ideas, associating one with the other. These verbs are like giant equal signs, equating the subject — which comes before the verb — with another idea after the verb. (See Chapter 2 for a full discussion of linking verbs.)

Sometimes a linking verb joins an adjective (or a couple of adjectives) and a noun:

> Lulu's favorite dress is *orange* and *purple.* (The adjectives *orange* and *purple* describe the noun *dress.*)
>
> The afternoon appears *gray* because of the nuclear fallout from Roger's cigar. (The adjective *gray* describes the noun *afternoon.*)
>
> George's latest jazz composition sounds *awful.* (The adjective *awful* describes the noun *composition.*)

Articles: Not just for magazines

If you ran a computer program that sorted and counted every word in this book, you'd be on the fast track for membership in the Get-a-Life Club. You'd also find that *articles,* a branch on the adjective family tree, are the most common words, even though the article-branch includes only *a, an,* and *the.*

> Melanie wants *the* answer, and you'd better be quick about it.

This statement means that Melanie is stuck on problem 12, and her mother won't let her go out until her homework is finished. A really good movie is playing at the cineplex, and now she's on the phone, demanding *the* answer to number 12.

> Melanie wants *an* answer, and you'd better be quick about it.

This statement means that Melanie simply has to have a date for the prom. She asked you a week ago, but if you're not going to be her escort, she'll ask someone else. She's lost patience, and she doesn't even care anymore whether you go or not. She just wants *an* answer.

To sum up: Use *the* when you're speaking specifically and *an* or *a* when you're speaking more generally.

A apple? An book? A precedes words that begin with consonant sounds (all the letters except *a, e, i, o,* and *u*). *An* precedes words beginning with the vowel sounds *a, e, i,* and *o.* The letter *u* is a special case. If the word sounds like *you,* choose *a.* If the word sounds like someone kicked you in the stomach — *uh* — choose *an.* Another special case is the letter *h.* If the word starts with a hard *h* sound, as in *horse,* choose *a.* If the word starts with a silent letter *h,* as in *herb,* choose *an.* Here are some examples:

> an aardvark (a = vowel)
>
> a belly (b = consonant)
>
> an egg (e = vowel)
>
> a UFO (*U* sounds like *you*)
>
> an unidentified flying object (*u* sounds like *uh*)
>
> a helmet (hard *h*)
>
> an hour (silent *h*)

Special note: Sticklers-for-rules say *an historic event.* The rest of us say *a historic event.*

Pop the question: Identifying adjectives

To find adjectives, go to the words they describe — nouns and pronouns. Start with the noun and ask it three questions. (Not "What's the new hot stock?" or "Will you marry me?" This is grammar, not life.) Here are the three questions:

✔ How many?

✔ Which one?

✔ What kind?

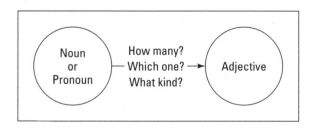

Take a look at this sentence:

> George placed three stolen atomic secrets inside his cheese burrito.

You see three nouns: *George, secrets,* and *burrito.* George has led a colorful life, but you can't find the answer to the following questions: How many *Georges?* Which *George?* What kind of *George?* No words in the sentence provide that information, so no adjectives describe *George.*

But try these three questions on *secrets* and *burrito* and you do come up with something: How many *secrets?* Answer: *three. Three* is an adjective. Which *secrets?* What kind of *secrets?* Answer: *stolen* and *atomic. Stolen* and *atomic* are adjectives. The same goes for *burrito:* What kind? Answer: *cheese. Cheese* is an adjective.

You may have noticed that *his* answers one of the questions. (Which *burrito?* Answer: *his burrito.*) *His* is working as an adjective, but *his* is also a pronoun. Normal people don't have to worry about whether *his* is a pronoun or an adjective. Only English teachers care, and they divide into two camps — the adjective camp and the pronoun camp. Needless to say, each group feels superior to the other. (I'm a noncombatant. As far as I'm concerned, you can call *his* a parakeet for all I care.)

Look at another sentence:

> The agonized glance thrilled George's rotten, little, hard heart.

This sentence has three nouns. One *(George's)* is possessive. If you ask how many *George's,* which *George's,* or what kind of *George's,* you get no answer. The other two nouns, *glance* and *heart,* do yield an answer. What kind of *glance? Agonized glance.* What kind of *heart? Rotten, little, hard heart.* So *agonized, rotten, little,* and *hard* are all adjectives.

You may notice that a word changes its part of speech depending upon how it's used in the sentence. In the last example sentence, *glance* is a noun because *glance* is clearly a thing. Compare that sentence to this one:

> George and Lulu *glance* casually at the giant television screen.

Here *glance* is not a thing; it is an action that George and Lulu are performing. In this example sentence, *glance* is a verb. Bottom line: read the sentence, see what the word is doing, and then — if you like — give it a name.

A common error changes nouns into adjectives — improperly! The word *quality,* for example, is a noun meaning *worth, condition,* or *characteristic.* Some people, especially ad-writers, use *quality* as an adjective meaning *good* or *luxurious.* Grammatically, you can't buy a *quality television.* You can buy a *high-quality television.*

Stalking the Common Adverb

Adjectives aren't the only descriptive words. Adverbs — words that alter the meaning of a verb, an adjective, or another adverb — are another type of description. Check these out:

The boss *regretfully* said no to Phil's request for a raise.

The boss *furiously* said no to Phil's request for a raise.

The boss *never* said no to Phil's request for a raise.

If you're Phil, you care whether the words *regretfully, furiously,* or *never* are in the sentence. *Regretfully, furiously,* and *never* are all adverbs. Notice how adverbs add meaning in these sentences:

Lola *sadly* sang George's latest song. (Perhaps Lola is in a bad mood.)

Lola sang George's latest song *reluctantly.* (Lola doesn't want to sing.)

Lola *hoarsely* sang George's latest song. (Lola has a cold.)

Lola sang George's latest song *quickly.* (Lola is in a hurry.)

Lola sang even George's latest song. (Lola sang everything, and with George's latest, she hit the bottom of the barrel.)

Pop the question: Finding the adverb

Adverbs mostly describe verbs, giving more information about an action. Nearly all adverbs — enough so that you don't have to worry about the ones that fall through the cracks — answer one of these four questions:

✔ How?

✔ When?

✔ Where?

✔ Why?

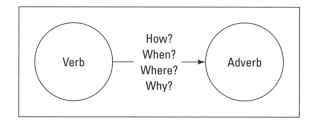

To find the adverb, go to the verb and pop the question. (See Chapter 2 for information on finding the verbs.) Look at this sentence:

> Ella secretly swiped Sandy's slippers yesterday and then happily went home.

You note two verbs: *swiped* and *went.* Take each one separately. *Swiped* how? Answer: *swiped secretly. Secretly* is an adverb. *Swiped* when? Answer: *swiped yesterday. Yesterday* is an adverb. *Swiped* where? No answer. *Swiped* why? Knowing Ella, I'd say she stole for the fun of it, but you find no answer in the sentence.

Go on to the second verb in the sentence. *Went* how? Answer: *went happily. Happily* is an adverb. *Went* when? Answer: *went then. Then* is an adverb. *Went* where? Answer: *went home. Home* is an adverb. *Went* why? Probably to drink champagne out of the slippers, but again, you find no answer in the sentence.

Here's another example:

> Eggworthy soon softly snored and delicately slipped away.

You identify two verbs again: *snored* and *slipped.* First one up: *snored. Snored* how? Answer: *snored softly. Softly* is an adverb. *Snored* when? Answer: *snored soon. Soon* is an adverb. *Snored* where? No answer. *Snored* why? No answer again. Now for *slipped. Slipped* how? Answer: *slipped delicately. Delicately* is an adverb. *Slipped* where? Answer: *slipped away. Away* is an adverb. *Slipped* when? No answer. *Slipped* why? No answer. The adverbs are *soon, delicately,* and *away.*

Adverbs can be lots of places in a sentence. If you're trying to find them, rely on the questions *how, when, where,* and *why,* not the location. Similarly, a word may be an adverb in one sentence and something else in another sentence. Check out this example:

> Gloria went *home* in a huff because of that slammed door.
>
> *Home* is where the heart is, unless you are in George's cabin.
>
> *Home* plate is the umpire's favorite spot.

In the first example, *home* tells you where Gloria went, so *home* is an adverb in that sentence. In the second example, *home* is a place, so *home* is a noun in that sentence. In the third example, *home* is an adjective, telling you what kind of *plate.*

Final answer: pop the question and see if you reveal an adverb, adjective, or another part of speech.

Adverbs describing adjectives and other adverbs

Adverbs also describe other descriptions, usually making the description more or less intense. (A description describing a description? Give me a break! But it's true.) Here's an example:

> An extremely unhappy Larry flipped when his trust fund tanked.

How *unhappy?* Answer: *extremely unhappy. Extremely* is an adverb describing the adjective *unhappy.*

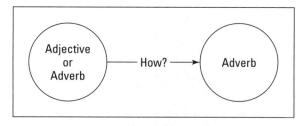

Sometimes the questions you pose to locate adjectives and adverbs are answered by more than one word in a sentence. In the previous example sentence, if you ask, "*Seemed* when?" the answer is *when his trust fund tanked.* Don't panic. These longer answers are just different members of the adjective and adverb families. For more information, see Chapters 8 and 24.

Now back to work. Here's another example:

> When he began to speak, Larry's very talkative pet frog *wouldn't stop.*

How *talkative?* Answer: *very talkative. Very* is an adverb describing the adjective *talkative.*

And another:

> Larry's frog croaked *quite hoarsely.*

This time an adverb is describing another adverb. *Hoarsely* is an adverb because it explains how the frog *croaked.* In other words, *hoarsely* describes the verb *croaked.* How *hoarsely?* Answer: *quite hoarsely. Quite* is an adverb describing the adverb *hoarsely,* which in turn describes the verb *croaked.*

Choosing Between Adjectives and Adverbs

Does it matter whether a word is an adjective or an adverb? Some of the time, no. In your crib, you demanded, "I want a bottle NOW, Mama." You didn't know you were adding an adverb to your sentence. For that matter, you didn't know you were making a sentence! You were just hungry. Now that you're past the crib stage, you should know the difference between these two parts of speech so you can select the form you need. Here are some guidelines:

- **Many adverbs end in –ly.** *Strictly* is an adverb, and *strict* is an adjective. *Nicely* is an adverb, and *nice* is an adjective. *Generally* is an adverb, and *general* is an adjective. *Lovely* is a . . . gotcha! You were going to say *adverb,* right? Wrong. *Lovely* is an adjective. (That's why I started this paragraph with *many,* not *all.*)

- **Some adverbs don't end in –ly.** *Soon, now, home, fast,* and many other words that don't end in *-ly* are adverbs, too.

- **One of the most common adverbs, *not*, doesn't end in ly.** *Not* is an adverb because it reverses the meaning of the verb from positive to negative. Loosely speaking, *not* answers the question *how.* (*How* are you going to the wedding? Oh, you're *not* going!)

While I'm speaking of *not,* I should remind you to avoid double negatives. In many languages (Spanish, for example), doubling or tripling the negative adjectives and adverbs or throwing in a negative pronoun or two simply makes your denial stronger. In Spanish, saying, "I did not kill no victim" is okay. In English, however, that sentence is a confession, because if you *did not* kill *no* victim, you killed at least *one* victim. (Other types of double negatives may trip you up. See Chapter 22 for more information.)

- **The best way to tell if a word is an adverb is to ask the four adverb questions: *how, when, where,* and *why.*** If the word answers one of those questions, it's an adverb.

Identify the adjectives and adverbs in the following sentences.

A. Thank you for the presents you gave us yesterday.

B. The lovely presents you gave us smell like old socks.

C. The presents you kindly gave us are very rotten.

Answers: In sentence A, *yesterday* is an adverb, describing when *you gave* the presents. In sentence B, *lovely* is an adjective describing the noun *presents*. *Old* is an adjective describing *socks*; sentence B has no adverbs. In sentence C, the adverb is *kindly* and it describes the verb *gave*. Also in sentence C, the adverb *very* describes the adjective *rotten*. *Rotten* is an adjective describing *presents*.

Try one more. Find the adjectives and adverbs.

> The carefully decorated purse that Bob knitted is already fraying around the edges.

Answers: The adverb *carefully* describes the adjective *decorated*. The verb *is fraying* is described by the adverb *already*.

Remember: Adjectives describe nouns or pronouns, and adverbs describe verbs, adjectives, or other adverbs.

Sorting out "good" and "well"

If I am ever elected president of the universe, one of the first things I'm going to do (after I get rid of apostrophes — see Chapter 11) is to drop all irregular forms. Until then, you may want to read about *good* and *well*.

Good is an adjective, and *well* is an adverb, except when you're talking about your health:

> I am *good.*

Good is an adjective here. The sentence means *I have the qualities of goodness* or *I am in a good mood.* Or, the sentence is a really bad pickup line.

> I am *well.*

Well is an adjective here. The sentence means *I am not sick.*

> I play the piano *well.*

This time *well* is an adverb. It describes how I play. In other words, the adverb well describes the verb *play.* The sentence means that I don't have to practice anymore.

Which sentence is correct?

A. When asked how he was feeling, Larry smiled at his ex-girlfriends and replied, "Not well."

B. When asked how he was feeling, Larry smiled at his ex-girlfriends and replied, "Not good."

Answer: Sentence A is correct because Larry's ex-girlfriends are inquiring about his health.

Try one more. Which sentence is correct?

A. Eggworthy did not perform good on the crash test.

B. Eggworthy did not perform well on the crash test.

Answer: Sentence B is correct because the adverb *well* describes the verb *did perform. Did perform* how? Answer: *did perform well.*

Dealing with "bad" and "badly"

Bad is a bad word, at least in terms of grammar. Confusing *bad* and *badly* is one of the most common errors. Check out these examples:

I felt badly.

I felt bad.

Remember the *–ly* test mentioned earlier in this chapter? If so, you know that *badly* is an adverb, and *bad* is an adjective. Which one should you use? Well, what are you trying to say? In the first sentence, you went to the park with your mittens on. The bench had a sign on it: "WET PAINT." The sign looked old, so you decided to check. You put your hand on the bench, but the mittens were in the way. You felt *badly* — that is, not very accurately. In the second sentence, you sat on the bench, messing up the back of your coat with dark green stripes. When you saw the stripes, you felt *bad* — that is, you were sad. In everyday speech, of course, you're not likely to express much about *feeling badly*. Few people walk around testing benches, and even fewer talk about their ability to feel something physically. So 99.99 percent of the time you feel *bad* — unless you're in a good mood.

Which sentence is correct?

A. Lola felt bad when she discovered a dent in her motorcycle.

B. Lola felt badly when she discovered a dent in her motorcycle.

Answer: Sentence A is correct. Lola loves her Harley, and every scratch and dent depresses her. Therefore "bad" is an adjective describing Lola (actually, Lola's state of mind). In sentence B, *badly* is an adverb, so it would have to describe Lola's ability to feel. That meaning makes no sense.

Try one more. Which sentence is correct?

A. Lola did bad in her negotiations with the insurance company.

B. Lola did badly in her negotiations with the insurance company.

Answer: Sentence B is correct because the adverb *badly* describes the verb *did. Did* how? Answer: *did badly.* (In other words, PayAll, Inc. stiffed Lola.)

Adjectives and adverbs that look the same

Odd words here and there (and they are odd) do double duty as both adjectives and adverbs. They look exactly the same, but they take their identity as adjectives or adverbs from the way that they function in the sentence. Take a look at these examples:

Upon seeing the stop sign, Abby stopped *short.* (adverb)

Abby did not notice the sign until the last minute because she is too *short* to see over the steering wheel. (adjective)

Lola's advice is *right:* Abby should not drive. (adjective)

Abby turned *right* after her last-minute stop. (adverb)

Abby came to a *hard* decision when she turned in her license. (adjective)

Lola tries *hard* to schedule some time for Abby, now that Abby's carless. (adverb)

The English language has too many adjectives and adverbs to list here. If you're unsure about a particular word, check the dictionary for the correct form.

Which sentence is correct?

A. It was real nice of you to send me that bouquet of poison ivy.

B. It was really nice of you to send me that bouquet of poison ivy.

Answer: B. How *nice? Really nice. Real* is an adjective and *really* is an adverb. Adverbs answer the question *how*.

Avoiding Common Mistakes with Adjectives and Adverbs

A few words — *even, almost, only, just, nearly* and others — often end up in the wrong spots. If these words aren't placed correctly, your sentence may say something that you didn't intend.

Standardized tests often include sentences misusing these adjectives and adverbs. Keep your eyes open and double-check every sentence with *even*, *almost*, *only*, *just*, and *nearly*.

Placing "even"

Even is one of the sneaky modifiers that can land any place in a sentence — and change the meaning of what you're saying. Take a look at this example:

It's two hours before the grand opening of the school show. Lulu and George have been rehearsing for weeks. They know all the dances, and Lulu has only one faint bruise left from George's tricky elbow maneuver. Suddenly, George's evil twin Lester, mad with jealousy, "accidentally" places his foot in George's path. George's down! His ankle is sprained! What will happen to the show?

✔ Possibility 1: Lulu shouts, "We can still go on! *Even Lester* knows the dances."

✔ Possibility 2: Lulu shouts, "We can still go on! Lester *even knows* the dances."

✔ Possibility 3: Lulu shouts, "We can still go on! Lester knows *even the dances.*"

What's going on here? These three statements look almost the same, but they aren't. Here's what each one means:

- ✔ Possibility 1: Lulu surveys the fifteen boys gathered around George. She knows that any one of them could step in at a moment's notice. After all, the dances are very easy. *Even Lester,* the clumsiest boy in the class, knows the dances. If *even Lester* can perform the role, it will be a piece of cake for everyone else.

- ✔ Possibility 2: Lulu surveys the fifteen boys gathered around George. It doesn't look good. Most of them would be willing, but they've been busy learning other parts. There's no time to teach them George's role. Then she spies Lester. With a gasp, she realizes that Lester has been watching George every minute of rehearsal. Although the curtain will go up very soon, the show can still be saved. Lester doesn't have to practice; he doesn't have to learn something new. Lester *even knows* the dances.

- ✔ Possibility 3: The whole group looks at Lester almost as soon as George hits the floor. Yes, Lester knows the words. He's been reciting George's lines for weeks now, helping George learn the part. Yes, Lester can sing; everyone's heard him. But what about the dances? There's no time to teach him. Just then, Lester begins to twirl around the stage. Lulu sighs with relief. Lester knows *even the dances.* The show will go on!

Got it? *Even* is a description; *even* describes the words that follow it. To put it another way, *even* begins a comparison:

- ✔ Possibility 1: *even* Lester (as well as everyone else)
- ✔ Possibility 2: *even* knows (doesn't have to learn)
- ✔ Possibility 3: *even* the dances (as well as the songs and words)

So here's the rule. Put *even* at the beginning of the comparison implied in the sentence.

Placing "almost" and "nearly"

Almost and nearly are tricky descriptions. Here's an example:

> Last night Lulu wrote for *almost* (or *nearly*) an hour and then went rollerblading.

and

> Last night Lulu *almost* (or *nearly*) wrote for an hour and then went rollerblading.

In the first sentence, Lulu wrote for 55 minutes and then stopped. In the second sentence, Lulu intended to write, but every time she sat down at the computer, she remembered that she hadn't watered the plants, called her best friend Lola, made a sandwich, and so forth. After an hour of wasted time and without one word on the screen, she grabbed her rollerblades and left.

Almost and *nearly* begin the comparison. Lulu *almost wrote* (or *nearly wrote*), but she didn't. Or Lulu wrote for *almost an hour* (or *nearly an hour*), but not for a *whole hour*. In deciding where to put these words, add the missing ideas and see whether the position of the word makes sense. (I discuss comparisons further in Chapter 20.)

Placing "only" and "just"

If only the word *only* were simpler to understand! If everyone thought about the word *just* for *just* a minute. Like the other tricky words in this section, *only* and *just* change the meaning of the sentence every time their positions are altered. Here are examples of *only* and *just* in action:

> *Only* (or *just*) Lex went to Iceland. (No one else went.)

> Lex *only* went to Iceland. (He didn't do anything else.)

> Lex *just* went to Iceland. (The ink on his passport is still wet. *Just* may mean *recently*.)

> Lex went *only* (or *just*) to Iceland. (He skipped Antarctica.)

Many people place *only* in front of a verb and assume that it applies to another idea in the sentence. I see t-shirts all the time with slogans like "My dad went to NYC and only bought me a lousy t-shirt." The *only* should be in front of *a lousy t-shirt* because the sentence implies that Dad should have bought more — the Empire State Building, perhaps. The original wording describes a terrible trip: zoom in from the airport, buy a t-shirt, and zoom back home.

Chapter 8

Small Words, Big Trouble: Prepositions

*H*ow does the proverb go? Little things mean a lot? Whoever said that was probably talking about prepositions. Some of the shortest words in the language — at least most of them — these little guys pack a punch in your sentences. Unfortunately, prepositions attract mistakes as powerfully as catnip captures the attention of the meow-set. In this chapter, I explain everything you always wanted to know about prepositions and show you how to avoid the pitfalls associated with them.

Proposing Relationships: Prepositions

Imagine that you encounter two nouns: *elephant* and *book*. (A *noun* is a word for a person, place, thing, or idea.) How many ways can you connect the two nouns to express different ideas?

the book *about* the elephant

the book *by* the elephant

the book *behind* the elephant

the book *in front of* the elephant

the book *near* the elephant

the book *under* the elephant

The italicized words relate two nouns to each other. These relationship words are called prepositions. *Prepositions* may be defined as any word or group of words that relates a noun or a pronoun to another word in the sentence.

Sometime during the last millennium when I was in grammar school, I had to memorize a list of prepositions. (How quaint, right? We had inkwells, too.) I was so terrified of Sister Saint Vincent, my seventh grade teacher, that not only did I learn the list, I made it part of my being. In fact, I can still recite it. I don't think memorizing prepositions is worth the time, but a familiarity would be nice. In other words, don't marry the preposition list. Just date it a few times. Take a look at Table 8-1 for a list of some common prepositions:

Table 8-1		Common Prepositions	
about	above	according to	across
after	against	along	amid
among	around	at	before
behind	below	beside	besides
between	beyond	by	concerning
down	during	except	for
from	in	into	like
of	off	on	over
past	since	through	toward
underneath	until	up	upon
with	within	without	

The Objects of My Affection: Prepositional Phrases and Their Objects

Prepositions never travel alone; they're always with an object. In the examples in the previous section, the object of each preposition is *elephant.* Just to get all the annoying terminology over with at once, a *prepositional phrase* consists of a preposition and an object. The object of a preposition is always a noun or a pronoun, or perhaps one or two of each. (A *pronoun* is a word that takes the place of a noun, such as *him* for *Eggworthy, it* for *omelet,* and so forth.)

Here's an example:

> In the afternoon the snow pelted Eggworthy on his little bald head.

This sentence has two prepositions: *in* and *on. Afternoon* is the object of the preposition *in,* and *head* is the object of the preposition *on.*

DEMONS

Different Than? From? a Preposition

How many times have you heard this sentence?

> Prepositions are different than other parts of speech.

Okay, never. But I bet you've heard (and maybe used) the expression *different than* lots of times. I hate to break the bad news, but I must. *Different than* is never correct. What you want is *different from*.

You can stop reading right here because now you have all the information you need. If you absolutely have to know why *different than* is a no-no, continue on. Just be aware that the explanation relies on some technical and therefore annoying grammar points. Here goes: *than* is not a preposition. It's a *conjunction* — the part of speech that links two ideas. The catch is that *than* joins two ideas containing subject-verb combos. (One more grammar term: anything with a subject-verb pair is called a *clause*.) Here's a sentence in which *than* is used correctly:

> Tracy knows more prepositions than I do.

Did you notice the subject-verb pairs? *Tracy knows* and *I do*, one on each side of *than*, make this sentence correct. Now take a look at the same sentence, which is also correct:

> Tracy knows more prepositions than I.

I imagine you're yelling at me right now. I don't blame you. The portion of the sentence following *than* appears to lack a subject-verb pair. But appearances, as we all know, may be deceiving. In the preceding example sentence, *do* is understood. Grammatically, both example sentences are exactly the same.

From, on the other hand, is a preposition. It has an object, a noun, or a pronoun. (In rare cases, a clause may be an object of a preposition, but that sort of sentence isn't relevant when you're creating a *different from* sentence.) Here are a few correct *different from* sentences, with the object of the preposition italicized:

> A preposition is different from other *parts* of speech.

> Lola's new tattoo will be different from her previous fifteen *tattoos*.

> In a break with tradition, Levon's flight path yesterday differed from his usual *pattern*.

As I'm sure you detected, the last sentence turned *different* into *differed*. I threw in that one on purpose to show you that *from* is appropriate whether you're *different* or *differing* — that is, whether you're using an adjective (*different*) or a verb (any form of *to differ*).

Why, you may ask, is the object *head* and not *little* or *bald?* Sigh. I was hoping you wouldn't notice. Okay, here's the explanation. You can throw a few other things inside a prepositional phrase — mainly descriptive words. Check out these variations on the plain phrase *of the elephant:*

> of the *apologetic* elephant

> of the *always apoplectic* elephant

> of the *antagonizingly argumentative* elephant

Despite the different descriptions, each phrase is still basically talking about an *elephant*. Also, *elephant* is a noun, and only nouns and pronouns are allowed to be objects of the preposition. So in the *Eggworthy* sentence, you need to choose the most important word as the object of the preposition. Also, you need to choose a noun, not an adjective. Examine *his little bald head* (the words, not Eggworthy's actual head, which is better seen from a distance). *Head* is clearly the important concept, and *head* is a noun. Thus *head* is the object of the preposition.

Pop the question: Questions that identify the objects of the prepositions

All objects — of a verb or of a preposition — answer the questions *whom?* or *what?* To find the object of a preposition, ask *whom?* or *what?* after the preposition.

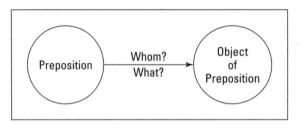

In this sentence you see two prepositional phrases:

> Marilyn thought that the selection of the elephant for the show was quite unfair.

The first preposition is *of. Of* what? *Of the elephant. Elephant* is the object of the preposition *of.* The second preposition is *for. For* what? For the *show. Show* is the object of the preposition *to.*

What is the object of the preposition in this sentence?

> The heroic teacher pounded the grammar rules into her students' tired brains.

Answer: *Brains* is the object of the preposition *into.* When you pop the question — *into* whom? or *into* what? — the answer is *her students' tired brains.* The most important word is *brains,* which is a noun.

In the group: Between/Among

Between and *among* are two tricky prepositions that are often used incorrectly. To choose the appropriate preposition, decide how many people or things you're talking about. If the answer is two, you want *between*, as in this sentence:

Lola was completely unable to choose *between* the biker magazine and *Poetry for Weightlifters*. (two magazines only)

If you're talking about more than two, *among* is the appropriate word:

Lola strolled *among* the parked motorcycles, reading poetry aloud. (more than two motorcycles)

One exception: Treaties are made *between* nations, even if more than two countries sign:

The treaty to outlaw bubble gum was negotiated *between* Libya, the United States, Russia, and Ecuador.

Why pay attention to prepositions?

When you're checking subject–verb pairs, you need to identify and then ignore the prepositional phrases. The prepositional phrases are distractions. If you don't ignore them, you may end up matching the verb to the wrong word. (See Chapter 10 for more information on subject–verb agreement.) You may also find it helpful to recognize prepositional phrases because sometimes, when you "pop the question" to find an adjective or an adverb, the answer is a prepositional phrase. Don't panic. You haven't done anything wrong. Simply know that a prepositional phrase may do the same job as a single-word adjective or adverb. (See Chapter 7 for more on adjectives and adverbs.)

You should also pay attention to prepositions because choosing the wrong one may be embarrassing:

Person 1: May I sit *next* to you?

Person 2: (smiling) Certainly.

Person 1: May I sit *under* you?

Person 2: (sound of slap) Help! Police!

A few questions in the SAT Writing and the ACT English tortures — sorry, I mean *tests* — revolve around prepositions. You may encounter a misused preposition (*to* instead of *with*, for example) or a situation in which another part of speech grabs a preposition's rightful spot (*different than* instead of *different from*, perhaps). The best preparation for preposition questions is

(a) a careful reading of this chapter and (b) general reading of good-quality writing. Why do I recommend quality writing? Language seeps into your brain when you read, and some of it stays there. If you're spending time with proper English, the correct use of prepositions simply sounds right. The reverse is also true. To heavy readers, preposition errors stand out like ukuleles in an opera.

Are You Talking to 1? Prepositions and Pronouns

A big preposition pitfall is pronouns. (Can you say that three times fast — without spitting?) A *pronoun* is a word that substitutes for a noun. The problem with pronouns is that only some pronouns are allowed to act as objects of prepositions; they're called *object pronouns*. (See Chapter 17 for details on pronoun-preposition rules.) Use the wrong pronoun as the object of a preposition — a non-object pronoun — and the grammar cops will be after you.

The object pronouns, cleared to act as objects of the preposition, are *me, you, him, her, it, us, them, whom,* and *whomever.*

Take a look at some sentences with *pronouns* as objects of the prepositions:

> Among Bill, Harry, and *me* there is no contest. (*Me* is one of the objects of the preposition *among.*)

> Without *them,* the bridge will fall out of Cedric's mouth. (*Them* is the object of the preposition *without* — also, in case you're wondering, it's a dental bridge, not the Golden Gate.)

> Lester added an amendment to the bill concerning us, but the bill did not pass. (*Us* is the object of the preposition *concerning.*)

What is one of the most common errors in the use of object pronouns? Is the correct prepositional phrase *between you and I* or *between you and me?* Answer: The correct expression is *between you and me. Between* = the preposition. *You and me* = the objects of the preposition. *Me* is an object pronoun. (*I* is a subject pronoun.) The next time you hear someone say *between you and I,* I expect you to recite the rule.

Which sentence is correct?

> A. According to Elton and she, the elephant's nose is simply too long.

> B. According to Elton and her, the elephant's nose is simply too long.

Answer: Sentence B is correct. *According to* is the preposition. The object of the preposition is *Elton and her. Her* is an object pronoun. (*She* is a subject pronoun.)

Most of the tough pronoun choices come when the sentence has more than one object of the preposition (*Elton and her,* for example, in the pop quiz). Your "ear" for grammar will probably tell you the correct pronoun when the sentence has a single pronoun object. You probably wouldn't say *according to she* because it sounds funny (to use a technical term).

If the sentence has more than one object of the preposition, try this rule of thumb — and I really mean thumb, at least when you're writing or looking for errors in someone else's writing. Take your thumb and cover one of the objects. Say the sentence. Does it sound right?

> According to Elton

Okay so far. Now take your thumb and cover the other object. Say the sentence. Does it sound right?

> According to she

Now do you hear the problem? Make the change:

> According to her

Now put the two back together:

> According to Elton and her

This method is not foolproof, but chances are good that you'll get a clue to the correct pronoun choices if you check the objects one by one.

A Good Part of Speech to End a Sentence With?

As I write this paragraph, global warming is increasing, the stock market is tanking, and the Yankees' pitching staff is in deep trouble. In the midst of all these earth-shattering events, some people still walk around worrying about where to put a preposition. Specifically, they (okay, I must admit that sometimes I, too) worry about whether or not ending a sentence with a preposition is acceptable. Let me illustrate the problem:

> Tell me whom he spoke *about.*

> Tell me *about* whom he spoke.

Interjections Are Easy!

If you've been reading *English Grammar For Dummies* in order and have gotten through this chapter, you've earned my undying devotion. You've also read something about every part of speech except one: interjections. I can't leave out one part of speech without giving up my membership in the Grammarians Club. *Interjections* are exclamations that often express intense emotion. These words or phrases aren't connected grammatically to the rest of the sentence. Check out these examples, in which the interjections are italicized:

Ouch. I caught my finger in the hatch of that submersible oceanographic vessel.

Curses, foiled again.

Yes! We've finally gotten to a topic that is foolproof.

Interjections may be followed by commas, but sometimes they're followed by exclamation points or periods. The separation by punctuation shows the reader that the interjection is a comment on the sentence, not a part of it. (Of course, in the case of the exclamation point or period, the punctuation mark also indicates that the interjection is not a part of the sentence at all.)

You can't do anything wrong with interjections, except perhaps overuse them. Interjections are like salt. A little salt sprinkled on dinner perks up the taste buds; too much sends you to the telephone to order take-out.

Here's the verdict: Both sentences are correct, at least for most people and even for most grammarians. But not, I must warn you, for all. If you're writing for someone who loves to tsk-tsk about the decline and fall of proper English, avoid placing a preposition at the end of a sentence. Otherwise, put the preposition wherever you like, including at the end of a sentence.

Chapter 9

Everyone Brought Their Homework: Pronoun Errors

In This Chapter

▶ Pairing pronouns with nouns

▶ Distinguishing between singular and plural pronouns

▶ Understanding possessive pronouns

▶ Selecting non-sexist pronouns

*P*ronouns are words that substitute for nouns. Even though they're useful, pronouns can also be pesky because English has many different types of pronouns, each governed by its own set of rules. (See Chapters 4 and 6 for information on subject and object pronouns.) In this chapter, I concentrate on how to avoid the most common errors associated with this part of speech.

Pairing Pronouns with Nouns

To get started on everything you need to know about pronouns, take a close look at how pronouns are paired with nouns. A pronoun's meaning can vary from sentence to sentence. Think of pronouns as the ultimate substitute teachers. One day they're solving quadratic equations, and the next they're doing push-ups in the gym. Such versatility comes from the fact that pronouns don't have identities of their own; instead, they stand in for nouns. In a few situations, pronouns stand in for other pronouns. I discuss pronoun–pronoun pairs later in this chapter.

To choose the appropriate pronoun, you must consider the word that the pronoun is replacing. The word that the pronoun replaces is called the pronoun's *antecedent*.

Identifying the pronoun–antecedent pair is really a matter of reading comprehension. If the sentence (or in some cases, the paragraph) doesn't make the pronoun–antecedent connection clear, the writing is faulty. Time to edit! But in most cases the meaning of the pronoun leaps off the page. Take a look at some examples:

> Hal stated *his* goals clearly: *He* wanted to take over the world. (The pronouns *his* and *he* refer to the noun *Hal.*)

> The lion with a thorn in *her* paw decided to wear sneakers the next time *she* went for a walk in the jungle. (The pronouns *her* and *she* in this sentence refer to the noun *lion.*)

> *Our* cause is just! Down with sugarless gum! *We* demand that all bubble gum be loaded with sugar! (The pronouns *our* and *we* refer to the speakers, who aren't named.)

> Tattered books will not be accepted because *they* are impossible to resell. (The pronoun *they* refers to the noun *books.*)

> Larry, *who* types five or six words a minute, is writing a new encyclopedia. (The pronoun *who* refers to *Larry.*)

> Ameba and *I* demand that the microscope be cleaned before *we* begin the exam. (The pronoun *I* refers to the speaker. The pronoun *we* refers to *Ameba and I.*)

When analyzing a sentence, you seldom find a noun that's been replaced by the pronouns *I* and *we*. The pronoun *I* always refers to the speaker and *we* refers to the speaker and someone else.

Similarly, the pronoun *it* sometimes has no antecedent:

> *It* is raining.

> *It* is obvious that Sylvia has not won the card-flipping contest.

In these sentences, *it* is just a place-filler, setting up the sentence for the true expression of meaning (First sample sentence: Take your umbrella and cancel the picnic. Second sample sentence: Sylvia's card-flipping hand is broken, and she has lost all her baseball cards.)

Sometimes the meaning of the pronoun is explained in a previous sentence:

> Ted's ice cream *cone* is cracked. I don't want *it*. (The pronoun *it* refers to the noun *cone*.)

Identify the pronouns and their antecedents in this paragraph:

Cedric arrived at his mother's charity ball, although it was snowing and no taxis had stopped to pick him up. When inside the ballroom, he glimpsed Lulu and her boyfriend dancing the tango. Their steps were strange indeed, for the orchestra was actually playing a waltz. As she sailed across the floor — her boyfriend had lost his grip — Lulu cried, "Help me!"

Answer: Cedric arrived at *his (Cedric's)* mother's charity ball, although *it* (no antecedent) was snowing and no taxis had stopped to pick *him (Cedric)* up. Once inside the ballroom, *he (Cedric)* glimpsed Lulu and *her (Lulu's)* boyfriend dancing the tango. *Their (Lulu and boyfriend's)* steps were strange indeed, for the orchestra was actually playing a waltz. As *she (Lulu)* sailed across the floor — *her (Lulu's)* boyfriend had lost *his (boyfriend's)* grip — Lulu cried, "Help *me!" (Lulu)*.

Choosing between Singular and Plural Pronouns

All pronouns are either singular or plural. Singular pronouns replace singular nouns, which are those that name *one* person, place, thing, or idea. Plural pronouns replace plural nouns — those that name *more than one* person, place, thing, or idea. (Grammar terminology has flair, doesn't it?) A few pronouns replace other pronouns; in those situations, singular pronouns replace other singular pronouns, and plurals replace plurals. You need to understand pronoun number — singulars and plurals — before you place them in sentences. Take a look at Table 9-1 for a list of some common singular and plural pronouns.

Table 9-1	Common Singular and Plural Pronouns
Singular	*Plural*
I	We
Me	Us
Myself	Ourselves
You	You
Yourself	Yourselves
He/She/It	They/Them
Himself/Herself/Itself	Themselves
Who	Who
Which	Which
That	That

Goldilocks and the three there's

They're putting all *their* bets on the horse over *there*. In other words, *there* is a place. *Their* shows ownership. *They're* is short for *they are*. Some examples:

"*They're* too short," muttered Eggworthy as he eyed the strips of bacon. (*They're* means *they are*.)

"Why don't you take some longer strips from *their* plates," suggested Lola. (The plates belong to *them* — expressed by the possessive pronoun *their*.)

"My arm is not long enough to reach over *there*," sighed Eggworthy. (*There* is a place.)

Notice that some of the pronouns in Table 9-1 do double duty; they take the place of both singular and plural nouns or pronouns. (You think this double duty is a good idea? Hah! Wait until you get to Chapter 10, when you have to match singular and plural subjects with their verbs.)

Most of the time choosing between singular and plural pronouns is easy. You're not likely to say

> Gordon tried to pick up the ski poles, but it was too heavy.

because *ski poles* (plural) and *it* (singular) don't match. Automatically you say

> Gordon tried to pick up the ski poles, but they were too heavy.

Matching *ski poles* with *they* should please your ear.

If you're learning English as a second language, your ear for the language is still in training. Put it on an exercise regimen of at least an hour a day of careful listening. A radio station or a television show in which reasonably educated people are speaking will help you to train your ear. You'll soon become comfortable hearing and choosing the proper pronouns.

Company and business names sometimes sound plural (Saks, Lord and Taylor, AT&T, and so forth). However, a company is just one company and is, therefore, a singular noun. When you refer to the company, use the singular pronoun *it* or *its*, not the plural pronouns *they* or *their*. Take a look at these sentences, in which the singular pronouns are italicized:

Dombey and Sons often sends *its* employees on business trips.

It is offering a free vacation in the Caribbean to all *its* clerks.

If a singular pronoun sounds strange, you may adjust the sentence to refer to the employees. Sometimes you cut the pronoun entirely. Here's an example:

STRANGE: I returned the sweater to Sheldon & Daughters Department Store, and it offered me a refund.

BETTER-SOUNDING BUT WRONG: I returned the sweater to Sheldon & Daughters Department Store, and they offered me a refund.

BETTER-SOUNDING AND RIGHT: I returned the sweater, and the sales representative offered me a refund.

Remember: pair singular pronouns with company names.

Two nouns — people and person — often confuse writers. *People* is plural and pairs with plural pronouns:

The people who scratched *their* names on the screen will be penalized.

Person is singular, as is any pronoun referring to *person*:

The person who left *his or her* chewing gum on the computer screen is in big trouble.

If you're writing a sentence similar to the preceding example, you may be tempted to match *their* with person. Resist the temptation. In Grammar World, singular and plural don't mingle, at least not legally. (Why *his or her*? Check out "Steering Clear of Sexist Pronouns" in this chapter for an explanation.)

Using Singular and Plural Possessive Pronouns

Possessive pronouns — those all-important words that indicate who owns what — also have singular and plural forms. You need to keep them straight. Table 9-2 helps you identify each type.

Do You Have an "Its" Problem?

I'm not talking about a poison-ivy rash that you need to scratch all the time. I'm talking about a possessive pronoun (*its*) and a contraction (*it's*). People who suffer from an *its* problem confuse the two words. Take heart: the remedy is simple. Just remember what each word means.

Its shows possession:

The computer has exploded, and *its* screen is now decorating the ceiling.

It's means *it is*:

It's raining cats and dogs, but I don't see any alligators.

So *it's* nice to know that grammar has *its* own rules. By the way, one of those rules is that *no possessive pronoun ever has an apostrophe.* Ever. Never. Never ever. Remember: If *it* owns something, dump the apostrophe.

Table 9-2	Singular and Plural Possessive Pronouns
Singular	*Plural*
my	our
mine	ours
your	your
yours	yours
his	their/theirs
her	their
hers	theirs
its	their
whose	whose

Positioning Pronoun–Antecedent Pairs

One way to lose a reader is to let your pronouns wander far from the words they refer to — their antecedents. To avoid confusion, keep a pronoun and its antecedent near each other. Often, but not always, they appear in the same sentence. Sometimes they're in different sentences. Either way, the idea is the same: If the antecedent of the pronoun is too far away, the reader or listener may become confused. Check out this example:

Bernie picked up the discarded *paper*. Enemy ships were all around, and the periscope's lenses were blurry. The sonar pings sounded like a Mozart sonata, and the captain's hangnails were acting up again. Yet even in the midst of such troubles, Bernie was neat. *It* made the deck look messy.

It? What's the meaning of *it?* You almost have to be an FBI decoder to find the partner of *it* (*paper*). Try the paragraph again.

Enemy ships were all around, and the periscope's lenses were blurry. The sonar pings sounded like a Mozart sonata, and the captain's hangnails were acting up again. Yet even in the midst of such troubles, Bernie was neat. He picked up the discarded *paper*. *It* made the deck look messy.

Now the antecedent and pronoun are next to each other. Much better!

Rewrite these sentences, moving the pronoun and antecedent closer together.

Bernie pulled out his handkerchief, given to him by Luella, the love of his life. He sniffed. His sinuses were acting up again. The air in the submarine was stale. He blew his nose. She was a treasure.

Answer: Several possibilities exist. The most important correction involves *Luella* and *she,* now too far apart. Here is one answer:

Bernie pulled out his handkerchief, given to him by Luella, the love of his life. She was a treasure. He sniffed. His sinuses were acting up again. The air in the submarine was stale. He blew his nose.

Some believe that position alone is enough to explain a pronoun–antecedent pairing. It's true that a pronoun is more likely to be understood if it's placed near the word it represents. In fact, you should form your sentences so that the pairs are neighbors. However, position isn't always enough to clarify the meaning of a pronoun. Standardized test writers want to know whether you can write clearly and express exact meaning, so they hit you with quite a few pronoun–antecedent problems.

The best way to clarify the meaning of a pronoun is to make sure that only one easily identifiable antecedent may be represented by each pronoun. If your sentence is about two females, don't use *she.* Provide an extra noun to clarify your meaning.

Look at this sentence:

Helena told her mother that she was out of cash.

Who is out of cash? The sentence has one pronoun — *she* — and two females (*Helena, Helena's mother*). *She* could refer to either of the two nouns.

The rule here is simple: Be sure that your sentence has a clear, understandable pronoun–antecedent pair. If you can interpret the sentence in more than one way, rewrite it, using one or more sentences until your meaning is clear:

> Helena said, "*Mom,* can I have your ATM card? I looked in the cookie jar and *you're* out of cash."

or

> Helena saw that her mother was out of cash and told her so.

What does this sentence mean?

> Alexander and his brother went to Arthur's birthday party, but he didn't have a good time.

  A. Alexander didn't have a good time.

  B. Alexander's brother didn't have a good time.

  C. Arthur didn't have a good time.

Answer: Who knows? Rewrite the sentence, unless you're talking to someone who was actually at the party and knows that Arthur got dumped by his girlfriend just before his chickenpox rash erupted and the cops arrived. If your listener knows all that, the sentence is fine. If not, here are a few possible rewrites:

> Alexander and his brother went to Arthur's party. Arthur didn't have a good time.

or

> Arthur didn't have a good time at his own birthday party, even though Alexander and his brother attended.

or

> Alexander and his brother went to Arthur's party, but Arthur didn't have a good time.

Matching Pronouns to Pronoun Antecedents

Most of the time, determining whether a pronoun should be singular or plural is easy. Just check the noun that acts as the antecedent, and bingo, you're done. But sometimes a pronoun takes the place of another pronoun. The pronouns being replaced are particularly confusing because they're singular, even though they look plural. In this section, I tackle the hard cases, showing you how to handle these tricky pronouns when they're antecedents. (The same pronouns sometimes cause problems with subject-verb agreement. Turn to Chapter 10 for the lowdown on this topic.)

Everyone, somebody, nothing, and similar pronouns

Everybody, somebody, and *no one* (not to mention *nothing* and *everyone*): These words should be barred from the English language. Why? Because matching these pronouns to other pronouns is a problem. If you match correctly, your choices sound wrong. But if you match incorrectly, you sound right. Sigh. Here's the deal. All of these pronouns are singular:

- The "ones": one, everyone, someone, anyone, no one.
- The "things": everything, something, anything, nothing.
- The "bodies": everybody, somebody, anybody, nobody.

These pronouns don't sound singular. *Everybody* and *everyone* appear to represent a crowd. Nevertheless, you're in singular territory with these pronouns. The logic (yes, logic applies, even though English grammar rules don't always bother with logic) is that *everyone* talks about the members of a group one by one. You follow this logic, probably unconsciously, when you choose a verb. You don't say,

> Everyone are here. Let the party begin!

You do say,

> Everyone is here. Let the party begin!

Picking the correct verb comes naturally, but picking the correct pronoun doesn't. Check out this pair:

> Everyone was asked to bring their bubble gum to the bubble-popping contest.

> Everyone was asked to bring his or her bubble gum to the bubble-popping contest.

Which one sounds right? The first one, I bet. Unfortunately, the second one is correct, formal English. The bottom line: When you need to refer to "ones," "things," "bodies" in formal English, choose singular pronouns to match (*he/she, his/her*) and avoid using *their*.

Which sentence is correct?

A. Matilda the lifeguard says that nobody should wear their earplugs in the pool in case shark warnings are broadcast.

B. Matilda the lifeguard says that nobody should wear his or her earplugs in the pool in case shark warnings are broadcast.

Answer: Sentence B is correct. *Nobody* is singular. *His or her* is singular. *Their* is plural. I know, I know, the sentence sounds horrible.

Once upon a time, sentence A would've been accepted, even by authors that English teachers love, such as Shakespeare and Jane Austen. A little more than 100 years ago, however, sentence A was arrested by the grammar police. Now B is correct and A is not. (In conversational English, sentence A abounds. Actually, it abounds in formal English also; it's wrong in both.)

Each and every

Each and every time I explain this rule, someone objects. As with *everybody*, which I explain in the preceding section, the proper use of *each* and *every* sounds wrong. These two pronouns are singular, and any pronouns that refer to *each* and *every* must be singular also. Check out these examples, in which I've italicized the pronouns referring to *each* and *every*:

> Each of the motorcycles should have *its* tires checked.

> Every motorcycle with leaky tires will have *its* inspection sticker removed.

> Every car, truck, and motorcycle on the road must display *its* inspection sticker on the windshield.

> Each of the owners must repair *his or her* motorcycle immediately.

Did you groan? Are you arguing with me? I understand. But I can't change the rule, which is based on the idea that *each* and *every* separate the members of the group into components. Any pronoun referring to *each* and *every* is actually referring to a member of the group, not to the group as a whole. Hence, you're in singular territory.

Which sentence is correct?

   A. Each of the computers popped its flash drive when the doughnut cream dripped in.

   B. Each of the computers popped their flash drives when the doughnut cream dripped in.

Answer: Sentence A is correct. The pronoun *its* refers to *each of the computers*. Think of *each* as converting a group of computers into *one computer*, followed by another, then another, and so on. Thus *its* — the singular pronoun — is correct.

Either and neither

These two pronouns sometimes share a park bench (sorry, I mean a *sentence*) with *or* and *nor*. In this section I don't deal with *either-or* and *neither-nor* combos. For that sort of sentence, turn to Chapter 10. Here I talk about *either* and *neither* alone, when these pronouns — and any pronouns referring to them — are always singular. In these sentences, the pronouns that refer to *either* and *neither* are italicized:

> Either of my daughters is willing to shave *her* head.

> Neither of the drill sergeants wants to deal with *his* fear of bald women.

> Either of the commanders must issue *his or her* order regulating hair length.

By the way, the last sentence assumes that you have a male and a female commander, or that you don't know whether the commanders are male, female, or a mixed pair. For more information on avoiding sexist pronouns, check out the next section.

Which sentence is correct?

   A. Neither of the shavers has had its battery changed.

   B. Neither of the shavers has had their battery changed.

Answer: Sentence A is correct. The pronoun *its* refers to *neither*, which is a singular pronoun.

Steering Clear of Sexist Pronouns

In preparing to write this section, I typed "pronoun + gender" into a Web search engine and then clicked "search." I wanted a tidbit or two from the Internet about the use of nonsexist language. I got more than a tidbit. In fact, I got over 700,000 hits. I can't believe that so many people are talking about pronouns! Actually, *talking* is not the appropriate word. *Arguing, warring, facing off, cursing,* and a few other less polite terms come to mind. Here's the problem. For many years, the official rule was that masculine terms (those that refer to men) could refer to men only or could be universal, referring to both men and women. This rule is referred to as the *masculine universal.* Here's an example. In an all-female gym class the teacher would say,

> Everyone must bring *her* gym shorts tomorrow.

and in an all-male gym class the teacher would say,

> Everyone must bring *his* gym shorts tomorrow.

Employing the masculine universal, in a mixed male and female gym class, the teacher would say,

> Everyone must bring *his* gym shorts tomorrow.

 Judging by the Internet, the battles over this pronoun issue aren't likely to be over in the near future. My advice? I think you should say *he or she* and *his or her* when grammar requires such terms. The masculine universal excludes females and may offend your audience.

To sum up: you may say,

> Everyone must bring *his or her* gym shorts.

or

> Everyone must bring *his* gym shorts.

or

> All the students must bring *their* gym shorts.

or

> Bring *your* gym shorts, *you* little creeps!

All these example sentences are grammatically correct.

Chapter 10

Just Nod Your Head: About Agreement

*H*ollywood filmmakers and about a million songwriters have tried to convince the public that opposites attract. Grammarians have clearly not gotten that message! Instead of opposites, the English language prefers matching pairs — singular with singular and plural with plural. Matching, in grammar terminology, is called *agreement*. In this chapter, I show you how to make subjects and verbs agree. I tackle this issue in a couple of tenses and in questions, and then I show you some special cases — treacherous nouns and pronouns that are often mismatched. By the way, this topic travels so often to the SAT Writing and ACT English tests that it should earn frequent flyer miles. Test-takers, take note!

Writing Singular and Plural Verbs

If you're a native speaker of English, your "ear" helps you correctly match singular and plural subjects to their verbs most of the time. But even if English isn't you're first language, you probably pair up lots of subjects and verbs correctly because most tenses use the same form for both singular and plural verbs. In this section, I show you the forms that don't change and the ones that do. (For more information on verb tenses, see Chapter 3.)

The unchangeables

When you're writing or speaking regular verbs in simple past, simple future, past perfect, and future perfect tense, this topic is almost a free pass. (Some of the progressive forms change; see the next section for more detail.) The non-progressive forms of these verbs don't change. Here are some examples, all with the regular verb *to snore,* of tenses that use the same form for both singular and plural subjects.

> Larry *snored* constantly, but his cousins *snored* only occasionally. (The simple past tense verb *snored* matches both the singular subject *Larry* and the plural subject *cousins.*)

> Ella *will snore* if she eats cheese before bedtime, but her bridesmaids *will snore* only after a meal containing sardines. (The simple future tense verb *will snore* matches both the singular subject *Ella* and the plural subject *bridesmaids.*)

> Cedric *had snored* long before his tonsils were removed. His pet tigers *had snored* nightly before Cedric upgraded their diet. (The past perfect verb *had snored* matches both the singular subject *Cedric* and the plural subject *tigers.*)

> By the time this chapter is over, Lola *will have snored* for at least an hour, and her friends *will have snored* for an even longer period. (The future perfect verb *will have snored* matches both the singular subject *Lola* and the plural subject *friends.*)

The changeables

Have you resolved to speak only in those unchanging tenses? Sorry! The other tenses are crucial to your communication skills. Fortunately, you need to know only a few principles to identify singular and plural verbs.

Simple present tenses

In simple present tense, nearly all the regular verb forms are the same for both singular and plural. If the subject of the sentence is *I, we,* or *you,* don't worry. They all use the same verb (*I snore, we snore, you snore*).

In choosing simple present tense verbs, you do have to be careful when the subject is a singular noun (*Lola, tribe, motorcycle,* or *loyalty,* for example) or a plural noun (such as *planes, trains,* and *automobiles*). You also have to be on your toes when the subject is a pronoun that replaces a singular noun (*he, she, it, another, someone,* and so forth). Finally, you have to take care when the subject is a pronoun that replaces a plural noun (perhaps *they, both,* or *several*). To boil all this down to a simpler rule: Be careful when your sentence is talking *about* someone or something.

When in Rome and Greece: Classical plurals

Granted, the Coliseum is a magnificent sight, and the Greek myths are pretty cool. But those languages! Thanks to the ancient Romans and Greeks, a number of English words form their plurals in an irregular way. Here are some singular/plural pairs:

✔ **Alumnus/alumni:** The singular, *alumnus,* is a masculine term. The plural, alumni, may refer to groups of males, or, if you accept the masculine term as universal, *alumni* may refer to both males and females. (See Chapter 9.)

✔ **Alumna/alumnae:** The singular, *alumna,* is a feminine term. The plural refers to groups of females.

✔ **Analysis/analyses:** *Analysis* is the singular, meaning "a course of psychological therapy" or, more generally, "a serious investigation or examination." The plural changes the *i* to *e.*

✔ **Parenthesis/parentheses:** (This sentence is in *parentheses,* but I try not to write with too many *parentheses* because readers find more than three *parentheses* confusing.)

✔ **Datum/data:** Technically, *data* is the plural of *datum* and takes a plural verb *(the data are clear).* However, more and more people are matching *data* with a singular verb *(the data is clear).* To impress all your grammarian friends, pair *data* with a plural verb.

✔ **Phenomenon/phenomena:** The singular term is *phenomenon,* a noun meaning "a marvel, a special occurrence or event." The plural term is *phenomena,* correct but so obscure nowadays that my computer thesaurus keeps trying to change it to *phenomenon.*

In sentences that talk about someone or something, the difference between the singular and plural forms of a regular verb is just one letter. The singular verb ends in *s* and the plural form doesn't. Here are some examples of simple present tense regular verbs:

Singular	*Plural*
the tiger *bites*	the tigers *bite*
Lulu *rides*	they *ride*
she *screams*	the boys *scream*
Lochness *burps*	both *burp*

Progressive tenses

Progressive tenses — those that contain an *-ing* verb form — may also cause singular/plural problems. These tenses rely on the verb *to be,* a grammatical weirdo that changes drastically depending on its subject. Just be sure to match the subject to the correct form of the verb *to be.* (See Chapter 3 for all the forms of *to be.*) Check out these examples — enough to satisfy a vampire — of progressive forms of the verb *to bite:*

- **Singular present progressive:** I *am biting,* you *are biting,* Dracula *is biting,* no one *is biting*

- **Plural present progressive:** We *are biting,* you *are biting,* the tigers *are biting,* they *are biting.*

- **Singular past progressive:** I *was biting,* you *were biting,* Dracula *was biting,* no one *was biting.*

- **Plural past progressive:** We *were biting,* you *were biting,* the tigers *were biting,* both *were biting.*

In case you're wondering about the future progressive, I'll mention the good news: This one never changes! Singular and plural forms are the same (I *will be biting,* we *will be biting,* and so on). No problems here.

Present perfect and future perfect tenses

The present perfect and future perfect tenses (both progressive and non-progressive) contain forms of the verb *to have.* Use *have* when the subject is *I, you,* or a plural noun or pronoun. Use *has* when you're talking about a singular noun or pronoun that may replace the singular noun. Some examples:

- **Singular present perfect:** I *have bitten,* I *have been biting,* you *have bitten,* you *have been biting,* Dracula *has bitten,* Lola *has been biting,* she *has bitten,* everyone *has been biting.*

- **Plural present perfect:** We *have bitten,* we *have been biting,* you *have bitten,* you *have been biting,* the tigers *have bitten,* the tigers *have been biting,* several *have bitten,* they *have been biting.*

You guys understand, don't you?

You may have noticed that the word *you* is both singular and plural. I can say, "You are crazy" to Eggworthy when he claims that bacon is low in fat. I can also say, "You are crazy" to all those people who think Martians constructed the pyramids. In either case, I use the plural form of the verb *(are).* The fact that *you* is both singular and plural may be responsible for the popularity of such terms as *you all, y'all, youse* (very big in New York City), *you guys* (ditto), and *you*

people. These terms are colorful but not correct in formal English. Use *you* for both singular and plural subjects, and if you care enough, make the meaning clear with context clues:

> Today you must all wear clothes to the Introduction to Nudism class because the heat is broken.

> "I must have you and only you!" cried Larry to his soon-to-be sixth wife.

Easier Than Marriage Counseling: Making Subjects and Verbs Agree

After you're able to tell a singular from a plural verb (see the previous section), you can concentrate on matchmaking. Remember that you must always pair singular subjects with singular verbs, and plural subjects with plural verbs. No mixing allowed. Check out these examples:

> The ugly duckling hates the mirrored room. (*duckling* = singular subject, *hates* = singular verb)

> The plastic elf is still sitting on the store shelf. (*elf* = singular subject, *is sitting* = singular verb)

> Hedge clippers are always a thoughtful gift. (*clippers* = plural subject, *are* = plural verb)

> We plan to redecorate next summer. (*we* = plural subject, *plan* = plural verb)

How did I know that the subject–verb pairs were either singular or plural? I determined the number of subjects performing the action and then matched the verbs.

Here are some steps to take in order to make sure that your subjects and verbs agree:

1. Pop the question to find the verb. (See Chapter 2.)
2. Pop the question to find the subject. (See Chapter 4.)
3. Determine whether the subject is singular or plural.
4. Match the appropriate verb: singular verb to singular subject, plural verb to plural subject.

Choosing Verbs for Two Subjects

Sentences with two subjects joined by *and* take a plural verb, even if each of the two subjects is singular. (Think of math: one + one = two. One subject + one subject = plural subject.)

Here are some sample sentences with subjects joined by the word *and:*

> The sofa and the pillow are very comfortable. (*sofa* + *pillow* = plural subject, *are* = plural verb)

The picture and its frame belong together. (*picture* + *frame* = plural subject, *belong* = plural verb)

Romance and garlic do not mix. (*romance* + *garlic* = plural subject, *do mix* = plural verb)

Which sentence is correct?

A. The judge and the jury have shown no mercy in these cases.

B. The judge and the jury has shown no mercy in these cases.

Answer: Sentence A is correct. The subject is plural (*judge and jury*) so a plural verb (*have shown*) is appropriate. In sentence B the verb (*has shown*) is singular.

The Question of Questions

Just to make subject–verb agreement even more complicated, English grammar shuffles a sentence around to form questions and often throws in a helping verb or two. (See Chapter 2 for more information on helping verbs.) More bad news: questions are formed differently in different tenses. In this section, I show you how to form singular and plural questions in each tense.

Present tense questions

Check out the italicized subjects and verbs in these questions:

Does the *ring* in Lulu's navel *rust* when she showers? (*ring* = singular subject, *does rust* = singular verb)

Do Larry and *Ella need* a good divorce lawyer? (*Larry* + *Ella* = plural subject, *do need* = plural verb)

You've probably figured out that the verbs in these questions are formed by adding *do* or *does* to the main verb. *Do* matches all plurals as well as the singular subjects *I* and *you*. *Does* is for all other singular subjects. That's the system for most present tense questions. (Questions formed with the verb *to be* don't need *do* or *does*.) When *do* or *does* is used to form a question, the main verb doesn't change. So when checking subject–verb agreement in present-tense questions, be sure to note the helping verb — *do* or *does*.

Just for comparison, here are a couple of questions with the verb *to be:*

Is grammar in style right now? (*grammar* = singular subject, *is* = singular verb)

Am I a good grammarian? (*I* = singular subject, *am* = singular verb)

Are the *grammarians analyzing* that sentence? (*grammarians* = plural subject, *are analyzing* = plural verb)

Change this statement into a question:

Ella meets Larry's parents today.

Answer: *Does* Ella *meet* Larry's parents today? *Ella* is a singular subject. To form the question, add the helping verb *does.*

Past tense questions

Past tense questions make use of the helping verb *did.* I imagine you'll cheer when you hear that *did* forms both singular and plural questions. Questions with the verb *to be* (always a maverick) don't need helping verbs, but the order changes. Here are some examples of past tense questions:

Did Zoe play the same song for eight hours? (*Zoe* = singular subject, *did play* = singular past tense verb)

Did the *grammarians complain* about that question? (*grammarians* = plural subject, *did complain* = plural past tense verb)

Was Lola on the Committee to Combat Body Piercing? (*Lola* = singular subject, *was* = singular past tense verb)

Were the villagers angry about the new tax? (*villagers* = plural subject, *were* = plural verb)

Change this statement into a question.

Ella and Larry *printed* the invitations.

Answer: *Did* Ella and Larry *print* the invitations? To form the past tense question, add the helping verb *did.*

Future tense questions

Once again, this topic is a free pass when it comes to singular and plural questions. The future tenses already have helping verbs, so no additions are necessary. Here's the best part: The helping verbs are the same for both singular and plural subjects. Read these sample future tense questions:

Will Lola and *Lulu* ever *see* the error of their ways? (*Lola* and *Lulu=* plural subject, *will see* = plural future tense verb)

Will George be seeing you in all the old familiar places? (*George* = singular subject, *will be seeing* = singular future tense verb)

Will both of you *be ordering* another dessert? (*both* = plural subject, *will be ordering* = plural future tense verb)

Negative Statements and Subject–Verb Agreement

Some present-tense negative statements are also formed by adding *do* or *does,* along with the word *not,* to a main verb. The *not* squeezes itself between the helper (*do* or *does*) and the main verb. Remember that *does* is always singular. The helping verb *do* may be paired with the singular subjects *I* and *you. Do* is also used with all plural subjects. Here are some examples:

Larry does not *drive* a sports car because he wants to project a wholesome image. (*Larry* = singular subject, *does drive* = singular present tense verb)

The killer *bees do* not *chase* Roger because they are afraid of him. (*bees* = plural subject, *do chase* = plural present tense verb)

I do not *want* to learn anything else about verbs ever again. (*I* = singular subject, *do want* = singular present tense verb)

You do not *dance* like that in this club! (*You* = singular or plural subject, *do dance* = singular or plural present tense verb.)

One more joyous thought: To form past tense negative statements, the helping verb *did* is all you need for both singular and plural subjects:

Roger did not *dance* all night. (*Roger* = singular subject, *did dance* = singular past tense verb*)*

Lola and *Lulu did* not *send* a package of killer bees to Roger. (*Lola* and *Lulu* = plural subject, *did send* = plural past tense verb)

Negative statements in the future tense questions are even easier. You don't need additional helping verbs, and the helping verbs (*shall* or *will*) are the same for both singular and plural:

Roger will not *write* a thank-you note to Lola. (*Roger* = singular subject, *will write* = singular future tense verb)

The killer *bees will* not *shy* away from Larry. (*bees* = plural subject, *will shy* = plural future tense verb)

Change this statement into a negative (opposite).

George gave me help during the grammar test.

Answer: George *did* not *give* me help during the grammar test. You form the negative with the helping verb *did*.

The Distractions: Prepositional Phrases and Other Irrelevant Words

Subjects and their verbs are like parents and babies on a stroll through the park; they always travel together. A passerby cooing at a baby may catch the kid's attention, but ultimately the passerby is a distraction — irrelevant to the essential parent-child bond. The sentence world has lots of passersby that show up, slip between a subject and its verb, and distract you. The best strategy is to identify distractions and then cross them out (at least mentally) to get to the bare bones of the sentence — the subject–verb pair.

The most common distractions, but not the only ones, are prepositional phrases. A *prepositional phrase* contains a preposition (*on, to, for, by,* and so on) and an object of the preposition (a noun or pronoun). These phrases may contain some descriptive words as well. Other distractions may be clauses or participles. (For more information on prepositional phrases, see Chapter 8. I cover clauses and participles in Chapter 24.)

In the following sentences, I added some camouflage. The distractions (not all prepositional phrases) are italicized.

> The accountant *with 10,000 clients and only two assistants* works way too hard. (*accountant* = subject, *works* = verb)

In this sentence, *accountant* is the singular subject. If you pay attention to the prepositional phrase, you may incorrectly focus on *clients* and *assistants* as the subject — both plural words.

> The FBI agent, *fascinated by my last three tax returns,* is ruining my vacation plans. (*agent*= subject, *is ruining* = verb)

By ignoring the distracting phrase about my tax returns in this sentence, you can easily pick out the singular subject–verb pair.

> The deductions, *not the tax rate,* are a problem. (*deductions* = subject, *are* = verb)

In this sentence, *deductions* is the plural subject. If you let yourself be distracted, you may incorrectly match your verb to *rate,* which is singular.

Final answer: Ignore all distracting phrases, and find the true subject–verb pair. Also, if any IRS employees are reading this book, please ignore my tax returns.

Which sentence is correct?

A. The boy in the first row, along with all the girls throwing spitballs, is ignoring the teacher.

B. The boy in the first row, along with all the girls throwing spitballs, are ignoring the teacher.

Answer: Sentence A is correct. The subject is *boy.* The boy *is ignoring. Along with all the girls throwing spitballs* is a distraction (in this case, a prepositional phrase).

Another: Which sentence is correct?

A. The girl in the last row, but not the football players in the hall, are firing spitballs at the teacher.

B. The girl in the last row, but not the football players in the hall, is firing spitballs at the teacher.

Answer: Sentence B is correct. The subject is *girl.* The verb must therefore be singular *(is firing).* Ignore the words between the commas; they're distractions and don't affect the subject–verb match.

Can't We All Just Get Along? Agreement with Difficult Subjects

Every family has at least one "difficult" relative — the one nobody wants to sit with on Thanksgiving. In this respect, English grammar resembles a family. Sadly, you can't dump your crazy relatives, nor can you ignore the difficult subject–verb scenarios I describe here.

Five puzzling pronouns as subjects

Earlier in this chapter, I told you to ignore prepositional phrases. Now I must confess that this rule has one small exception — well, five small exceptions. Five pronouns — five little words that just have to stir up trouble — change from singular to plural because of the prepositional phrases that follow them. The five troublemaking pronouns are

- ✔ any
- ✔ all
- ✔ most
- ✔ none
- ✔ some

A good way to remember these five important words is with this nonsense sentence. (What? You say all the sentences in *English Grammar For Dummies* are nonsense sentences? Thanks for the compliment.) Anyway, remember these pronouns, if you like, with this sentence:

> Alice's aunt makes nice salads. (*Alice's* = any, *aunt*= all, *makes* = most, *nice* = none, *salads* = some)

Here they are with some prepositional phrases and verbs. Notice how the prepositional phrase affects the verb number.

Singular	**Plural**
any of the information is	*any* of the magazines are
all of the pie is	*all* of the shoes are
most of the city is	*most* of the pencils are
none of the pollution is	*none* of the toenails are
some of the speech is	*some* of the politicians are

See the pattern? For these five words, the prepositional phrase is the determining factor. If the phrase refers to a plural idea, the verb is plural. If the phrase refers to a singular idea, the verb is singular.

Here and there you find problems

A variation on unusual word order is a sentence beginning with *here* or *there*. In the examples below, the subject–verb pairs are italicized:

> Here *is* the *baby parakeet* that just bumped his head on the window.

> There *are* no flying *schools* for birds.

As you see, the words *here* and *there* aren't italicized. These words are never subjects! The true subject in this type of sentence comes after the verb, so that's where you look when you're making a subject–verb match.

The ones, the things, and the bodies

In Chapter 9, I explain how to pair up the *ones,* the *things,* and the *bodies* — families of pronouns that delight in mischief-making — with other pronouns. Here I concentrate on verbs. Take a peek at the family tree:

The ones: *one, everyone, someone, anyone, no one*

The things: *everything, something, anything, nothing*

The bodies: *everybody, somebody, anybody, nobody*

These pronouns are always singular, even if they're surrounded by prepositional phrases that express plurals. These pronouns must be matched with singular verbs. Take a look at these examples:

So everybody *is* happy because *no one has caused* any trouble, and *anything goes.*

Anyone in the pool of candidates for dogcatcher *speaks* better than Lulu.

One of the million reasons to hate you *is* your tendency to split infinitives.

Not *one* out of a million spies *creates* as much distraction as George.

Each and every mistake is painful

Two other pronouns, which I explain in relation to pronoun/antecedent agreement in Chapter 9, are also a pain when the issue is subject/verb agreement. *Each* and *every* are very powerful words; they're strong enough to change any subject following them into a singular idea. Sneak a peek at these examples:

Each shoe and sock *is* in need of mending, but Larry refuses to pick up a needle and thread.

Every dress and skirt in that store *is* on sale, and Lulu's in a spending mood.

Do these sentences look wrong to you? Granted, they appear to have plural subjects: two things *(shoe and sock)* in sentence one, and another two things *(dress and skirt)* in sentence two. But when *each* or *every* is placed in front of a group, you take the items in the group one at a time. In the first sample sentence, the subject consists of one *shoe,* one *sock,* another *shoe,* another *sock,* and so on. Therefore, the sentence needs a singular verb to match the singular subject. Ditto for the *dress and skirt* reference in the second example.

Either and neither: Alone or with partners

If you're reading this chapter in order, by now you've probably figured out that the same pronouns causing you grief in antecedent agreement also present subject/verb agreement problems. (Chapter 9 tells you all you need to know about pronouns and their antecedents.) Two more pain-in-the-pick-your-body-part pronouns are *either* and *neither*, when they're without their partners *or* and *nor*. When they're alone, *either* and *neither* are always singular, even if you insert a huge group (or just a group of two) between them and their verbs. Hence

> *Either* of the two armies *is* strong enough to take over the entire planet.

> *Neither* of the football captains *has shown* any willingness to accept Lola as quarterback.

Because the sample sentences are about armies and captains, you may be tempted to choose plural verbs. Resist the temptation! No matter what the sentence says, if the subject is *either* or *neither,* singular is the correct way to go.

When *either* and *neither* appear with their best buds, *or* and *nor,* two things happen. First, *either* and *neither* turn into conjunctions (joining words). Second, if they're joining two subjects, the subject that is closer to the verb determines whether the verb is singular or plural. Yes, that's right! This is a grammar problem you can solve with a ruler. Check out these examples:

> Either *Ella* or *her bridesmaids have eaten* the icing on the cake. (*brides-maids* = closest subject, a plural; *have eaten* = plural verb)

> Neither *the waiters* nor *Larry is planning* to eat the leftovers. (*Larry* = closest subject, a singular; *is planning* = singular verb)

Most sentences that are questions have helping verbs, and the helpers are the part of the verb that changes. Never fear: this is still grammar by ruler. The subject closest to the part of the verb that changes governs the singular/plural decision. Take a look at these examples:

> *Does* either *Ella* or *her cousins want* antacids? (*Ella* = subject closest to the helping verb *does*; *Ella* = singular subject, *does want* = singular verb)

> *Do* neither *her cousins* nor *Ella know* how to cook? (*cousins* = subject closest to the helping verb *do*; *cousins* = plural subject, *do know* = plural verb)

Politics and other irregular subjects

Besides dirty tricks and spin masters, the problem with politics is agreement. Specifically, *politics* looks plural because it ends in *s.* So do *mathematics, tactics, news, economics, civics, physics, athletics, measles, mumps,* and *analysis.* Surprise! all these words are singular and pair with singular verbs:

> *Politics is* a dirty sport, very much suited to Bob's view of the world.

> Roger thinks that *mathematics is* overrated. *Civics hasn't captured* his attention either. *Physics,* however, *has been* his favorite subject since second grade.

> *Athletics is* not my strong point.

> I may have to change my diet because the *news* about doughnuts *is* not encouraging.

> "*Economics is* my thing," commented Cedric as he stuffed money into his pockets.

> "Do you think that *measles is* a serious disease?" asked Eggworthy.

> "No, *mumps is* a lot worse," replied Michael.

> "Your troubles are all in your mind," said Lola. "*Analysis is* the answer."

Another word — *statistics* — may be either singular or plural. If you're talking about numbers, you're in plural territory:

> *Statistics show* that grammar knowledge is declining.

If you're talking about a course or a field of study, *statistics* is singular:

> *Statistics is* a difficult course.

The English language also has words that are always *plural.* Here are a few of them: *eyeglasses, pants, trousers, jeans, shorts* and *scissors.* (Did you notice how many of those words refer to clothing? Strange.) Other common plural-only words are *credentials, acoustics, earnings, headquarters,* and *ceramics.*

When in doubt, check your dictionary and remember to match singular nouns with singular verbs and plural nouns with plural verbs.

Part III
No Garage, but Plenty of Mechanics

The 5th Wave   By Rich Tennant

"C'mon Fogelman-talk! And I don't want to hear any of your non-parallel sentence structures, incomplete sentences or dangling participles!"

In this part . . .

Passed any construction sites lately? If so, you've probably noticed giant piles of lumber, steel, or bricks — all very useful and very noticeable parts of the new building. Off to the side, you've probably also seen some of the little things that also make the building possible — the nails, the nuts, and the bolts.

In this part I explain the nails, nuts, and bolts of writing: apostrophes, quotation marks, and other punctuation, as well as the rules for capitalization. Just like the construction industry, the "grammar industry" is constantly updating its products. Punctuation and capitalization customs have changed quite a bit in the last few years, probably to fit more smoothly with electronic communication. At the risk of sending hordes of traditional grammarians spinning in their graves, I devote an entire chapter to e-mail, texting, presentation slides, and the like. By the time you finish reading this part, you'll understand why little things — what English teachers call *mechanics* — are an essential part of the package that carries your meaning to the reader, and you'll be up-to-date on the rules for 21st century writing.

Chapter 11

Punctuation Law That Should Be Repealed: Apostrophes

• •

• •

*I*t happens every time I take a walk. I stroll along, thinking (in perfect grammar, of course), and a sign catches my eye.

> Bagel's Sold Here
>
> Mens Suits — the Best Deals in Town!

I hear a thud as the apostrophe rule bites the dust yet again. *Apostrophes* are those little curved marks you see suspended between certain letters — as in the *bagels* sign example. Why do those signs upset me? Because in both signs, the apostrophe (or lack thereof) is a problem. The signs should read:

> Bagels Sold Here
>
> Men's Suits — the Best Deals in Town!

Why don't they? Beats me. For some reason, even educated people throw apostrophes where they don't belong and leave them out where they're needed. So I favor repealing the apostrophe rule. Wipe it off the books. Pry the apostrophe key off computer keyboards. Erase the apostrophe from the collective mind of English teachers. Done, over, finito.

Until that happy day when apostrophes disappear, you have to learn the rules. In this chapter, I explain how to use apostrophes to show ownership and to shorten words.

The Pen of My Aunt or My Aunt's Pen? Using Apostrophes to Show Possession

Most other languages are smarter than English. To show possession in French, for example, you say

the pen of my aunt (la plume du ma tante)

the fine wines of that corner bar

the letters of the lovers

and so on. You can say the same thing in English, too, but English has added another option — the apostrophe. Take a look at these same phrases — with the same meaning — using apostrophes:

my *aunt's* pen

that corner *bar's* fine wines

the *lovers'* letters

All of these phrases include nouns that express ownership. I like to think of the apostrophe as a little hand, holding on to an *s* to indicate ownership or possession. In the first two examples, you notice that the apostrophe shows singular nouns that own something (*aunt's, bar's*). In the third example the apostrophe indicates that a plural noun (*lovers'*) owns something.

Ownership for singles

No, I'm not talking about the ownership of real estate or singles who sit in bars asking, "What's your sign?" or "Come here often?" I'm talking about using apostrophes to show ownership with singular nouns. Here's the bottom line: To show possession by one owner, add an apostrophe and the letter *s* to the owner:

the *dragon's* burnt tooth (the burnt tooth belongs to the dragon)

Lulu's pierced tooth (the pierced tooth belongs to Lulu)

Michael's gold-filled tooth (the gold-filled tooth belongs to Michael)

Another way to think about this rule is to see whether the word *of* expresses what you're trying to say. With the *of* method, you note the sharp tooth *of* the crocodile = the *crocodile's* sharp tooth

the peanut-stained tooth *of* the elephant = the *elephant's* peanut-stained tooth

and so on.

Sometimes, no clear owner appears in the phrase. Such a situation arises mostly when you're talking about time. If you can insert *of* into the sentence, you may need an apostrophe. For an idea of how to run the "of test," read these phrases:

one week's tooth cleaning = one week *of* tooth cleaning

a year's dental care = one year *of* dental care

Here's the bottom line: When you're talking about time, give your sentence the "of test." If it passes, insert an apostrophe.

Which sentence is correct?

A. Lulu told Lola that Roger needs a years work on his gum disease.

B. Lulu told Lola that Roger needs a year's work on his gum disease.

Answer. Sentence B is correct because Roger needs *a year of work* on his mouth. (Actually, he needs false teeth and maybe a nose job, but the year's gum work is a start.)

Sharing the wealth: Plural possessives

You'd be finished figuring out apostrophes now if everything belonged to only one owner. Bill Gates is close, but even he hasn't taken over everything (yet). So for now, you need to deal with plural owners. The plurals of most English nouns — anything greater than one — already end with the letter *s*. To show ownership, all you do is add an apostrophe after the *s.* Take a look at these examples:

ten *gerbils'* tiny teeth (the tiny teeth belong to ten gerbils)

many *dinosaurs'* petrified teeth (the petrified teeth belong to a herd of dinosaurs)

a thousand sword swallowers' sliced teeth (the sliced teeth belong to a thousand sword swallowers)

The owl rule: Who's, whose

Whose shows ownership. It seldom causes any problems, except when it's confused with another word: *who's*. *Who's* is a contraction that is short for *who is*. In other words

> The boy *whose* hat was burning was last seen running down the street screaming,

"*Who's* in charge of fire fighting in this town?"

and

Whose box of firecrackers is on the radiator? *Who's* going to tell Eggworthy that his living room looks like the Fourth of July?

The *of* test works for plurals, too. If you can rephrase the expression using the word *of,* you may need an apostrophe. Remember to add the apostrophe after the letter *s*.

> three *days'* dental work on those false teeth = three days *of* dental work

> sixteen *years'* neglect on the part of Lulu's dentist = sixteen years *of* neglect

> two *centuries'* pain of rotten teeth = two centuries *of* pain

Which is correct?

A. The dentist has only one goal in life: to clean the Yankee's teeth.

B. The dentist has only one goal in life: to clean the Yankees' teeth.

Answer: Sentence A is correct if you're talking about one player. Sentence B is correct if you're talking about 24 sets of teeth, or all the choppers on the team.

Try another. Which sentence is correct?

A. The Halloween decorations are decaying, especially the pumpkins teeth. Sam carved all ten jack-o-lanterns, and he can't bear to throw them away.

B. The Halloween decorations are decaying, especially the pumpkins' teeth. Sam carved all ten jack-o-lanterns, and he can't bear to throw them away.

C. The Halloween decorations are decaying, especially the pumpkin's teeth. Sam carved all ten jack-o-lanterns, and he can't bear to throw them away.

Answer: Sentence B is correct. The context of the sentence *(all ten jack-o-lanterns)* makes clear the fact that more than one pumpkin is rotting away. In sentence B, *pumpkins'* expresses a plural possessive. In sentence A, *pumpkins* has no apostrophe, though it clearly shows possession. In sentence C, the apostrophe is placed before the *s,* showing a single pumpkin.

Irregular plural possessives

In many of my examples in this chapter, I use the word "teeth." (You're hearing chomping in your sleep, right?) The word *teeth* is plural, but *teeth* doesn't end with the letter *s.* In other words, *teeth* is an irregular plural. To show ownership for an irregular plural, add an apostrophe and then the letter *s* (*teeth's*). Check out these examples:

> *teeth's* cavities (The cavities belong to the teeth.)
>
> *children's* erupting teeth (The erupting teeth belong to the children.)
>
> the three blind *mice's* imaginary teeth (The imaginary teeth belong to the three blind mice.)
>
> the *women's* lipstick-stained teeth (The lipstick-stained teeth belong to the women.)
>
> the *mice's* cheesy teeth (The cheesy teeth belong to the mice.)
>
> *geese's* missing teeth (No teeth belong to the geese because, as of course you know, birds have beaks instead.)

Compound plural possessives

What happens when two single people own something? In real life they go to court and fight it out. In grammar, they (or you) add one or two apostrophes, depending upon the type of ownership. If two people own something together, as a couple, use only one apostrophe.

> George and Martha *Washington's* home (The home belongs to the two of them.)
>
> Larry and *Ella's* wedding (The wedding was for both the blushing groom and the frightful bride.)
>
> Lulu and *Lola's* new set of nose rings (The set was too expensive for either one alone, so Lulu and Lola each paid half and agreed to an every-other-week wearing schedule.)
>
> Roger and the superspy's secret (Roger told it to the superspy, so now they're sharing the secret, which concerns doughnuts and explosives.)

If two people own things separately, as individuals, use two apostrophes:

George's and *Martha's* teeth (He has his set of teeth — false, by the way — and she has her own set.)

Lulu's and *Gary's* new shoes. (She wears size 2, and he wears size 12. Hers are lizard skin with four-inch heels. His are plastic with five-inch heels.)

Eggworthy's and *Roy's* attitudes towards dieting. (Eggworthy doesn't worry about cholesterol. Roy monitors every scrap of food he eats.)

Lester's and *Archie's* sleeping habits (You don't want to know. I'll just say that Lester sleeps all night, and Archie sleeps all day.)

Cedric's and *Lola's* fingernails. (He has his; she has her own; both sets are polished and quite long.)

Speaking of plurals: Remember that an apostrophe shows ownership. Don't use an apostrophe when you have a plural that is *not* expressing ownership. Here are some examples:

RIGHT: Bagels stick to your teeth.

WRONG: Bagel's stick to your teeth.

ALSO WRONG: Bagels' stick to your teeth.

Look at another set:

RIGHT: The gnus gnashed their teeth when they heard the news.

WRONG: The gnus' gnashed their teeth when they heard the news.

ALSO WRONG: The gnu's gnashed their teeth when they heard the news.

To sum up the rule on plurals and apostrophes: If the plural noun is not showing ownership, *don't* use an apostrophe. If the plural noun shows ownership, *do* add an apostrophe after the *s* (for regular plurals). For irregular plurals showing ownership, add *'s*.

I have to admit that in two special cases, apostrophes do show up in plurals. If you're writing the plural of a lowercase letter, you add an apostrophe and an *s*. To help the reader along, you should italicize the letter but not the apostrophe or the *s*. If you're writing the plural of a word used as a word (not for what it means), italicize the word and add a nonitalicized s (with no apostrophe). If you're writing with a pen, not a computer, italics aren't possible. Pen-writers should place the plural of the word used as a word or the letter in quotation marks and add an apostrophe and an *s*. Take a peek at these examples:

You have too many *f*'s in that word, young lady!

The boss throws "impossible's" into every discussion of my raise.

Up until a few years ago, the plurals of capital letters, numbers and symbols were also formed with apostrophes (*F's, 1960's*, and *&'s* , for example). Most writers now omit the apostrophe in these cases (*Fs, 1960s* and *&s*). So far, civilization hasn't crumbled from the shock. Stay tuned!

Possession with Proper Nouns

Companies, stores, and organizations also own things, so these proper nouns — singular or plural — also require apostrophes. Put the apostrophe at the end of the name:

> *Macy's* finest shoes
>
> *Microsoft's* finest operating system
>
> *McGillicuddy, Pinch, and Cinch's* finest lawsuit
>
> *Grammar, Inc.'s* finest apostrophe rule

Special note: Some stores have apostrophes in their names, even without a sense of possession:

> *Macy's* occupies an entire city block.

Macy's is always written with an apostrophe, even when there's no noun after the store name. *Macy's* implies a shortened version of a longer name (perhaps *Macy's Department Store*).

Place apostrophes where they're needed in this paragraph.

> Jeff went to Macys Department Store to buy a suit for Lolas party. His shopping list also included a heart for the Valentines Day dinner and a card for his brothers next anniversary. Jeffs shopping spree was successful, in spite of Lulus and Lolas attempts to puncture his tires.

Answer: Jeff went to *Macy's* Department Store to buy a suit for *Lola's* party. His shopping list also included a heart for the *Valentine's* Day dinner and a card for his *brother's* next anniversary. *Jeff's* shopping spree was successful, in spite of *Lulu's* and *Lola's* attempts to puncture his tires. (***Note:*** Lulu and Lola made separate stabs at the tires.)

Ownership with Hyphenated Words

Other special cases of possession involve compound words — son-in-law, mother-of-pearl, and all the other words with *hyphens* (those little horizontal lines). The rule is simple: Put the apostrophe at the end of the word. Never put an apostrophe inside a word. Here are some examples of singular compound nouns:

> the *secretary-treasurer's* report on teeth (The report belongs to the secretary-treasurer.)
>
> the *dogcatcher-in-chief's* canine teeth (The canine teeth belong to the dogcatcher-in-chief.)
>
> my *mother-in-law's* elderly teeth (The elderly teeth belong to my mother-in-law. Hi, Mom!)

The same rule applies to plural compound nouns that are hyphenated. Take a look at these examples:

> the *doctors-of-philosophy's* study lounge (The study lounge is owned by all the doctors-of philosophy.)
>
> my *fathers-in-law's* wedding present (The wedding present was from both fathers-in-law.)

Possessive Nouns That End in S

Singular nouns that end in *s* present special problems. Let me explain: My last name is Woods. My name is singular, because I am only one person. When students talk about me, they may say,

> Ms. Woods's grammar lessons can't be beat.

or

> Ms. Woods' grammar lessons can't be beat.

(Okay, they say a lot of other things, too, but this is a positive, family-friendly book. I'll omit the other comments.)

Both of the sentences about me and my grammar lessons (sounds like an old song: "Me and my grammar lessons / down in the good old school / where we learned apostrophes / so we wouldn't drool") are correct. Why are there two options — *Ms. Woods's* and *Ms. Woods'*? The answer has to do with sound. If you say the first sentence above, by the time you get to the word *grammar*

you're hissing and spitting all over your listener. Not a good idea. The second sentence sounds better. So the grammar police have given in on this one. If the name of a singular owner ends in the letter *s,* you may add only an apostrophe, not an apostrophe and another *s.* But if you like hissing and spitting, feel free to add an apostrophe *and* an *s.* Both versions are acceptable.

Which sentence is correct?

A. The walrus' tusk gleamed because the walrus brushed it for ten minutes after every meal.

B. The walrus's tusk gleamed because the walrus brushed it for ten minutes after every meal.

Answer: Both are correct. Sentence B calls for more saliva, but it follows the rule. Sentence A breaks the old rule, but nowadays breaking that rule is acceptable. (Yes, it was a trick question. You know how teachers are.)

Try another set. Which sentence is correct?

A. My whole family got together for Thanksgiving. The Woods' are a large group.

B. My whole family got together for Thanksgiving. The Woodses are a large group.

Answer: Another trick question. Sentence B is correct because Woodses is a plural, not a possessive. In sentence A, the apostrophe is incorrect because plurals shouldn't have apostrophes unless they express ownership.

Common Apostrophe Errors with Pronouns

English also supplies pronouns — words that take the place of a noun — for ownership. Some possessive pronouns are *my, your, his, her, its, our,* and *their.* Here's a rule so important — and so often broken — that you should consider tattooing it on your pinky finger: No possessive pronoun ever has an apostrophe. A few examples of possessive pronouns in action:

> *your* completely unruly child — not your' completely unruly child (also wrong: that completely unruly child of yours')

> *our* extremely well-behaved youngster — not our' extremely well-behaved youngster (also wrong: the extremely well-behaved youngster of ours')

their tendency to fight — not their' tendency to fight (also wrong: the tendency of theirs' not to fight)

his call to the police — not his' call to the police

Which sentence is correct?

A. Roy stole Jenny's mouthwash because of their' ancient feud.

B. Roy stole Jenny's mouthwash because of their ancient feud.

C. Roy stole Jennys mouthwash because of their ancient feud.

Answer: Sentence B is correct. In sentence A, the apostrophe is needed in *Jenny's* because Jenny owns the mouthwash. However, *their* should not have an apostrophe because no possessive pronoun ever has an apostrophe. In sentence C, *their* is written correctly, but *Jennys* lacks the apostrophe.

Just one more. Which sentence is correct?

A. Eggworthy claims that a weeks mouthwash is not worth fighting over and has pledged his support to Roy.

B. Eggworthy claims that a week's mouthwash is not worth fighting over and has pledged his' support to Roy.

C. Eggworthy claims that a week's mouthwash is not worth fighting over and has pledged his support to Roy.

Answer: Sentence C is correct. In sentence A, *a weeks* needs an apostrophe because the phrase means *a week of.* In sentence B, *his'* shouldn't have an apostrophe because (say it aloud — bellow it!) no possessive pronoun ever has an apostrophe.

For more information on possessive pronouns, see Chapter 9.

Shortened Words for Busy People: Contractions

Are you in a hurry? Probably. So like just about everyone in our society, you probably use contractions when you speak. A *contraction* shortens a word by removing one letter or more and substituting an apostrophe in the same spot. For example, chop *wi* out of *I will,* throw in an apostrophe, and you have *I'll.* The resulting word is shorter and faster to say, with only one syllable (sound) instead of two.

Take a look at Table 11-1 for a list of common contractions. Notice that a couple of contractions are irregular. (*Won't,* for example, is short for *will not.*)

Table 11-1		**Contractions**	
Phrase	*Contraction*	*Phrase*	*Contraction*
are not	aren't	she is	she's
cannot	can't	that is	that's
could not	couldn't	they are	they're
do not	don't	they will	they'll
does not	doesn't	they would	they'd
did not	didn't	we are	we're
he will	he'll	we will	we'll
he would	he'd	we would	we'd
he is	he's	we have	we've
is not	isn't	what is	what's
it is	it's	who is	who's
I am	I'm	will not	won't
I will	I'll	would not	wouldn't
I would	I'd	you are	you're
I have	I've	you have	you've
she will	she'll	you will	you'll
she would	she'd	you would	you'd

If you'd like to make a contraction that isn't in Table 11-1, check your dictionary to make sure it's legal!

Your right to use apostrophes

You're in trouble if *your* apostrophes are in the wrong place, especially when you're writing in the second person. (The second person is the form that uses *you, your, yours*, both singular and plural.) *You're* means *you are. Your* shows possession. These two words are not interchangeable. Some examples:

"*You're* not going to eat that rotten pumpkin," declared Rachel. *(You are not going to eat.)*

"*Your* refusal to eat the pumpkin means that you will be given mystery meat instead," commented Dean. *(The refusal comes from you,* so you need a possessive word.)

"*You're* going to wear that pumpkin if you threaten me," said Lola. *(You are going to wear.)*

"I'm not afraid of *your* threats!" stated Art. (The threats come from *you,* so you need a possessive word.)

Common Contraction Mistakes

If you've gone to the mall — any mall — chances are you've seen a sign like this:

Doughnuts 'N Coffee

or

Broken Grammar Rules

Okay, I doubt you've seen the last one, at least as a sign, but you've seen 'n as a contraction of *and*. And therefore, you've witnessed broken grammar rules at the mall. I know I'm fighting a losing battle here, and I know I should be worried about much more important issues, like the economy and the environment. Even so, I also care about the grammatical environment, and thus I make a plea to the store owners and sign painters of the English-speaking world. Please don't put 'n in anything. It's a grunt, not a word. Thank you.

Woulda, coulda, shoulda. These three "verbs" are potholes on the road to better grammar. Why? Because they don't exist. Here's the recipe for a grammatical felony. Start with three real verb phrases: *would have*, *could have*, and *should have*.

And turn them into contractions: *would've*, *could've*, and *should've*.

Now turn them back into words. But don't turn them back into the words they actually represent. Instead, let your ears be your guide. (It helps if you have a lot of wax in your ears because the sounds don't quite match.) Now you say the following: *would of, could of, and should of.*

These three phrases are never correct. Don't use them! Take a look at these examples:

WRONG: If George had asked me to join the spy ring, I would of said, "No way."

RIGHT: If George had asked me to join the spy ring, I would have said, "No way."

ALSO RIGHT: If George had asked me to join the spy ring, I would've said, "No way."

Here's another set:

WRONG: When I heard about the spy ring, I should of told the Central Intelligence Agency.

RIGHT: When I heard about the spy ring, I should have told the Central Intelligence Agency.

ALSO RIGHT: When I heard about the spy ring, I should've told the Central Intelligence Agency.

Which is correct?

A. Jane wouldnt go to the dentist even though she needed a new tooth.

B. Jane wouldn't go to the dentist, even though she needed a new tooth.

Answer: Sentence B is correct. *Wouldn't* is short for *would not.*

Chapter 12

Quotations: More Rules Than the Internal Revenue Service

. . . .

. . . .

*W*hen I correct quotations in students' papers, I field many questions, such as "Why did you move that period?" or Do I really need a capital letter?" I counter with a question of my own. (Not "Do you know the way to detention?" I'm much nicer than that.) I ask the students what rules they were following when they wrote those quotations. Their answers reveal many myths about the proper way to quote.

This chapter is a myth-buster. It explains the real rules of quotations — unfortunately, a list even longer than the nation's tax laws. Lucky for you, quotation rules aren't as hard to follow as the regulations set by that beloved government agency, the Internal Revenue Service.

And I Quote

A *quotation* is a written repetition of someone else's words — just one word or a whole statement or passage. Quotations pop up in almost all writing: newspapers, magazines, novels, essays, letters, and so on. To get an idea how to identify a quotation, take a look at the following story:

One day, while Betsy was on her way to a music lesson, she gazed through a shop window at a gleaming grand piano. Her heart beating wildly at the thought of playing such a marvel, she neglected to look up when everyone around her began to shout. Seconds later, another piano — an upright, not a grand — came whizzing through the air. One of the movers had taken a bite of his tuna fish sandwich, allowing the piano to break loose from the ropes hoisting it to the third floor. The piano landed a mere inch away from Betsy. What did Betsy say?

> She said that she was relieved.

This sentence tells you about Betsy and her feelings, but it doesn't give her exact words. It's a report of someone's ideas, but not a record of the words actually spoken or written. You can write that sentence if you heard Betsy say, "I am relieved." You can also write the same sentence if you heard Betsy say, "Thank goodness it missed me. My knees are shaking! I could have been killed."

As an observer, you can also record Betsy's reaction by writing:

> She said that she was "relieved."

This account of Betsy's reaction is a little more exact. Some of the sentence is general, but the reader knows that Betsy actually said the word "relieved" because it's in quotation marks. The quotation marks are signs for the reader; they mean that the material inside the marks is exactly what was said.

> Betsy said, "I am so relieved that I could cry."
>
> "I am so relieved that I could cry," Betsy said.

These two sentences quote Betsy. The words enclosed by quotation marks are exactly what Betsy said. The only thing added is a *speaker tag* — an identifying phrase that tells you who said the words (in this case, Betsy). As you see in the example, you can place the speaker tag in the beginning of the sentence or at the end. (It can also land in the middle, but I talk about that situation later in this chapter.) The quotation marks enclose the words that were said or written.

Which sentences are quotations? Which sentences are general reports of what was said?

A. Bob doesn't get along with the conductor of the school orchestra, according to Lulu.

B. Besides placing exploding cushions on the conductor's chair, Bob has talked about the conductor's "sentimental" choices of music for the next concert.

C. "I refuse to play anything that was composed before the twenty-first century," declared Bob.

Answer: Sentence A is a general report with none of Bob's exact words. Sentence B tells the reader that Bob said the word "sentimental." Sentence C is a quotation.

Punctuating Quotations

Here's a math problem for you: Quotation + Punctuation =? Answer: A million dumb rules. Yes, I'm brave in calling the rules "dumb," even though I risk being expelled from the grammarians' union. In general, the rules for quotations are simply customs. Put a period inside, put a period outside — what difference does it make to your reader? Not much. But to write proper English, you need to follow all the rules, even the illogical ones.

Quotations with speaker tags

DUMB RULE 1: When the speaker tag comes first, put a comma after the speaker tag. The period at the end of the sentence goes *inside* the quotation marks.

> The gang remarked, "Lola's candidate is a sure bet."
>
> Lola replied, "He's not my candidate."

DUMB RULE 2: When the speaker tag comes last, put a comma *inside* the quotation marks and a period at the end of the sentence.

> "Lola's candidate isn't a sure bet now," the gang continued.
>
> "I support a different candidate," screamed Lola.

Now you know the first two (of far too many) quotation rules. Keep in mind that it doesn't matter where you put the speaker tag as long as you punctuate the sentence correctly.

Which sentence is correct?

A. Alonzo muttered, "I don't want to practice the piano".

B. Alonzo muttered, "I don't want to practice the piano."

Answer: Sentence B is correct, because the period is inside the quotation marks.

Here's another pair. Which sentence is correct?

A. "The equation that Al wrote on the board is incorrect," trilled Anna.

B. "The equation that Al wrote on the board is incorrect", trilled Anna.

Answer: Sentence A is correct, because the comma is inside the quotation marks.

How rude! Punctuating interrupted quotations with speaker tags

Sometimes a speaker tag lands in the middle of a sentence. To give you an example of this sort of placement, I revisit Betsy. Her saga continues with a visit to her lawyer.

"I think I'll sue," Betsy explained, "for emotional distress."

"You can't imagine," she added, "what I felt."

"The brush of the piano against my nose," she sighed, "will be with me forever."

"The scent of tuna," she continued, "brings it all back."

"I can't go to the cafeteria," she concluded, "without suffering post-piano stress syndrome."

In each of these sample sentences, the speaker tag interrupts the quotation. Time for some more dumb rules for interrupted quotations.

DUMB RULE 3: In a sentence with an interrupted quotation, the comma is *inside* the quotation marks for the first half of a quotation.

DUMB RULE 4: In a sentence with an interrupted quotation, the speaker tag is followed by a comma *before* the quotation marks.

DUMB RULE 5: In a sentence with an interrupted quotation, the period at the end of the sentence is *inside* the quotation marks.

DUMB RULE 6: In a sentence with an interrupted quotation, the second half of a quotation does *not* begin with a capital letter.

Which sentence is correct?

A. "After the concert", said Lulu, "the piano goes to the third floor."

B. "After the concert," said Lulu, "The piano goes to the third floor."

Answer: Neither is correct. In sentence A, the comma after *concert* is in the wrong place. In sentence B, the second half of the quotation should not begin with a capital letter. Here is the correct sentence:

"After the concert," said Lulu, "the piano goes to the third floor."

Try another. Which sentence is correct?

A. "Although I am only a humble musician, said Betsy, "I have the right to a piano-free sidewalk."

B. "Although I am only a humble musician," said Betsy "I have the right to a piano-free sidewalk."

C. "Although I am only a humble musician," said Betsy, I have the right to a piano-free sidewalk."

D. "Although I am only a humble musician," said Betsy, "I have the right to a piano-free sidewalk."

Answer: Sentence D is correct. In sentence A, there should be a quotation mark after *musician.* In sentence B, a comma should be placed after *Betsy.* In sentence C, a quotation mark should be placed before *I.* (Annoying rules, aren't they? So many things can go wrong with this type of sentence.)

Notice that in all the interrupted quotations I supply in this section, the quoted material adds up to only one sentence, even though it's written in two separate parts.

Avoiding run-on sentences with interrupted quotations

When you plop a speaker tag right in the middle of someone's conversation, make sure that you don't create a run-on sentence. A *run-on sentence* is actually two sentences that have been stuck together (that is, *run* together) without a conjunction (a word that joins grammatical elements) or a semicolon. (For more information on run-on sentences, see Chapter 5.) Just because you're quoting is no reason to ignore the rules about joining sentences. Check out this set of examples:

WRONG: "When you move a piano, you must be careful," squeaked Al, "I could have been killed."

RIGHT: "When you move a piano, you must be careful," squeaked Al. "I could have been killed."

The quoted material forms two complete sentences:

SENTENCE 1: When you move a piano, you must be careful.

SENTENCE 2: I could have been killed.

Because the quoted material forms two complete sentences, you must write two separate sentences. If you cram this quoted material into one sentence, you've got a run-on.

Remove the speaker tag and check the quoted material. What is left? Enough for half a sentence? That's okay. Quoted material doesn't need to express a complete thought. Enough material for one sentence? Also okay. Enough material for two sentences? Not okay, unless you write two sentences.

Which is correct?

A. "A piano hits the ground with tremendous force," explained the physicist. "I would move to the side if I were you."

B. "A piano hits the ground with tremendous force," explained the physicist, "I would move to the side if I were you."

Answer: Sentence A is correct. The quoted material forms two complete sentences and you must quote it that way. Sentence 1 = *A piano hits the ground with tremendous force*. Sentence 2 = *I would move to the side if I were you*.

Here's another. Which is correct?

A. "I insist that you repeal the laws of physics, demanded Lola. "Pianos should not kill people."

B. "I insist that you repeal the laws of physics," demanded Lola, "Pianos should not kill people."

C. "I insist that you repeal the laws of physics," demanded Lola. "Pianos should not kill people."

Answer: C is correct. In A, a quotation mark is missing after the word *physics*. Choice B is a run-on. In C, the two complete thoughts are expressed in two sentences and punctuated correctly.

Quotations without speaker tags

Not all sentences with quotations include speaker tags. The punctuation and capitalization rules for these sentences are a little different, though not more logical than other types of quotation rules. Check out these examples:

> According to the blurb on the book jacket, Anna's history of geometry is said to be "thrilling and unbelievable" by all who read it.

When Michael said that the book "wasn't as exciting as watching paint dry," Anna threw a pie in his face.

Michael's lawyer is planning a lawsuit for "grievous injury to face and ego."

DUMB RULE 7: If the quotation doesn't have a speaker tag, the first word of the quotation is not capitalized.

DUMB RULE 8: No comma separates the quotation from the rest of the sentence if the quotation doesn't have a speaker tag.

Actually, rules 7 and 8 aren't completely dumb. Quotations without speaker tags aren't set off from the sentence; they're tucked into the sentence. You don't want to put a capital letter in the middle of the sentence, which is where nonspeaker-tag quotations usually end up. Also, omitting the comma preserves the flow of the sentence.

Notice that quotations without speaker tags tend to be short — a few words rather than an entire statement. If you're reporting a lengthy statement, you're probably better off with a speaker tag and the complete quotation. If you want to extract only a few, relevant words from someone's speech, you can probably do without a speaker tag.

Which is correct?

A. Eggworthy said that the latest nutritional research was "Suspect" because the laboratory was "Unfair."

B. Eggworthy said that the latest nutritional research was, "suspect" because the laboratory was, "unfair."

C. Eggworthy said that the latest nutritional research was "suspect" because the laboratory was "unfair."

Sentence C is correct. In sentence A, *suspect* and *unfair* should not be capitalized. In sentence B, no comma should be placed after *was*.

Quotations with question marks

Remember Betsy's piano from earlier in this chapter? When the piano nearly squashed Betsy, she said a few more things. (Not all of them are printable, but we'll ignore those remarks.) Here are her other remarks:

"How can you eat a tuna sandwich while hoisting a piano?" Betsy asked as she eyed his lunch.

"May I have a bite?" she queried.

Let me put it another way:

> As she eyed his lunch Betsy asked, "How can you eat a tuna sandwich while hoisting a piano?"
>
> She queried, "May I have a bite?"

What do you notice about these two sets of quotations? That's right! The quoted words are questions. (Okay, I didn't actually hear your answer, but I'm assuming that because you were smart enough to buy this book, you're smart enough to notice these things.) And quotations that include questions follow the

NOT-SO-DUMB RULE 9: If you quote a question, put the question mark *inside* the quotation marks.

This rule makes good sense; it distinguishes a quoted question from a quotation embedded in a question. Time to look at one more part of Betsy's encounter with the falling piano. The piano mover answered Betsy, but no one could understand his words. (He had a mouthful of tuna fish.) I wonder what he said.

> Did he say, "I can't give you a bite of my sandwich because I ate it all"?
>
> Did he really declare, "It was just a piano"?

The quoted words in this set are not questions. However, each entire sentence is a question. Now it's time for more rules:

SLIGHTLY LESS-DUMB RULE 10: If the quoted words aren't a question but the entire sentence is a question, the question mark goes *outside* the quotation marks. (This rule makes sense too, don't you think?)

To sum up the rules on question marks:

- ✔ If the quoted words are a question, put the question mark *inside* the quotation marks.
- ✔ If the entire sentence is a question, put the question mark *outside* the quotation marks.

Some of you detail-oriented (okay, picky) people may want to know what to do when the quotation and the sentence are both questions. Read on.

DUMB RULE 11: For those rare occasions when both the quoted words and the sentence are questions, put the question mark *inside* the quotation marks.

Here's an example of this rule:

> Did the mover really ask, "Is that lady for real?"

No matter what, don't use two question marks:

> WRONG: Did Betsy ask, "What's the number of a good lawyer?"?
>
> RIGHT: Did Betsy ask, "What's the number of a good lawyer?"

Which sentence is correct?

> A. Did Lulu say, "I wish a piano would drop on me so that I could sue?"
>
> B. Did Lulu say, "I wish a piano would drop on me so that I could sue"?

Answer: Sentence B is correct. Because the quoted words are not a question and the entire sentence is a question, the question mark goes outside the quotation marks.

Quotations with exclamation points

A word about exclamation points: These punctuation marks follow the same general rules as question marks. In other words,

NOT-SO-DUMB RULE 12: If the entire sentence is an exclamation, but the quoted words aren't, put the exclamation point *outside* the quotation marks.

NOT-SO-DUMB RULE 13: If the quoted words are an exclamation, put the exclamation point *inside* the quotation marks.

Here are some sample sentences with exclamation points:

> Gene said, "I can't believe it's not butter!" (The quoted words are an exclamation but the entire sentence is not.)
>
> I simply cannot believe that Gene actually said, "No, thank you"! (Now the entire sentence is an exclamation but the quoted words are not.)

For those of you who like to dot every *i* and cross every *t*:

DUMB RULE 14: If both the sentence and the quotation are exclamations, put the exclamation point *inside* the quotation marks.

Take a look at this example:

> I cannot believe that Gene actually said, "No way would I run for president!"

No matter what, don't use two exclamation points:

> WRONG: I refuse to believe that Gene said, "In your dreams!"!
>
> RIGHT: I refuse to believe that Gene said, "In your dreams!"

Quotations with semicolons

Every hundred years or so you may write a sentence that has both a quotation and a semicolon. (In Chapter 5, I explain semicolons in detail.) Here's how to combine semicolons and quotations.

DUMB RULE 15: When writing a sentence that includes a quotation and a semicolon, put the semicolon *outside* the quotation marks.

Sneak a peek at this example:

> Cedric thinks that vending-machine snacks are a food group; "I can't imagine eating anything else," he said.

and

> Cedric said, "I can't imagine eating anything but vending-machine snacks"; he must have the IQ of a sea slug.

Okay, maybe that last sentence was a bit nasty. I apologize to sea slugs everywhere.

Quotations inside quotations

Now the topic of quotations becomes a little complicated. Sometimes you need to place a quotation inside a quotation. Consider this situation:

Al, President of the Future Engineers of America, sees himself as a paragon of popularity. He doesn't want Archie to join the club because Archie wears a plastic pocket-protector filled with pens and pencils. Al wants Archie to dump the pocket-protector, but Archie is outraged by the demand. You're writing a story about Archie and the Future Engineers of America. You're quoting Archie, who is quoting Al. How do you punctuate this quotation?

Archie says, "Al had the nerve to tell me, 'Your pocket protector is nerd-city and dumpster-ready.'"

A sentence like this has to be sorted out. Without any punctuation, here's what Al said:

Your pocket protector is nerd-city and dumpster-ready.

Without any punctuation, here are all the words that Archie said:

Al had the nerve to tell me your pocket protector is nerd-city and dumpster-ready.

Al's words are a quotation inside another quotation. So Al's words are enclosed in single-quotation marks, and Archie's are enclosed (in the usual way) in double quotation marks. Which brings me to

DUMB RULE 16: A quotation inside another quotation gets single quotation marks.

Another example: Lola says, "I'm thinking of piercing my tongue." Lulu tells Lola's mom about Lola's plan, adding a comment as she does so. Here's the complete statement:

Lulu says, "As a strong opponent of piercing, I am sorry to tell you that Lola told me, 'I'm thinking of piercing my tongue.'"

Lola's words are inside single quotation marks and Lulu's complete statement is in double quotation marks.

Commas and periods follow the same rules in both double and single quotations.

Which sentence is correct?

A. Angel complained, "He said to me, 'You are a devil.'"

B. Angel complained, "He said to me, "You are a devil."

Answer: Sentence A is correct. You must enclose *You are a devil* in single quotation marks and the larger statement *He said to me you are a devil* in double quotation marks. The period at the end of the sentence goes inside both marks.

British English alert!

Despite having settled their differences shortly after the Boston Tea Party, Britain and America are still fighting over grammar rules. Everything I've told you about quotation rules is true for American English grammar. The reverse is often true for British English grammar. The British frequently use single quotation marks when they're quoting, and double marks for a quotation inside another quotation. Thus a British book might punctuate Lulu's comment in this way:

Lulu says, 'As a strong opponent of piercing, I am sorry to tell you that Lola told me, "I'm thinking of piercing my tongue."'

The name of the quotations marks is also different. In British English, the little squiggles are called "inverted commas." What's a puzzled grammarian to do? Follow the custom of the country he or she is in.

Who Said That? Identifying Speaker Changes

In a conversation, people take turns speaking. Take a look at this extremely mature discussion:

"You sat on my tuna fish sandwich," Michael said. "It's flatter than a pancake, and I hate pancakes, unless they're covered with maple syrup."

"No, I didn't sit on your sandwich," Ella said. "I am afraid of mayonnaise, so I sat ten feet away from your lunch bag."

"Did too," Michael said.

"Did not!" Ella said.

Notice that every time the speaker changes, a new paragraph is formed. By starting a new paragraph every time the speaker changes, the conversation is easy to follow; the reader always knows who is talking. Here's another version of the tuna fight:

"You sat on my tuna fish sandwich," Michael said. "It's flatter than a pancake, and I hate pancakes, unless they're covered with maple syrup."

"No, I didn't sit on your sandwich," Ella said. "I am afraid of mayonnaise, so I sat ten feet away from your lunch bag."

"Did too."

"Did not!"

Although the speaker tags are left out after the first exchange, you can still figure out who is speaking because of the paragraph breaks.

DUMB RULE 17: Every change of speaker is signaled by a new paragraph.

The new-speaker/new paragraph rule applies even if the argument deteriorates into single-word statements such as *yes* or *no* or some other single-word statements. (I won't specify because this is a family-friendly book.)

Who said what? Label each statement, using the paragraph clues.

"Are you in favor of piano-tossing?" asked Roger curiously.

"Not really," replied Cedric. "I like my pianos to have all four feet on the floor."

"But there's something about music in the air that appeals to me."

"There's something about no broken bones, no concussions, and no flattened bodies that appeals to me."

"You really have no artistic instinct!"

Answer: Here's the passage again, with the speakers' names inserted. (Note the punctuation.)

"Are you in favor of piano-tossing?" asked Roger curiously.

"Not really," replied Cedric. "I like my pianos to have all four feet on the floor."

Roger continued, "But there's something about music in the air that appeals to me."

Cedric countered, "There's something about no broken bones, no concussions, and no flattened bodies that appeals to me."

"You really have no artistic instinct!" shouted Roger.

If you're quoting someone who's very longwinded, you may want to leave out some extra words. No problem, as long as you don't change the meaning of the quotation. Simply replace the missing words with an *ellipsis* (three spaced dots). If you're cutting out more than one sentence, insert four spaced dots — one is the period, and the other three are the ellipsis. If you need to add a word to a quotation to clarify meaning, put *brackets* — these symbols [ ] — around the addition. Here's what I mean:

ORIGINAL STATEMENT: "I must practice the piano, the whole piano, and nothing but the piano in order to keep my notes sharp."

STATEMENT WITH WORDS OMITTED: "I must practice . . . in order to keep my notes sharp. (The ellipsis takes the place of *the piano, the whole piano, and nothing but the piano.*)

ORIGINAL STATEMENT: "He doesn't like flat-screen televisions either."

STATEMENT WITH CLARIFICATION: "He [Ollie] doesn't like flat-screen televisions either."

Germ-free Quotations: Using Sanitizing Quotation Marks

Sanitizing quotation marks (also known as *apologetic quotation marks*) tell the reader that you don't completely approve of the words inside the quotation marks. You often see sanitizing quotation marks enclosing slang, highly informal speech that falls outside standard English. (For more information on slang, see Chapter 1.) Check out this example:

Archie knew that the guys thought him "nerd-city," but he was determined not to abandon his beloved pocket protector just because it was considered "uncool."

The writer knows that "nerd-city" and "uncool" aren't correct, but those words show the ideas (but not the exact remarks) of Archie's co-workers.

Don't overuse sanitizing quotation marks. Think of them as plutonium; a little goes a long way. Or, to sanitize that statement, a little goes a "long" way. Annoying, right?

A useful little word is *sic*. *Sic* (a Latin word that literally mean "thus"), indicates that you're quoting exactly what was said or written, even though you know something is wrong. In other words, you put a little distance between yourself and the error by showing the reader that the person you're quoting made the mistake, not you. For example, if you're quoting from the works of Dan Quayle, former Vice President of the United States (and a *very* poor speller) you may write

"I would like a potatoe [sic] for supper."

"Potato," of course, is the correct spelling.

Punctuating Titles: When to Use Quotation Marks

In your writing, sometimes you may need to include the title of a magazine, the headline of a newspaper article, the title of a song or movie, and so on. When punctuating these magazine titles, headlines, and song or movie titles, keep in mind these two options:

1. **Put the title in quotation marks. Quotation marks enclose titles of smaller works or parts of a whole.**

or

2. **Set the title off from the rest of the writing with italic or underlining. By using italic or underlining, you set off titles of larger works or complete works.**

These options aren't interchangeable. Each option has a different use. To put it another way, quotation marks are for jockeys. Italic and underlining are for basketball players. One is for little, the other for big.

Use quotation marks for the titles of

- ✔ Poems
- ✔ Stories
- ✔ Essays
- ✔ Songs
- ✔ Chapter titles
- ✔ Magazine or newspaper articles
- ✔ Individual episodes of a television series
- ✔ Page of a Web site

Use italic or underlining for the titles of

- ✔ Collections of poetry, stories, or essays
- ✔ Titles of books
- ✔ Titles of CDs or tapes or records (Do they still make records?)
- ✔ Magazines or newspapers

✔ Television and radio shows

✔ Plays

✔ The title of the entire Web site

Here are some examples:

✔ "A Thousand Excuses for Missing the Tax Deadline" (a newspaper article) in *The Ticker Tape Journal* (a newspaper)

✔ "Ode to Taxes Uncalculated" (a poem) in *The Tax Poems* (a book of poetry)

✔ "I Got the W2 Blues" (a song title) on *Me and My Taxes* (a CD containing many songs)

✔ "On the Art of Deductions" (an essay) in *Getting Rich and Staying Rich* (a magazine)

✔ "Small Business Expenses" (an individual episode) on *The IRS Report* (a television series)

✔ *April 15th* (a play)

✔ "Deductions Unlimited" (a page in a Web site) in *Beat the IRS* (the title of a Web site)

You may be wondering which letters you should capitalize in a title. For information on capitalization, see Chapter 15.

Add quotation marks and italic to the following paragraph.

Gloria slumped slowly into her chair as the teacher read The Homework Manifesto aloud in class. Gloria's essay, expressing her heartfelt dislike of any and all assignments, was never intended for her teacher's eyes. Gloria had hidden the essay inside the cover of her textbook, The Land and People of Continents You Never Heard Of. Sadly, the textbook company, which also publishes The Most Boring Mathematics Possible, had recently switched to thinner paper, and the essay was clearly visible. The teacher ripped the essay from Gloria's frightened hands. Gloria had not been so embarrassed since the publication of her poem I Hate Homework in the school magazine, Happy Thoughts.

Answer: Put "The Homework Manifesto" and "I Hate Homework" in quotation marks, because they're titles of an essay and a poem. Italicize *The Land and People of Continents You Never Heard Of* and *The Most Boring Mathematics Possible* and *Happy Thoughts,* because they're titles of books and a magazine.

When a title is alone on a line — on a title page or simply at the top of page one of a paper — don't use italic or quotation marks. Don't underline the title either. The centering calls attention to the title. Nothing else is needed. One exception: If part of the title is the name of another work, treat that part as you would any other title. For example, suppose you've written a brilliant essay about Gloria's poem, "I Hate Homework." The title page contains this line, centered:

Freudian Imagery in "I Hate Homework"

If your brilliant essay is about the magazine *Happy Thoughts*, the title page includes this line (also centered):

The Decline of the School Magazine: A Case Study of *Happy Thoughts*

Chapter 13

The Pause That Refreshes: Commas

Aloud, commas are the sounds of silence — short pauses that contrast with the longer pause at the end of each sentence. Commas are signals for your reader. Stop here, they say, but not for too long. Commas also cut parts of your sentence away from the whole, separating something from whatever's around it in order to change the meaning of the sentence. When you're speaking, you do the same thing with your tone of voice and the timing of your breaths.

The rules concerning commas aren't very hard. In fact, after you grasp the underlying logic, placing commas correctly is a piece of cake. In this chapter, I guide you through that logic so you know where to put commas in common situations.

Distinguishing Items: Commas in Series

Imagine that you text a shopping list to your roommate Charlie, who's at the store shopping for your birthday party. (If you're curious about texting and grammar rules, turn to Chapter 16.) Everything's on one line.

flashlight batteries butter cookies ice cream cake

How many things does Charlie have to buy? Perhaps only three:

> flashlight batteries
>
> butter cookies
>
> ice cream cake

Or five:

> flashlight
>
> batteries
>
> butter cookies
>
> ice cream
>
> cake

How does Charlie know? He doesn't, unless you use commas. Here's what Charlie actually needs to buy — all four items:

> flashlight batteries, butter cookies, ice cream, cake

To put it in a sentence:

> Charlie has to buy flashlight batteries, butter cookies, ice cream, and cake.

The commas between these items are signals. When you read the list aloud, the commas emerge as breaths:

> Charlie has to buy flashlight batteries [breath] butter cookies [breath] ice cream [breath] and cake.

You need commas between each item on the list, with one important exception. The comma in front of the word *and* is optional. Why? Because when you say *and,* you've already separated the last two items. But if you want to throw an extra comma there, you're welcome to do so. It's your choice.

Never put a comma in front of the first item on the list.

> WRONG: Charlie has to buy, flashlight batteries, butter cookies, ice cream and cake.

> RIGHT: Charlie has to buy flashlight batteries, butter cookies, ice cream and cake.

> ALSO RIGHT: Charlie has to buy flashlight batteries, butter cookies, ice cream, and cake.

> ALSO RIGHT, BUT NOT A GOOD IDEA: Charlie has to buy flashlight batteries and butter cookies and ice cream and cake.

You don't need commas at all in the last sentence because the word *and* does the job. Grammatically, that sentence is fine. In reality, if you write a sentence with three *ands,* your reader will think you sound like a little kid or a tape on continuous rewind.

Punctuate the following sentence.

> Belle requested a jelly doughnut a silk dress four sports cars and a race-horse in exchange for the rights to the computer code she had written.

Answer: Belle requested a jelly doughnut, a silk dress, four sports cars, and a racehorse in exchange for the rights to the computer code she had written. ***Note:*** You may omit the comma before the *and.*

Using "Comma Sense" to Add Information to Your Sentence

Your writing relies on nouns and verbs to get your point across. But if you're like most people, you also enrich your sentences with descriptions. In grammar terminology, you add adjectives and adverbs, participles and clauses, and an occasional appositive. Before you hyperventilate, let me explain that you don't have to know any of those terms in order to write — and punctuate — a good sentence. You just have to keep a couple of key ideas in your head. In this section, I explain how to place commas so that your writing expresses what you mean.

Separating a list of descriptions

Writers often string together a bunch of single-word descriptions, *adjectives,* in grammar lingo. (For more information on adjectives, turn to Chapter 5.) If you have a set of descriptions, you probably have a set of commas also. Take a look at the following sentences:

> "What do you think of me?" Belle asked Jill in an idle moment.

> Jill took a deep breath, "I think you are a sniffling, smelly, pimple-tongued, frizzy-haired monster."

> "Thank you," said Belle, who was trying out for the part of the wicked witch in the school play. "Do you think I should paint my teeth black too?"

Notice the commas in Jill's answer. Four descriptions are listed: *sniffling, smelly, pimple-tongued, frizzy-haired.*

A comma separates each of the descriptions from the next, but there is no comma between the last description (*frizzy-haired*) and the word that it's describing (*monster*).

Here's a little more of Belle and Jill's conversation:

"So do I get the part?" asked Belle.

"Maybe," answered Jill. "I have four sniffling, smelly, pimple-tongued, frizzy-haired monsters waiting to audition. I'll let you know."

Now look closely at Jill's answer. This time there are five descriptions of the word *monster: four, sniffling, smelly, pimple-tongued, frizzy-haired*.

There are commas after *sniffling, smelly,* and *pimple-tongued*. As previously stated, no comma follows *frizzy-haired* because you shouldn't put a comma between the last description and the word that it describes. But why is there no comma after *four*? Here's why: *sniffling, smelly, pimple-tongued*, and *frizzy-haired* are more or less equal in importance in the sentence. They have different meanings, but they all do the same job — telling you how disgusting Belle's costume is. *Four* is in a different category. It gives you different information, telling you how many monsters are waiting, not how they look. Therefore, it's not jumbled into the rest of the list.

Numbers aren't separated from other descriptions or from the word(s) that they describe. Don't put a comma after a number. Also, don't use commas to separate other descriptions from words that indicate number or amount — *many, more, few, less,* and so forth. More descriptive words that you shouldn't separate from other descriptions or from the words that they describe include *other, another, this, that, these, those.* Examine these correctly punctuated sentences:

Sixteen smelly, bedraggled, stained hats were lined up on the shelf marked, "WITCH COSTUME."

Additional stinky, mud-splattered, toeless shoes sat on the shelf marked, "GOBLIN SHOES."

No drippy, disgusting, artificial wounds were in stock.

This green, glossy, licorice-flavored lipstick belongs in the witch's makeup kit.

Those shiny, battery-powered, factory-sealed witches' wands are great.

Punctuate this sentence.

Jill was worried about the musical number in which one hundred scraggly fluorescent flowing beards come to life and dance around the stage.

Answer: Jill was worried about the musical number in which one hundred scraggly, fluorescent, flowing beards come to life and dance around the stage.

Note: Don't put a comma after a number *(one hundred)* or after the last description *(flowing)*.

In your writing, you may create other sentences in which the descriptions should not be separated by commas. For example, sometimes a few descriptive words seem to blend into each other to create one larger description in which one word is clearly more important than the rest. Technically the list of descriptions may provide two or three separate facts about the word that you're describing, but in practice, they don't deserve equal attention. Take a look at this example;

> Jill just bought that funny little French hat.

You already know that you should not separate *that* from *funny* with a comma. But what about *funny, little,* and *French*? If you write

> Jill just bought that funny, little, French hat.

you're giving equal weight to each of the three descriptions. Do you really want to emphasize all three qualities? Probably not. In fact, you're probably not making a big deal out of the fact that the hat is *funny* and *little.* Instead, you're emphasizing that the hat is *French.* So you don't need to put commas between the other descriptions.

Sentences like the example require judgment calls. Use this rule as a guide: If the items in a description are not of equal importance, don't separate them with commas.

Essential or extra? Commas tell the tale

The descriptions in a sentence may be longer than one word. You may have a subject-verb expression (which grammarians call a *clause*) or a verb form (in technical terms, a *participle*). No matter what they're called, these longer descriptions follow one simple rule: If a description is essential to the meaning of the sentence, don't put commas around it. If the description provides extra, nonessential information, set it off with commas.

If you expect to darken little ovals with a #2 pencil (and by the way, what's wrong with a #1 pencil anyway?), spend a little extra time in this section and the next, "Commas with appositive influence." Both the SAT and the ACT gauge your knowledge of essential and nonessential commas.

Consider this situation:

In her quest to reform Larry's government, Ella made this statement:

> Taxes, which are a hardship for the people, are not acceptable.

Lou, who is a member of Larry's Parliament, declared himself in complete agreement with Ella's statement. However, his version had no commas:

> Taxes which are a hardship for the people are not acceptable.

Do the commas really matter? Yes. They matter a lot. Here's the deal. If the description *which are a hardship for the people* is set off from the rest of the sentence by commas, the description is extra — not essential to the meaning of the sentence. You can cross it out and the sentence still means the same thing. If commas do not set off the description, however, the description is essential to the meaning of the sentence. It may not be removed without altering what you are saying. Can you now see the difference between Ella's statement and Lou's? Here's the expanded version of each statement:

> ELLA'S EXPANDED STATEMENT: The government should not impose taxes. We can run the government perfectly well by selling postage stamps to foreign tourists. I suggest a tasteful portrait of the royal bride (me) on a new stamp. No taxes — that's the bottom line.

Because Ella's original sentence includes commas, the description *which are a hardship for the people* is extra information. You can omit it from the sentence. Thus Ella is against all taxes.

> LOU'S EXPANDED STATEMENT: The government is against any taxes which are a hardship for the people. No one wants to place a burden on the working families of our great nation. However, a 90 percent income tax is not a hardship; it pays my salary. This particular tax is acceptable.

Lou's proposal is much less extreme than Ella's. Without commas the description is a necessary part of the sentence. It gives the reader essential information about the meaning of *taxes*. Lou opposes only some taxes — those he believes are a burden. He isn't against all taxes. This description doesn't simply add a reason, as Ella's does. Instead it identifies which taxes Lou opposes.

The pronouns *which* and *that* may help you decide whether or not you need commas. *That* generally introduces information that the sentence can't do without — essential information that isn't set off by commas. The pronoun *which,* on the other hand, often introduces nonessential information that may be surrounded by commas. Keep in mind, however, that these distinctions are not true 100 percent of the time. Sometimes *which* introduces a description that is essential and therefore needs no commas. On rare occasions, the pronoun *that* introduces nonessential material.

Check out these additional examples, with the description in italic:

> SENTENCE: The students *who are planning a sit-in tomorrow* want to be paid for doing homework.

> PUNCTUATION ANALYSIS: The description is not set off by commas, so you may not omit it.

> WHAT THE SENTENCE MEANS: Some of the students — those planning a sit-in — want to be paid for doing homework. Not all the students want to be paid. The rest are perfectly content to do math problems for free.

> SENTENCE: The senators, planning to revolt, have given the television network exclusive rights to cover their rebellion.

> PUNCTUATION ANALYSIS: The commas indicate that the description is extra, nonessential information.

> WHAT THE SENTENCE MEANS: All the senators are involved. They're quite upset, and all have prepared sound bites and scheduled press conferences.

Which sentence means that you can't fly to Cincinnati for your cousin's wedding?

A. The pilots who are going on strike demand that soft music be piped into the cockpit.

B. The pilots, who are going on strike, demand that soft music be piped into the cockpit.

Answer: Sentence B talks about *all* the pilots. They all demand that soft music be piped into the cockpit, and they're all going on strike. The description between the commas adds that little bit of information. In sentence A, only the pilots who like soft music are going on strike.

The word "because" generally introduces a reason. At the beginning of a sentence, the "because" statement acts as an introductory remark is always set off by a comma.

> Because the tattoo was on sale, Lulu whipped out her credit card and rolled up her sleeve.

At the end of a sentence, the "because" statement is sometimes set off by commas, in which case it may be lifted out of the sentence without changing the meaning. Without commas, it's essential to the meaning. Take a look at these two statements:

WITH COMMAS: Lulu didn't get that tattoo, because it was in bad taste.

MEANING: No tattoos for Lulu! The "because" information is extra, explaining why Lulu passed on the design.

WITHOUT COMMAS: Lulu didn't get that tattoo because it was in bad taste.

MEANING: Lulu got the tattoo, but not because it was in bad taste. She got it for another reason (perhaps the sale). The fact that the tattoo grossed out everyone who saw it was just an extra added attraction to Lulu, who enjoys looking strange.

Commas with appositive influence

If you're seeing double when you read a sentence, you've probably encountered an *appositive*. Strictly speaking, appositives aren't descriptions, though they do give you information about something else in the sentence. Appositives are nouns or pronouns that are exactly the same as the noun or pronoun preceding them in the sentence. Some appositives are set off by commas, and some aren't. The rule concerning commas and appositives: If you're sure that your readers will know what you're talking about before they get to the appositive, set off the appositive with commas. If you're not sure your readers will know exactly what you're talking about by the time they arrive at the appositive, you should not use commas. (This rule is a variation of the rule that I explain in the preceding section.)

Now put the rule into practice: What's the difference between these two sentences?

Michael's play *Dinner at the Diner* won the Drama Critics' "Most Boring Play Award."

Dinner at the Diner, Michael's play, won the Drama Critics' "Most Boring Play Award."

In the first example sentence, *Dinner at the Diner* is the appositive of *Michael's play.* When you get to *play,* you don't know which of Michael's plays is being discussed. The appositive supplies the name. Hence, the appositive is essential and isn't set off by commas. In the second example sentence, *Michael's play* is the appositive of *Dinner at the Diner.* Because *Dinner at the Diner* comes first, the reader already knows the name of the play. The fact that Michael wrote the play is extra information and must therefore be surrounded by commas.

Here are a two more examples. In each sentence, *Mary* is the appositive of *sister*.

> Lulu has five sisters, but her sister Mary is definitely her favorite.

Because Lulu has five sisters, you don't know which sister is being discussed until you have the name. *Mary* identifies the sister and shouldn't be placed between commas.

> Roger has only one sibling. His sister, Mary, does not approve of Roger's espionage.

Because Roger has only one sibling, the reader knows that he has only one sister. Thus the words *his sister* pinpoint the person being discussed in the sentence. The name is extra information, not identifying information, and is set off by commas.

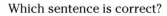

Which sentence is correct?

A. Lola's mother, Lala, doesn't approve of her daughter's pierced toe.

B. Lola's mother Lala doesn't approve of her daughter's pierced toe.

Answer: Sentence A is correct. Lola has only one mother, so the name is extra, not identifying information.

You Talkin' to Me? Direct Address

When writing a message to someone, you need to separate the person's name from the rest of the sentence with a comma. Otherwise, your reader may misread the intention of the message. Take a look at the following note that Michael left on the door:

> Roger wants to kill Wendy. I locked him in this room.

You think: Wendy is in danger. That's a shame. Oh well, I guess I'm safe. However, when you unlock the door and sit down for a cup of tea, Roger jumps up and starts chasing you around the room. You escape and run screaming to Michael. "Why didn't you tell me that Roger was violent!" Michael pleads guilty to a grammatical crime. He forgot to put in the comma! Here's what he meant:

> Roger wants to kill, Wendy. I locked him in this room.

It was your bad luck to read a note intended for Wendy. In grammarspeak, *Wendy* is in a *direct-address* sentence. Because the writer was directing his comments to Wendy, her name should be cut her off from the rest of the sentence with a comma. Direct address is also possible at the beginning or in the middle of a sentence:

> Wendy, Roger wants to kill, so I locked him in this room.

> Roger wants to kill, Wendy, so I locked him in this room.

Which sentence is correct?

    A. The teacher called, Emma, but I answered.

    B. The teacher called Emma, but I answered.

Answer: It depends. If you're talking to Emma, telling her that Miss Sharkface phoned your house to report missing homework but you, not your mom, picked up the phone, then sentence A is correct. However, if you're explaining that the teacher screamed to Emma, "Bring your homework up here *this minute!*" and instead you replied, "Miss Sharkface, Emma asked me to tell you that a dog ate her homework," sentence B is correct.

Using Commas in Addresses and Dates

Commas are good, all-purpose separators. They won't keep you and your worst enemy apart, but they do a fine job on addresses and dates — especially when items that are usually placed on individual lines are put next to each other on the same line.

Addressing addresses

Where are you from? Jill is from Mars. Belle is from a small town called Venus. Here's her (fictional) address, the way you see it on an envelope:

> Ms. Belle Planet
>
> 223 Center Street
>
> Venus, New York 10001

In the body of a letter, you can insert an address in "envelope form" like this:

> Please send a dozen rockets to the following address:
>
> > Ms. Belle Planet
> >
> > 223 Center Street
> >
> > Venus, New York 10001

The introductory words (*Please send a dozen rockets to the following address*) end with a colon (:) if they express a complete unit of thought. If the introductory words leave you hanging (*Please send a dozen rockets to*, for example), don't use a colon.

If you put Belle's address into a sentence, you have to separate each item of the address, as you see here:

> Belle Planet lives at 223 Center Street, Venus, New York 10001.

Here's the address (envelope style) for her best friend Jill:

> Jill Willis
>
> 53 Asimov Court
>
> Mars, California 90210

And now the sentence version:

> Jill Willis lives at 53 Asimov Court, Mars, California 90210.

Notice that the house number and street are not separated by a comma, nor are the state and zip code.

If the sentence continues, you must separate the last item in the address from the rest of the sentence with another comma:

> Belle Planet lives at 223 Center Street, Venus, New York 10001, but she is thinking of moving to Mars in order to be closer to her friend Jill.

If there is no street address — just a city and a state — put a comma between the city and the state. If the sentence continues after the state name, place a comma after the state.

> Belle Planet lives in Venus, New York, but she is thinking of moving to Mars.

Commas also separate countries from the city/state/province:

> Roger lives in Edinburgh, Scotland, near a large body of water. His brother Michael just built a house in Zilda, Wisconsin.

Punctuate the following sentence.

> Police believe that the missing salamander ran away from his home at 77 Main Street Zilda Wisconsin because of a dispute over the number of insects he would receive for each meal.

Answer: Police believe that the missing salamander ran away from his home at 77 Main Street, Zilda, Wisconsin, because of a dispute over the number of insects he would receive for each meal.

Punctuating dates

Confession time: The rules for placing commas in dates aren't very stable these days. What was once carved into stone (and I mean that literally) is now sometimes viewed as old-fashioned. To make matters even more complicated, writers from different areas (science, literature, and the like) favor different systems. In this section, I tell you the traditional form and show you some possible variations. If you're writing for business or school, the traditional form should get you through. If you're up for publication, check with your editor about the publisher's preferred style.

If the date is alone on a line (perhaps at the top of a letter), these formats are fine:

> September 28, 2060 (traditional)
>
> Sept. 28, 2060 (traditional)
>
> 28 September 2060 (modern in the United States, traditional in many other countries)

When dates appear in a sentence, the format changes depending upon (a) how traditional you want to be and (b) how much information you want to give. Take a look at the commas — or the lack of commas — in these sentences:

> On September 28, 2060, Lulu ate several thousand gummy candies. (Traditional: commas separate the day and year and the year from the rest of the sentence.)
>
> In October, 2060, Lulu gave up sugary snacks. (Traditional: a comma separates the month from the year and the year from the rest of the sentence.)
>
> Lulu pigs out every October 31st. (Timeless: both the traditional and modern camp omit commas in this format.)
>
> In October 2060 Lulu suffered from severe indigestion. (Modern: no commas appear.)
>
> Lulu visited a nutritionist on 20 October 2060. (Modern: no commas appear.)

Punctuate this sentence.

> Lola testified under oath that on December 18 2011 she saw Lulu place a carton of gummy bears under the counter without paying for them.

Traditional Answer: Lola testified under oath that on December 18, 2011, she saw Lulu place a carton of gummy bears under the counter without paying for them.

Modern Answer: Lola testified under oath that on 18 December 2011 she saw Lulu place a carton of gummy bears under the counter without paying for them.

Flying Solo: Introductory Words

Yes, this section introduces a comma rule. No, it's not optional. Well, you probably know it already. Oh, I'll explain it anyway. Okay, the rule is that you must separate words that aren't part of the sentence but instead comment on the meaning of the sentence. I'll put it another way: *introductory words* that appear at the beginning of a sentence are set off from what follows by commas. If you omit these words, the sentence still means the same thing. Common introductory words include *yes*, *no*, *well*, *oh*, and *okay*.

Read these examples twice, once with the introductory words and once without. See how the meaning stays the same?

> Yes, you are allowed to chew gum balls during class, but don't complain to me if you break a tooth.

> No, you are not allowed to write the exam in blood as a protest against the amount of studying you need to do in order to pass this course.

> Well, you may consider moving on to another topic if you have exhausted the creative possibilities of "My Favorite Lightbulb."

> Oh, I didn't know that you needed your intestines today.

To sum up the rule on introductory words: Use commas to separate them from the rest of the sentence, or omit them entirely.

Which sentence is correct?

A. Well Ella plays the piano well when she is in the mood.

B. Well, Ella plays the piano, well, when she is in the mood.

C. Well, Ella plays the piano well when she is in the mood.

Answer: Sentence C is correct. If you omit the first word, the sentence means exactly the same thing. *Well* is an introductory word that a comma should separate from the rest of the sentence. In sentence A, there is no comma after *well*. In sentence B, the first comma is correct, but the second *well* shouldn't be separated from the rest of the sentence because it's not an introductory word.

Punctuating Independently

When you join two complete sentences with the conjunctions (joining words) *and, or, but, nor, yet, so,* or *for,* place a comma before the conjunction. Some examples include:

> Agnes robbed the bank, and then she went out for a hamburger.

> James spies, but apart from that lapse he is not a bad fellow.

> Sam bribed the judges of this year's state spitball contest, for he is determined to qualify for the national tournament.

For more information on conjunctions and complete sentences, see Chapter 5.

Some sentences have one subject (who or what you're talking about) and two verbs joined by *and, but, or,* and *nor.* Don't put commas between the two verbs. You aren't joining two complete sentences, just two words or groups of words. Here are some examples:

> WRONG: Ella wrote a statement for the media, and then screamed at her press agent for an hour.

> WHY IT IS WRONG: The sentence has one subject *(Ella)* and two verbs *(wrote, screamed).* You aren't joining two complete sentences, so you shouldn't place a comma before *and.* Either way, Ella should learn to control her temper.

> RIGHT: Ella wrote a statement for the media and then screamed at Larry for an hour.

> WRONG: Larry has proposed a toast to his bride, but has given her nothing but a headache.

> WHY IT IS WRONG: The sentence has one subject *(Larry)* and two verbs *(has proposed, has given).* The word *but* joins the two verbs, not two complete sentences. You don't need a comma. Also, if she's putting up with Larry, she deserves a wedding gift.

> RIGHT: Larry has proposed a toast to his bride but has given her nothing but a headache.

Which sentence is correct?

A. Al slits envelopes with his teeth, but Dorothy opens the mail with a fork.

B. Al answers every letter on the day he receives it but doesn't pay any bills.

Answer: Both sentences are correct. In sentence A, the conjunction *but* joins two complete sentences. A comma must precede the conjunction *but*. In sentence B, *but* joins two verbs (*answers, does pay*). No comma precedes the conjunction.

Chapter 14

Useful Little Marks: Dashes, Hyphens, and Colons

In This Chapter

▶ Inserting dashes for maximum effect

▶ Using long and short dashes correctly

▶ Placing hyphens in compounds and interrupted words

▶ Knowing where to place a colon in a business letter, list, and quotation

*I*n a classic episode of an old detective show, the hero's sidekick writes a book. The entire thing has no punctuation whatsoever. The author explains that he's going to put in "all that stuff" later. Many writers sympathize with the sidekick. Who has time to worry about punctuation when the fire of creativity burns? But the truth is that the three little marks I explain in this chapter — dashes, hyphens, and colons — go a long way toward getting your point across.

Inserting Information with Dashes

Long dashes — what grammarians call "em dashes" — are dramatic. Those long straight lines draw your eye and hold your attention. But long dashes aren't just show-offs. They insert information into a sentence and introduce lists. Short dashes — technically, "en dashes" — aren't as showy as their wider cousins, but they're still useful. Short dashes show a range or connect words when the word *to* or *and* is implied.

Long dashes

A long dash's primary job is to tell the reader that you've jumped tracks onto a new (though related) subject, just for a moment. Here are some examples:

> After we buy toenail clippers — the dinosaur in that exhibit could use a trim, you know — we'll stop at the doughnut shop.

> Standing on one manicured claw, the dinosaur — delivered to the museum only an hour before the grand opening — is the star of the exhibit.

The information inside the dashes is off-topic. Take it out, and the sentence makes sense. The material inside the dashes relates to the information in the rest of the sentence, but it acts as an interruption to the main point that you're making.

The words between a pair of dashes may or may not form a complete sentence. Fine. However, some people use only one dash to tack a complete sentence onto another complete sentence. Not fine! (Also, an issue you may encounter on standardized tests.) Here's what I mean:

> WRONG: The curator painted the dinosaur orange — everyone hates the color.

> RIGHT: The curator painted the dinosaur orange — everyone hates the color — because she wanted to "liven the place up."

> ALSO RIGHT: The curator painted the dinosaur orange; everyone hates the color.

> ALSO RIGHT: The curator painted the dinosaur orange — a color hated by everyone.

The first example sentence is wrong because a dash can't link two complete sentences. The second example is okay because a pair of dashes can surround a complete sentence embedded inside another complete sentence. The third example avoids the problem by linking the two sentences with a semicolon. The fourth example is correct because a dash may add extra information at the end of a sentence, as long as the extra information isn't a complete sentence. (*A color hated by everyone* isn't a complete sentence.)

Is the following sentence legal or grounds for arrest by the grammar police?

> The sweet sounds of a thousand tubas wafted through the air — she fell asleep.

Answer: If you said legal, you get five to ten in the punctuation penitentiary. You need a period after *air* because *The sweet sounds of a thousand tubas wafted through the air* is a complete sentence. *She fell asleep* is also a complete sentence. You may not connect two complete sentences with a dash. The correct version reads

> The sweet sounds of a thousand tubas wafted through the air. She fell asleep.

A dash's second job is to move the reader from general to specific, often by supplying a definition. Check out the following examples:

> I think I have everything I need for the first day of camp — bug spray, hair spray, sun block, and DVD player.

Everything I need is general; *bug spray, hair spray, sun block, and DVD player* are the specifics.

> Louie said that he would perform the *ugu-ug-ba* — the ritual unwrapping of the season's first piece of chewing gum.

The definition of *ugu-ug-ba* is *the ritual unwrapping of the season's first piece of chewing gum*.

Long dashes may be fun to write, but they're not always fun to read. For a little change of pace, dash a new idea into your sentence. Just don't dash in too often or your reader will be tempted to dash away.

Short dashes

If you master this punctuation mark, you deserve an official grammarian's badge — very attractive at cocktail parties! Short dashes show a range:

> From May – September, the convicts prune commas from literature written over the winter.

Short dashes also show up when you're omitting the word *to* between two elements:

> The New York – Philadelphia train is always on time.

Finally, a short dash links two or more equal elements when *and* is implied:

> The catcher – pitcher relationship is crucial to the success of the Yankees. (Sorry, can't resist rooting for my favorite team.)

Don't confuse short dashes with hyphens, an even shorter punctuation mark that I cover in the next section.

H-y-p-h-e-n-a-t-i-n-g Made Easy

Think of a hyphen as a dash that's been on a diet. You need these short, horizontal lines to help you maneuver through unexpected line breaks and for a couple of other reasons as well — to separate parts of compound words, to write certain numbers, and to create one description from two words. This section provides you with a guide to the care and feeding of the humble hyphen.

Understanding the great divide

Computer users have to worry about hyphens less often than other writers. Most of the time, the word processing program moves a word to a new line if there isn't enough room at the end of a line for the entire word. But when you're writing by hand or typing on an old-fashioned typewriter (do they still exist?), you may need to divide a word at the end of a line to avoid a long blank space along the right-hand margin. If you have to divide a word, follow these simple rules:

- ✔ Place the hyphen between the *syllables,* or sounds, of a word. (If you're not sure where the syllable breaks are in a word, check the dictionary.)
- ✔ Don't leave only one letter of a divided word on a line. If you have a choice, divide the word more or less in the middle.
- ✔ Don't divide words that have only one syllable.

Web addresses can be very long. Don't divide them with a hyphen. Either place the Web address on its own line or, if you absolutely have to divide, chop the address at a period or slash mark.

Using hyphens for compound words

Hyphens also separate parts of compound words, such as *ex-wife*, *pro-choice*, *mother-in-law*, and so forth. When you type or write these words, don't put a space before or after the hyphen.

The British system

The practice of dividing a word between syllables is American. In Britain, words are often divided according to the derivation (family tree) of the word, not according to sound. For example, in the American system, *democracy* is divided into four parts — *de-moc-ra-cy* — because that's how it sounds. In the British system, the same word is divided into two parts — *demo-cracy* — because the word is derived from two ancient Greek forms, *demos (people)* and *kratia (power)*. Let the dictionary of the country you're in be the final authority on dividing words.

I should mention that the trend in modern writing is toward fewer punctuation marks. Thus, many words that used to be hyphenated compounds are now written as single words. *Semi-colon*, for instance, has morphed into *semicolon.* As always, the dictionary is your friend when you're figuring out whether a particular expression is a compound, a single word, or two separate words.

One cap or two? The answer is complicated. All the parts of a person's title are capitalized, except for prepositions and articles (*Secretary-Treasurer, Commander-in-Chief,* and so forth). Don't capitalize the prefix *ex-* (as in *ex-President Carter, ex-Attorney-General Meese*). Words that are capitalized for some other reason (perhaps because they're part of a book title or a headline) follow a different rule. Always capitalize the first half. Capitalize the second half of the compound if it's a noun, or if the second half of the compound is equal in importance to the first half: *Secretary-General Lola, President-elect Lulu.* (For more information on capitalization, see Chapter 15.)

Hyphens also show up when a single word might be misunderstood. I once received an e-mail from a student. "I resent the draft," she wrote. I spent ten minutes worrying about her feelings before I realized that she sent the draft of a paper twice because the e-mail didn't go through the first time. To avoid misinterpretation, she should have written *re-sent.*

Placing hyphens in numbers

Decisions about whether to write a numeral or a word are questions of style, not of grammar. The authority figure in your life — teacher, boss, parole officer, whatever — will tell you what he or she prefers. In general, larger numbers are usually represented by numerals:

Roger has been arrested 683 times, counting last night.

However, on various occasions you may need to write the word, not the numeral. If the number falls at the beginning of a sentence, for example, you must use words because no sentence may begin with a numeral. You may also need to write about a fractional amount. Here's how to hyphenate:

- ✔ Hyphenate all the numbers from twenty-one to ninety-nine.
- ✔ Hyphenate all fractions used as descriptions (*three-quarters full*, for example).
- ✔ Don't hyphenate fractions used as nouns (*three quarters of the money; one third of all registered voters*).

Utilizing the well-placed hyphen

If two words create a single description, put a hyphen between them if the description comes before the word that it's describing. For example:

a *well-placed* hyphen — BUT — the hyphen is *well placed.*

Don't hyphenate two-word descriptions if the first word ends in *-ly:*

nicely drawn rectangle

completely ridiculous grammar rule

Place hyphens where they're needed.

Lulu was recently elected secretary treasurer of her club, the All Star Athletes of Antarctica. Lulu ran on an anti ice platform that was accepted by two thirds of the members.

Answer: Here's the paragraph with the hyphens inserted, along explanations in parentheses:

Lulu was recently elected secretary-treasurer (hyphen needed for compound title) of her club, the All-Star (hyphen needed for two-word description) Athletes of Antarctica. Lulu ran on an anti-ice (hyphen needed for two-word description) platform that was accepted by two thirds (no hyphen for fractions not used as descriptions) of the members.

Creating a Stopping Point: Colons

A colon is one dot on top of another (:). It appears when a simple comma isn't strong enough. (It also shows up in those smiley faces — the so-called *emoticons* — that people write in their e-mails.) In this section, I look at the colon in a few of its natural habitats: business letters, lists, and quotations.

Addressing a business letter

Colons appear in business letters, as you see in the following examples.

Dear Mr. Ganglia:

You are getting on my nerves. You're fired.

Sincerely,

I.M. Incharj

To Whom It May Concern:

Everyone in the division is fired also.

Sincerely,

I.M. Incharj

 The colon makes a business letter more formal. The opposite of a business letter is what English teachers call a *friendly letter,* even if it says something like "I hate you." When you write a friendly letter, put a comma after the name of the person who will receive the letter.

Introducing lists

When you insert a short list of items into a sentence, you don't need a colon. (For more information on how to use commas in lists, see Chapter 13.) When you're inserting a long list into a sentence, however, you may sometimes use a colon to introduce the list. Think of the colon as a gulp of air that readies the reader for a good-sized list. The colon precedes the first item. Here are some sentences using colons to introduce lists:

> General Parker needed quite a few things: a horse, an army, a suit of armor, a few million arrows, a map, and a battle plan.

> Roger sent each spy away with several items: an excerpt from the encyclopedia entry on espionage, a collection of the essays of Mata Hari, a photocopy of the nation's policy on treason, and a poison pill.

If you put a colon in front of a list, check the beginning of the sentence — the part before the colon. Can it stand alone? If so, no problem. The words before the colon must form a complete thought. If not, don't use a colon. Take a look at these examples:

> WRONG: The problems with Parker's battle plan are: no understanding of enemy troop movements, a lack of shelter and food for the troops, and a faulty trigger for the retreat signal. (The words before the colon — *The problems with Parker's battle plan are* — don't form a complete thought.)

> RIGHT: The problems with Parker's battle plan are numerous: no under-standing of enemy troop movements, a lack of shelter and food for the troops, and a faulty trigger for the retreat signal. (Now the words before the colon — *The problems with Parker's battle plan are numerous* — form a complete thought.

For more information on complete sentences, see Chapter 5.

Introducing long quotations

The rule concerning colons with quotations is fairly easy. If the quotation is short, introduce it with a comma. If the quotation is long, introduce it with a colon. Take a look at the following two examples for comparison.

What did Lola say at the meeting? Not much, so a comma does the job.

> Lola stated, "I have no comment on the squirrel incident."

What did General Parker say at the press conference? Too much, so a colon is better.

> Parker explained: "The media has been entirely too critical of my prepa-rations for war. Despite the fact that I have spent the last ten years and two million gold coins perfecting new and improved armor, I have been told that I am unready to fight."

When you write a paper for school, you may put some short quotations (up to three lines) into the text. If a quotation is longer than three lines, you should double-indent and single-space the quoted material so that it looks like a sepa-rate block of print. Such quotations are called *block quotations*. Introduce the block quotation with a colon, and don't use quotation marks. (The blocking shows that you're quoting, so you don't need the marks.) Here's an example:

Flugle, in his essay entitled, "Why Homework is Useless," makes the following point:

> Studies show that students who have no time to rest are not as efficient as those who do. When a thousand teens were surveyed, they all indicated that sleeping, listening to music, talking on the phone, and watching television were more valuable than schoolwork.

If you're writing about poetry, you may use the same block format:

> The post-modern imagery of this stanza is in stark contrast to the imagery of the Romantic period:
>
> > Roses are red,
> > Violets are blue,
> > Eggworthy is sweet,
> > And stupid, too.

Colons sometimes show up inside sentences, joining one complete sentence to another. A colon may be used this way only when the second sentence explains the meaning of the first sentence, as in this example:

> Lola has refused to take the job: She believes the media will investigate every aspect of her life.

The second half of the sentence explains why Lola doesn't want to run for president. Actually, it explains why almost no Americans want to run for president. Notice that I've capitalized the first word after the colon. Some writers prefer lowercase for that spot. This decision is a matter of style, not grammar. Check with the authority figure in charge of your writing (teacher, boss, warden, and so on) for his or her preference.

Chapter 15

CAPITAL LETTERS

In This Chapter

▶ Understanding the basics of capital letters

▶ Capitalizing names, places, and things

▶ Knowing when capital letters are needed in ordinary writing

---

*E*very teacher has at least one pet peeve. I've got a good-sized set of usage errors that set my teeth on edge. One is *lowercase* — what kindergarteners call "small letters" — for the personal pronoun *I*. It's not that I have anything against lowercase letters. It's just that I believe *i* and *I* should follow tradition because, well . . . capitalization is all about tradition. So don't look for logic in this chapter. All you'll find here is what's up (as in *uppercase*, or capitals) with capitalization rules.

Browsing the Basics of Capital Letters

Fortunately, the rules for capital letters are easy. Here are the basics:

✔ **Begin every sentence with a capital letter**. What's that you asked? What about sentences that begin with a numeral? Caught you! You're not supposed to begin a sentence with a numeral. Ever. If a number is needed in that spot, you have to write the word and capitalize it. So if you're a star pitcher and the Yankees make an offer, don't send this text:

> $10,000,000 per game is not enough.

Instead, type one of these messages:

> A mere $10,000,000 per game is not enough.

> Ten million dollars per game is not enough.

Traditionally, the first letter of each line of a poem is capitalized, even if it isn't the beginning of a sentence. However, poets enjoy trashing (sorry, I meant *reinterpreting*) rules. In poetry, anything goes — including capitalization rules.

- **Capitalize *I*.** My pet peeve, as I explain in the beginning of this chapter. I have no idea why the personal pronoun *I* — the word you use to refer to yourself — must be capitalized. The reason probably has something to do with psychology, but I'm not a shrink. I'm a grammarian. So go for caps when you write *I*, and save lowercase for other pronouns (*he, she, us, them,* and so on).

- **Capitalize names.** This rule applies when you're using an actual name, not a category. Write about *Elizabeth*, not *elizabeth*, when you're discussing the cutest baby ever (my granddaughter). She's a *girl*, not a *Girl*, because *girl* is a category, not a name. Elizabeth lives in *Washington*, not *washington* (her *state*, not *State,* because *state* is a general category, not a name). You also capitalize brand names (*Sony*, for example) unless the company itself uses lowercase letters (the *iPod*, for instance).

- **Capitalize words that refer to the deity.** Traditionally, believers capitalize all words that refer to the being they worship, as in this line from a famous hymn:

  God works in mysterious ways *His* wonders to perform.

  Capitalize mythological gods only when giving their names:

  The ancient Greeks built temples in honor of *Zeus* and other *gods.*

- **Begin most quotations with a capital letter.** When quotation marks appear, so do capitals — most of the time. (For exceptions to this rule, turn to Chapter 13.)

That's it for the basics. For the picky stuff, keep reading.

Capitalizing (or Not) References to People

If human beings were called only by their names, life would be much simpler, at least in terms of capital letters. But most people pick up a few titles and some relatives as they journey through life. In this section, I tell you what to capitalize when you're referring to people.

Sorting out titles

Allow me to introduce myself. I'm *Ms.* Woods, *Chief Grammarian* Woods, and *Apostrophe-Hater-in-Chief* Woods (see Chapter 11). All these titles start with capital letters because they're attached to the front of my name. In a sense, they've become part of my name.

Allow me to introduce my friend Eggworthy. He's *Mr.* Eggworthy Henhuff, *director of poultry* at a nearby farm. Next year *Director of Poultry* Henhuff plans to run for *state senator,* unless he cracks under the pressure of a major campaign, in which case he'll run for *sheriff.*

Now what's going on with the capitals? The title *Mr.* is capitalized because it's attached to Eggworthy's last name. Other titles — *state senator* and *sheriff* — are not. In general, lowercase titles are those not connected to a name.

Notice that *Director of Poultry* is capitalized when it precedes Eggworthy's last name but not capitalized when it follows Eggworthy's name. *Director of Poultry Henhuff* functions as a unit. If you were talking to Eggworthy, you might address him as *Director of Poultry Henhuff.* So the first *Director of Poultry* in the paragraph above functions as part of the name. When the title follows the name, it gives the reader more information about Eggworthy, but it no longer acts as part of Eggworthy's name. Hence, the second *director of poultry* in the previous paragraph is in lowercase.

No self-respecting rule allows itself be taken for granted, so this capitalization rule has an exception or two, just to make sure that you're paying attention. You must capitalize very important titles even when they appear without the name of the person who holds them. What's very important? Definitely these:

- ✔ President of the United States
- ✔ Secretary General of the United Nations
- ✔ Chief Justice of the Supreme Court
- ✔ Vice President of the United States
- ✔ Prime Minister of Great Britain

Here's an example of one of these titles, President of the United States, in action:

> The President of the United States addressed the nation tonight. In her address, the President called for the repeal of all illogical grammar rules.

Of course, there's some leeway with the rule on titles, with the boss or editor or teacher making the final decision. (When in doubt, check with the authority in question.) The following titles are often but not always lowercase when they appear without a name:

- ✔ representative

- ✔ ambassador

- ✔ consul

- ✔ justice

- ✔ cabinet secretary

- ✔ judge

- ✔ mayor

Nameless titles that are even lower on the importance ladder are strictly lowercase:

- ✔ assistant secretary

- ✔ dogcatcher-in-chief

- ✔ officer

- ✔ ensign

When capitalizing a hyphenated title, capitalize both words (*Chief Justice*) or neither *(assistant secretary).* One exception (sigh) to the rule is for *exes* and *elects:*

- ✔ ex-President

- ✔ President-elect

Writing about family relationships

It's not true that Elizabeth's *grandma* was imprisoned for felonious sentence structure. I know for a fact that *Uncle Bart* took the rap, although his *brother* Alfred tried desperately to convince *Grandma* to make a full confession. "My *son* deserves to do time," said *Grandma,* "because he split an infinitive when he was little and got away with it."

What do you notice about the family titles in the preceding paragraph? Some of them are capitalized, and some are not. The rules for capitalizing the titles of family members are simple. If you're labeling a relative, don't capitalize. (I'm talking about kinship — *aunt, sister, son,* and so on — not appearance or personality flaws — *tubby, sweet-faced, dishonest,* and so on.) If the titles take the place of names (as in *Uncle Bart and Grandma*), capitalize them. For example:

Lulu's *stepsister* Sarah took care to pour exactly one cup of ink into every load of wash that Lulu did. (*stepsister* = label)

Sarah told *Mother* about the gallon of paint thinner that Lulu had dripped over Sarah's favorite rose bush. (*Mother* = name)

I was surprised when my *father* took no action; fortunately *Aunt Aggie* stepped in with a pail of bleach for Lulu. (*father* — label; *Aunt Aggie* — name)

If you can substitute a real name — Mabel or Jonas, for example — in the sentence, you probably need a capital letter:

I told *Father* that he needed to shave off his handlebar moustache and put it on his bicycle. (original sentence)

I told *Jonas* that he needed to shave off his handlebar moustache and put it on his bicycle. (The substitution sounds fine, so capitalize *Father.*)

If the substitution sounds strange, you probably need lowercase:

I told my *grandmother* not to shave off her moustache. (original sentence)

I told my *Mabel* not to shave off her moustache. (The substitution doesn't work because you don't say *my Mabel.* Use lowercase for *grandmother.*)

The word *my* and other possessive pronouns (*your, his, her, our, their*) often indicate that you should lowercase the title. (For more information on possessive pronouns, see Chapter 17.)

Which sentence is correct?

A. Ever since he heard that housework causes acute inflammation of elbow grease, Archie helps mother around the house as little as possible.

B. Ever since he heard that housework causes acute inflammation of elbow grease, Archie helps Mother around the house as little as possible.

Answer: Sentence B is correct. *Mother* is used as a name, not a label, so you must capitalize it. (Try the *Mabel* test; it works!)

Tackling race and ethnicity

If you come from Tasmania, you're Tasmanian. If you come from New York, you're a New Yorker. (Don't ask me about Connecticut; I've never been able to get an answer, though I've asked everyone I know from that state.) Those examples of capitalization are easy. But what about race and ethnicity? Like everyone else, grammarians struggle to overcome the legacy of a racist society and its language. Here are some guidelines concerning capitalization and race:

✔ White and Black (or white and black) are acceptable descriptions, but be consistent. Don't capitalize one and not the other. Always capitalize *Asian* because the term is derived from the name of a continent.

✔ European American, Asian American, African American (and the less popular Afro-American) are all in capitals.

✔ Mexican American, Polish American, and other descriptions of national origin are written with capital letters because the terms are derived from country names.

✔ To hyphenate or not to hyphenate, that is the question. *Afro-American* is generally written with a hyphen. As for terms such as Asian American, Mexican American, African American, and the like, the answer depends on your politics. Without the hyphen, *American* is the primary word, described by the word that precedes it. So without the hyphen, you emphasize the identity of *American.* With the hyphen, both words are equal, so both parts of the identity have equal importance.

Capitalizing Geography: Directions, Places, and Languages

Even if nothing more than your imagination leaves the living room, you still need to know the rules for capitalizing the names of places, languages, geographical features, regions, and directions. Here's a complete guide to capitalizing geography.

Directions and areas of a country

Robbie and Levon, my parakeets, don't migrate for the winter. (Instead, they sit on the window frame and squawk at their friends, the pigeons of New York.) If they did fly away, though, where would they go — south or South? It depends. The direction of flight is *south* (lowercase). The area of the country where they work on a tan, grow a few new feathers, and generally enjoy themselves is the *South* (uppercase). Got it? From New York City you drive *west* to visit the *West* (or the *Midwest*).

The names of other, smaller areas are often capitalized too. Plopped in the center of New York City is Central Park, which the West Side and the East Side flank. Chicago has a South Side and London has Bloomsbury. Note the capital letters for the names of these areas.

Capitalizing geographic features

Capitalize locations within a country when the proper name is given (the name of a city or region, such as the *Mississippi River*, *the Congo*, or *Los Angeles*, for example).

Is *the* part of the name? Usually not, even when it's hard to imagine the name without it. In general, don't capitalize *the*.

When the name doesn't appear, lowercase geographical features (*mountain*, *valley*, *gorge* or *beach*, for instance).

In general, you should capitalize the names of countries and languages. One exception to this rule: common objects with a country or nationality as part of the name (*french fries*, *scotch whiskey*, *venetian blinds,* and so forth). By attaching itself to a common object, the language or country name takes on a new meaning. The name no longer makes the reader think of the country or language. Instead, the reader simply thinks of an everyday object. If you're not sure whether or not to capitalize the geographical part of a common item, check the dictionary.

Correct the capitalization in this paragraph.

> When Alex sent his little brother Abner to Italy, Abner vowed to visit mount Vesuvius. Alex asked Abner to bring back some venetian blinds, but Abner returned empty-handed. "Let's go out for chinese food," said Abner when he returned. "Some sesame noodles will cheer me up."

Here is the answer, with explanations in parentheses:

> When Alex sent his little brother Abner to Italy (correct — country name), Abner vowed to visit Mount Vesuvius (capitalize the entire name of the mountain). Alex asked Abner to bring back some venetian blinds (correct — lowercase for the name of a common object), but Abner returned empty-handed. "Let's go out for Chinese food (because this isn't the name of one specific item, such as french fries, capitals are better)," said Abner when he returned. "Some sesame noodles will cheer me up."

Marking Seasons and Other Times

Lochness hates the *summer* because of all the tourists who try to snap pictures of what he calls "an imaginary monster." He's been known to roar something about *"winter's* peaceful *mornings,"* even though he never wakes up before *3 p.m.*

After reading the preceding example, you can probably figure out this rule without me. Write the seasons of the year in lowercase, as well as the times of day.

Some books tell you to capitalize the abbreviations for morning and afternoon (A.M. and P.M.) and some specify lowercase (a.m. and p.m.). So no matter what you do, half your readers will think you're right (the good news) and half will think you're wrong (the bad news). Your best bet is to check with the authority overseeing your writing. If you're the authority, do what you wish.

Schooling: Courses, Years, and Subjects

As every student knows, school is complicated. So is the rule concerning the capitalization of school-related terms. Don't capitalize subjects and subject areas (*history, science, physics, phys ed*, for example) unless the name refers to a language (*Spanish, Latin, English,* and so on). On the other hand, capitalize the titles of courses (*Economics 101, Math for Poets, Paper Clips in American History*, and the like).

The years in school, while interminable and incredibly important, are not capitalized (*seventh grader, freshman, sophomore,* for instance).

Correct the capitalization in this paragraph.

> Hurrying to his Chemistry class, Kneejerk slipped on the ice on the very first day of his Senior year. He was carrying a small jar of purple crystals, which, when added to water, were guaranteed to produce dense, purple smoke. Kneejerk wanted to impress the love of his life, Freshman Lilac Jones, who had enrolled in history of the ancient world with Professor Krater. Lilac's class, deep in the study of history, never knew the peril they had escaped.

Answer: Here's the correct version, with the reasons in parentheses:

> Hurrying to his chemistry (don't capitalize subjects) class, Kneejerk slipped on the ice on the very first day of his senior year (never capitalize years in school). He was carrying a small jar of purple crystals, which, when added to water, were guaranteed to produce dense, purple smoke. Kneejerk wanted to impress the love of his life, freshman (never capitalize years in school) Lilac Jones, who had enrolled in History of the Ancient World (capitalize course titles) with Professor Krater. Lilac's class, deep in the study of history (this one is correct — lowercase for subject areas), never knew the peril they had escaped.

Writing Capitals in Titles

Lochness is hosting a party to celebrate the publication of his new book, *I AM NOT A MONSTER*. He has postponed the party three times because he can't decide how to capitalize the title. What should he do? Actually, he should scrap the book, which consists of 540 pages of unbelievably boring detail about his humdrum life. Apart from that issue, here's what Lochness should do:

- Capitalize *I* and *Monster*. *I* is always uppercase and *Monster* is an important word. Also, *I* is the first word of the title, and the first word of the title is always capitalized.

- Capitalize *Am* because it's a verb, and verbs are at the heart of the title's meaning. (See Chapter 2.)

- Capitalize *Not* because it changes the meaning of the verb and thus has an important job to do in the sentence.

- Lowercase the only word left — *a*. Never capitalize articles (*a*, *an*, and *the*) unless they're the first words in the title.

Do you see the general principles that I've applied? Here is a summary of the rules for all sorts of titles:

- Capitalize the first word in the title.

- Capitalize verbs and other important words.

- Lowercase unimportant words — articles (*a*, *an*, *the*), conjunctions (words that connect, such as *and*, *or*, *nor*, and the like), and prepositions (*of*, *with*, *by*, and other words that express a relationship between two elements in the sentence).

The resulting book title is *I Am Not a Monster*.

Some grammarians capitalize long prepositions — those with more than four letters. Others tell you to lowercase all prepositions, even the huge ones — *concerning*, *according to*, and so on. (See Chapter 8 for a list of common prepositions.) Your best bet is to check with your immediate authority (editor, boss, teacher, and so on) to make sure that you write in the style to which he or she is accustomed.

When writing the title of a magazine or newspaper, should you capitalize the word *the?* Yes, if *the* is part of the official name, as in *The New York Times*. No, if the publication doesn't include *the* in its official name, as in the *Daily News*.

Which words should you capitalize in these titles?

> the importance of being lochness
>
> romeo and lulu
>
> slouching toward homework

Answers:

> The Importance of Being Lochness (*The* is the first word of the title. *Importance, Being,* and *Lochness* are important words. Lowercase *of* because it's not an important word.)
>
> Romeo and Lulu (*Romeo* is the first word of the title and is also a name. Similarly, *Lulu* is a name. Lowercase *and* because it's not an important word.)
>
> Slouching Toward Homework (*Slouching* is the first word of the title. *Homework* is important. *Toward* can go either way. It's a preposition — a relationship word — and thus may be lowercase, at least according to some grammarians. It's also a long word, which makes it suitable for capitalization in the opinion of other grammarians.)

Concerning Historic Capitals: Events and Eras

Jane entered her time machine and set the dial for the *Middle Ages.* Because of a tiny glitch in the power supply, Jane instead ended up right in the middle of the *Industrial Revolution.* Fortunately for Jane, the *Industrial Revolution* did not involve a real *war.* Jane still shudders when she remembers her brief stint in the *Civil War.* She is simply not cut out to be a fighter, especially not a fighter in the *nineteenth century.* On the next *Fourth of July,* Jane plans to fly the bullet-ridden flag she brought back from the *Battle of Gettysburg.*

The story of Jane's adventures should make the rules concerning the capitalization of historic events and eras easy. Capitalize the names of specific time periods and events but not general words. Hence

✔ Capitals: Middle Ages, Industrial Revolution, Civil War, Fourth of July, Battle of Gettysburg

✔ Lowercase: war, nineteenth century

Some grammarians capitalize *Nineteenth Century* because they see it as a specific time period. Others say that you should lowercase numbered centuries. I prefer to lowercase the century.

Correct the capitalization in this paragraph.

> Jane has never met Marie Antoinette, but Jane is quite interested in the French revolution. With her trusty time-travel machine, Jane tried to arrive in the Eighteenth Century, just in time for Bastille Day. However, once again she missed her target and landed in the middle of the first crusade.

Answer, with explanations in parentheses:

> Jane has never met Marie Antoinette, but Jane is quite interested in the French Revolution. (Capitalize the name of a war.) With her trusty time-travel machine, Jane tried to arrive in the eighteenth century, (Optional, but most grammarians write numbered centuries in lower case.) just in time for Bastille Day. (Correct. Capitalize the names of important days.) However, once again she missed her target and landed in the middle of the First Crusade. (Capitalize the name of the war.)

If U Cn Rd Ths, U Cn Abbreviate

I can't cite a historical source, but I suspect that abbreviations stem from the need for speed. Why type eleven letters when two will do the job? Texting, twittering, and instant-messaging, which may have strict character limits, also encourage abbreviations.

I discourage them, most of the time. Why? Well, for several reasons. First of all, you want people to understand you. The first time you saw *e.g.,* did you know that it meant *for example?* If so, fine. If not, you probably didn't understand what the author was trying to say. Second, abbreviations clash with formal writing. Formal writing implies thought and care, not haste. (Yes, I know things are different when you're thumbing in a message. Check out Chapter 16 for more on electronic media and grammar.)

Sometimes, however, you do want to abbreviate. Here's how to do so correctly:

- ✔ Capitalize abbreviations for titles and end the abbreviation with a period. For example, *Mrs.* Snodgrass, *Rev.* Tawkalot, *Sen.* Veto, Jeremiah Jones, *Jr.,* and *St.* Lucy.

- ✔ Capitalize geographic abbreviations when they're part of a name but not when they're alone. Put a period at the end of the abbreviation: Appalachian *Mts.* or Amazon *R.,* for example. On a map you may write *mt.* (mountain).

> ✔ The United States Postal Service has devised a list of two-letter state abbreviations. Don't put periods in these abbreviations. Examples: *AZ* (Arizona), *CO* (Colorado), *WY* (Wyoming), and so on.
>
> ✔ Write most measurements in lowercase and end the abbreviation with a period (*yds.* for *yards* or *lbs.* for *pounds*). Metric abbreviations are sometimes written without periods (*km* for *kilometer* or *g* for *gram*).

Don't confuse abbreviations with acronyms. Abbreviations generally chop some letters out of a single word. Acronyms are new words made from the first letters of each word in a multiword title. Some common acronyms include the following:

NATO: North Atlantic Treaty Organization

OPEC: Organization of Petroleum Exporting Countries

AIDS: Acquired Immune Deficiency Syndrome

Want to drive your teacher crazy? Write a formal essay with &, w/, w/o, or b/c. (For the abbreviation-deprived, & means *and,* w/ means *with,* w/o means *without,* b/c means *because.*) These symbols are fine for your notes but not for your finished product. Similarly, save *brb* (*be right back*), *lol* (*laugh out loud*), and other texting abbreviations for your friends, not for authority figures. (For more on texting and electronic media, turn to Chapter 16.)

Correct Legghorn's homework.

> Yesterday (Tues.) I went in the a.m. to CO. I saw Mr. Pimple, who told me that the EPA had outlawed his favorite pesticide. I have three gal. in the basement, & I'll have to discard it.

Answer:

> Yesterday (Tuesday) I went in the morning to Colorado. I saw Mr. Pimple, who told me that the EPA had outlawed his favorite pesticide. I have three gallons in the basement, and I'll have to discard it.

Explanation: Don't abbreviate in homework assignments except for titles (*Mr. Pimple*) and easily understood acronyms (*EPA,* or *Environmental Protection Agency*). If you're writing about an acronym that your reader may not understand, write the whole thing out the first time you use it and place the acronym in parentheses. Thereafter, the acronym alone is fine. Also, if this had been a note to a friend, the abbreviations would have been perfectly acceptable.

Chapter 16

New Media, New Grammar Rules

During my childhood — so long ago that George Washington was still in diapers — communication was limited. I went to my friends' houses and screamed, "Wanna play?" until somebody said yes. Occasionally I picked up the phone (needless to say, a landline) and confided the latest gossip.

Technology has given you many more communication options — texting, tweeting, instant-messaging, e-mails, blogs, and PowerPoint-style presentations. But these new media have created confusion, too. Which grammar rules stay the same? Which ones should you adapt in the name of practicality? This area of English usage resembles the Old West, except that instead of sheriffs and outlaws shooting at each other, grammarians are facing off — and they're a lot less polite than the guys with guns. In this chapter, I explain the most commonly accepted guidelines for twenty-first-century media.

Thumb Wrestling with Grammar: Text and Instant Messages

Do you want to read this section now, or save it for *L8R*? If that last "word" is a mystery to you, I'm guessing that your thumbs are rested and relaxed because you haven't been using them to type on a Blackberry, a cell phone, or a similar device. In other words, you're not into tweeting or texting (sending short notes) or instant messaging (having a real-time, written "chat"). But if you easily decoded "L8R" as "later" and you thumb much of your communication with the outside world, this section is for you.

The distinction between traditional e-mail (isn't it amazing that a medium only a couple of decades old is already "traditional"?) and text messages is blurry; some text messages arrive in my computer's inbox, and the people I write to from my desktop computer often receive my e-mails on a handheld device, such as a cell phone or iPod. In this section, I deal with messages that are generally short (sometimes really short!) and written without benefit of a desk, coffee cart, miniature basketball hoop, and other accessories that accompany a traditional work space. The next section, "E-Mailing Your Way to Good Grammar," explains how to apply proper English to longer messages, presumably typed under more pleasant, less rushed conditions.

Choosing formal or informal language

In Chapter 1, I talk about *friendspeak*, my term for deliberately informal English that you use with your hangout crowd. I also discuss *conversational English* — the casual language exchanged with friends and acquaintances. These two types of English don't follow all the rules of grammar, as *formal English* does.

I've seen text messages written in all these styles, and under the right circumstances, I think all of them work well. (As a grammarian, however, I have to use proper English in all circumstances — at rock concerts, during arguments with my husband, for conversations with traffic cops, and — well, *everything*. Normal people have more leeway.) When you're deciding how formal to be, try these guidelines:

- ✓ Consider the identity of the person receiving the message. If he or she is a friend who can practically read your mind, formal English isn't necessary. Abbreviations and half-sentences are probably fine, and you don't need to worry about capitalization and punctuation. The less friendly the relationship, the more correct your language and grammar should be. If you're writing to someone you've met once or twice, don't chop out letters or words unless you know that the recipient appreciates informality. Stick to the normal rules for capitalization and punctuation unless you're sure that the message-receiver is comfortable with non-standard English.

- ✓ Power matters also. If you're the boss, you make the rules. Your subordinates aren't going to point out that you lowercased a word that should be in caps — not if they want to keep working for you! But if your message is going up the chain of command, choose formal English.

With the possible exception of dudes wearing tie-dyed t-shirts and love beads because they're stuck in the "cool" sixties, most teachers favor formal English. Follow grammar rules when you write to anyone in the academic world.

✔ Think about the impression you're trying to make. If you're writing to a potential client, formal language may show respect and care. On the other hand, if you've got an antsy client — the type who wants the work done yesterday, if not sooner — a few dropped words or characters may give the impression that you're speeding along on the client's behalf, too busy for such niceties as commas and periods.

✔ Save abbreviations such as "ttyl" (*talk to you later*), lol (*laugh out loud,* indicating a joke), and "ctn" (*can't talk now*) for someone who is your "bff" (*best friend forever*). However, some abbreviations are acceptable in business or academic writing. For example, you may begin a message with "FYI" (*for your information*) and ask for a reply "ASAP" (*as soon as possible*). If the abbreviation appears in a dictionary, it's probably okay unless you're writing in an extremely formal situation.

No matter who the recipient is, you have to get your point across. Check out the next section for some tips on writing understandable messages.

Being clear but concise

The screens and keyboards of handhelds and smartphones are as tiny as a low-calorie cookie, so sending or reading a long letter isn't comfortable. Plus, depending upon the device and cost structure of your carrier, you may pay extra if you're not concise. Some formats even have a character limit. The conclusion is obvious: Make your messages as short as possible in order to avoid eye and finger fatigue.

Compressing your thoughts into the smallest space doesn't get you off the hook when it comes to grammar, however. Remember one rule, no matter what you're writing with, on, or to:

Be clear!

Your reader has to understand what you mean, or your message is a failure. Period, end of story. With that principle in mind, check out these guidelines:

Dropping words

Because every character counts, you may at times break the "complete sentence" rule when you're texting. The most common cut is the subject of a sentence. (See Chapter 4 for more information on subjects.) For example, you may type

Left meeting early. No progress.

to someone who knows that despite having an early dinner date, you attended a session of that learned (and imaginary) society, Grammarians for Punctuation Reform. However, don't omit a subject unless you're absolutely sure that no confusion may result. For instance, suppose you and a colleague spoke about the meeting and decided that the key figure was the leader of a pro-apostrophe lobby. His support for punctuation reform is guaranteed to convince everyone else. His disapproval means that any proposal is dead on arrival. Upon receiving the previous text message, will your colleague know who left the meeting early? Perhaps she will think you left because the situation was going nowhere and you'd rather be nibbling an appetizer. Or she may believe that the apostrophe fan skipped out, leading you to conclude that nothing was going to change. In such a situation, it's better to type

> President left meeting early. No progress.

or

> I left the meeting early. No progress.

so your colleague understands what happened.

Articles (*a, an, the*) and conjunctions (words that join, such as *and, or, but,* and so forth) can often be omitted. Just be aware that the resulting message sounds rushed and at times strange. Can you imagine typing, "I went to bar"? Somehow *the* makes a big difference.

Dropping punctuation and capital letters

Some handhelds automatically correct your typing by inserting capital letters and a period after you've typed two spaces. Others don't, and I realize that capital letters may be a pain to type when you're on the go. Nevertheless, I'm in favor of that little extra effort. Ditto for periods. Yes, some people text

> saw helen after the meeting

and civilization as we know it hasn't yet crumbled. But don't you like this version better?

> Saw Helen after the meeting.

Or

> I saw Helen after the meeting.

Okay, maybe you don't. But some people, including me, do. Why take a chance on offending your reader?

Dropping a comma or a period usually isn't crucial. However, don't skip anything that adds meaning, such as question marks. Take a look at these two text messages:

> Dinner at 5
>
> Dinner at 5?

Obviously, they express two different ideas. The first assumes attendance, and the second is an invitation.

Making a text and checking it twice

Type carefully, and reread what you typed before sending the message. Some people easily decode mistyped words as they read, but do you want to risk having your wrods — oops, I mean *words* — turn into a puzzle? It's worth an extra secod of your time. Er, that's *second*.

Wireless messages often include a little phrase saying something like "sent from a ___ " (fill in the name of your device). I've heard a number of arguments about this phrase. One side believes that readers accept mistakes when they see it because they know that texts and instant messages are written quickly, without proofreading. The other side believes that if you're writing, you should write with care. You can probably guess my stance. I don't give get-out-of-grammar-jail-free cards!

E-Mailing Your Way to Good Grammar

In this section, I talk about electronic messages that can be considerably longer than the usual text message. (Yes, I know that e-mails can be short also. When a student asks to be excused from homework, usually in a *very* long message, I reply with a one-word e-mail: "No.") Here I discuss e-mails that are a little more structured than text-messages — closer to a traditional, paper-printed letter than to a 140-character message (the current limit for "tweets" — short messages sent via Twitter). I take you through the parts of the e-mail, explaining the best format to use when you're writing to someone who expects good grammar.

The heading

Atop every e-mail is a little box with a heading, which includes a "From," "To," and "Subject" line. You don't have to worry about the grammar of the "To" and "From" boxes. The "To" contains the e-mail address of the recipient (no choices there!), and the e-mail program automatically slots your address into the "From" line.

The subject line is the "title" of your e-mail. Most people follow standard capitalization rules for the subject line. (See Chapter 15 for a complete explanation of how to capitalize a title.)

The greeting

The message often begins with a greeting (in English-teacher terminology, a *salutation*). These are all acceptable greetings, complete with punctuation:

> **Dear Ms. Snodgrass,** or **Dear Ms. Snodgrass:** (The one with the comma is less formal. Begin the message on the following line.)

> **To Whom It May Concern:** (This one always has a colon and is ultra-formal. Begin the message on the following line.)

> **Hi, Lola.** or **Hi, Ms. Snodgrass.** (Use these forms for friends and acquaintances. Begin the message right after the period, not on the next line.)

> **Hi, Lola!** (This one is for friends only. Begin the message right after the exclamation point.)

> **Lola,** (Informal messages need nothing more than the name. The message begins on the following line.)

> **Ms. Snodgrass,** (This greeting can be a bit stern, as if you couldn't be bothered with the *Dear*.) Start the message one line below this greeting.

> **Hi, Everyone.** or **Hi, Everyone!** (Use these when you write to a group of friends or colleagues. Begin the message on the same line.)

Some writers drop the greeting altogether. No problem, unless you happen to be writing to traditionalists, who prefer the time-honored formats, or egotists, who love seeing their names in print.

The body

The body contains what you want to communicate — words, links to Web sites, images, whatever. If you're a traditionalist, your e-mails probably mimic paper, mailed-in-envelopes letters. I should probably say, "try to mimic" because what you see when you're typing isn't necessarily what the reader sees on his or her screen. Some e-mail programs automatically delete spaces between paragraphs when they zap the message to wherever it's going. Plus, different operating systems don't always play nicely together. A quotation mark may show up as a strange symbol (@ or a box, perhaps), and margins may wander in and out. Sigh. If you really care about how the document looks, you can attach the message as a text file. That last maneuver isn't perfect because not every bit of formatting comes through properly. But most of your document will look the way you want it to. The only surefire method to preserve every bit of formatting is to send your message as a Portable Document Format (.pdf) file, which is a "picture" of your document.

Regardless of method, follow the grammar rules outlined in the rest of *English Grammar For Dummies*, matching your level of formality to the identity of the person you're writing to. (See "Choosing formal or informal language" in this chapter for more information.)

The closing

If you haven't bothered with a greeting (which I explain earlier in this section), don't worry about a closing either, unless you want to "sign" your name at the end of the message. If you like a big send-off, try one of these:

> **Best,** (short for "best regards" and good for formal and informal e-mails)
>
> **Sincerely,** (formal)
>
> **See you soon,** (informal)
>
> **Hope to hear from you,** (somewhere between formal and informal)
>
> **Regards,** (formal and a little old-fashioned)

 All of the preceding closings contain commas. You can also close your message simply by typing your name (*Lola* or *Ms. Snodgrass*) or with your initials (*LS* for "Lola Snodgrass"), in which case no commas are needed.

Handling Grammar on the Internet

Is your passion peanut butter and marshmallow sandwiches? Films of the 1990s? Knitting? If something revs you up, chances are you're blogging or posting a paragraph or two about it on Facebook or another social-networking site. As you explain to your readers the merits of chunky versus smooth or the symbolism of Indiana Jones' hat, should you worry about grammar? Yes! And no, too. Confused? Read on.

Blogging for fun and (sometimes) profit

As I write, *Julie and Julia* is drawing crowds at my local theater. One character is based on a real person, Julie Powell, who cooked her way through a massive cookbook in one year and wrote about her experience in a blog. (A blog is a kind of diary, posted on the Internet. It may include photos, video clips, and links to other sites. Generally, blogs allow readers to post comments, so the "diary" becomes an extended conversation.) The real Julie Powell turned her blog into a book, which, as you already know, became a movie. Powell approached her blog as a *writer*. She paid attention to structure, tone — and yes, grammar — though she allowed herself the freedom of conversational English. (See Chapter 1 for more information on conversational English.)

Not every blogger is aiming for a book deal, and lots of bloggers are perfectly comfortable typing "cuz" instead of "because." Some bloggers avoid proper grammar as if it were a contagious disease, and their readers may not mind at all! When you blog, you have to consider the impression you want to make on your readers. Do you want them to see you as friends sitting in the living room with shoes off and feet up? Break a few grammar rules, and you're there. Do you want readers to accept your authority — to see you as someone who truly understands the care and feeding of boa constrictors or the significance of every single name in the Harry Potter series? Then you should probably put on your game face and pull out your best grammar.

Blogs are as varied as the people who create them. Some blogs place a title on each entry (see Chapter 15 for help with capitalizing titles), and some don't bother. Whatever level of grammar you choose, remember that communication is a two-way street. You've got readers, not mind readers. Be sure that your intended audience can decode your message.

Navigating social networks

Friendster, MySpace, Facebook, and other social networking sites allow you to interact with 3,450 of your closest friends (or any number!) and to connect with members who have similar interests. Each social networking site is a little different from the others, but all generally include a "profile," in which you cover basic biographical information, post fake photos — okay, sometimes they're real — and indicate your areas of interest. You can update your profile as often as you want, and you may be allowed to comment on others' sites (on a user's "wall" on Facebook, for example). Some social networks allow you to import blogs from other sites or to create your own blog.

Social networks used to be, well, purely social. Thus the language in them reflected the writer at his or her most casual. (Pause for a grammatical shudder.) Because they've become so popular, companies, politicians, and celebrities now use social networks to get their message out to a wide range of people. Writing to strangers — and writing to sell — usually raises the level of formality. Proper grammar may not take a starring role, but it's not completely absent.

As with all writing, think about your audience, your message, and yourself. How do you want readers to see you? Too cool for school? Smart enough to be President? When you know the context, you can decide how correct you need to be.

This is life, not grammar, but I can't resist telling you that social networks can be dangerous places. I'm not talking about crazy stalkers (though they do exist); I'm talking about the fact that teachers, potential employers, and date-worthy acquaintances may look at your profile unless you've limited access to it. If you've blogged about hacking into a teacher's e-mail, going to work with an epic hangover, or stalking an ex-friend, you may not get the recommendation, the job, or the date you're hoping for. Networker beware!

PowerPoint to the People

I teach a class in which students are required to make presentations about their research projects. Most of the presenters are a bit nervous, but PowerPoint and similar computer programs help a lot. After they've created a series of slides containing text and visuals — charts, graphs, diagrams, photos and the like — their information is organized and accessible. All the presenters have to do is speak a little about each slide as it flashes in front of the audience. Oh, and they have to follow some simple grammar rules. (You knew there was a catch, right?) In this section, I tell you everything you need to know about presentation slides.

If you're not making an oral presentation, you may still find useful material in this section. The format for bullet points remains the same whether those points are on a ten-foot screen or a standard sheet of paper. Check out "Biting the Bulleted List" in this section for more information.

Writing titles

Your presentation should have a title, and so may individual slides: *The Care and Feeding of Fleas, Foods That Fleas Fear, Your Little Pets' Nesting Material,* and so on. Guidelines for presentation titles include:

✔ **Place the title alone on a slide or on a line.** The title needs to stand out. When you're typing a standard paragraph, the title may be italicized or placed in quotation marks. On a presentation slide, however, neither italic nor quotation marks are needed. Why? Because the title's position calls attention to it, so you don't need anything else, in terms of grammar, at least. (Check out Chapter 12 for title-punctuation guidelines.) If you want the title to fade in, fade out, swirl around, or dance to the latest rap song, go ahead. The laws of taste are not mine to make. Just be sure that your message isn't lost in a sea of special effects.

✔ **Generally, don't place punctuation at the end of a title.** If the title is a complete sentence, it's probably too long. Cut it down! For example, you can change

> Fleas crave many types of food.

to

> Foods Fleas Crave

✔ **If the title is a question, you need a question mark.** Continuing the example from the previous bullet point, you may write,

> What Foods Do Fleas Crave?

✔ **Follow the standard capitalization rules for titles.** I explain these rules in detail in Chapter 15.

With your sharp eyes, you probably noticed that the title of some sections (including this one) don't follow the rules of capitalization I set forth in Chapter 15. *For Dummies* style calls for standard caps for chapter and section titles but a variation for subsections — capital letters for the first word only. If your presentation has subsections, you can differentiate larger and smaller units in the same way.

Biting the bulleted list

Bullets are the newest punctuation mark. Their job is to introduce each item in a list. The bullets in *For Dummies* books are check marks, but other publishers and writers favor dark circles, little stars, arrows, and similar symbols. A bulleted list has two parts — the introduction and the bullet texts.

Bullet introductions

If the introduction to your bullet list is a complete thought, end it with a colon, as in these sample introductions:

Fleas divert themselves with many exercises:

Fleas' favorite pastimes are as follows:

If the introduction to a bullet list is not a complete thought, don't place any punctuation mark at the end of the introduction. Check out these examples:

Fleas love to play with

Fleas' pet peeves are

If the introduction line ends with a linking verb as in the second example above, no punctuation follows the verb. See Chapter 2 for more information on linking verbs.

If the introduction line begins a series of quotations, place a comma at the end, as in these examples,

Simon Flea always says,

The flea trainer explains,

In *English Grammar For Dummies*, and all *For Dummies* books, bulleted lists are introduced and punctuated properly. Keep your eyes open to see the rules in action.

Bullet texts

The text for each bullet point is usually fairly short — sometimes just one or two words, and sometimes a bit more. Follow these guidelines in writing bullet points:

- ✔ If the text is a complete sentence, begin with a capital letter and end with a period (unless of course the sentence is a question, in which case you end with a question mark).

- ✔ If the text isn't a complete sentence, don't use any endmarks. You may capitalize the first word of each bullet point, but most people prefer lower case, especially if the introduction line isn't a complete sentence. Whatever style you choose, be consistent. Don't leave half of your bullet points capitalized and half lowercased.

- ✔ Each bullet point on a slide or in a list should have the same grammatical identity. If the first bullet point is a complete sentence, all the bullet points should be complete sentences. If you've begun one bullet point with a noun, begin all of them with nouns. Here's a "before and after" bullet list, illustrating a common mistake and its correction:

INCORRECT

- table tennis

- playing air guitar

- to swing from a trapeze

CORRECT

- table tennis

- air guitar

- trapeze swinging

This grammatical principle is called *parallelism*. (For more information on parallelism, check out Chapter 21.)

Many presentations, especially in the academic world, require a slide listing sources (books, Web sites, articles, films, and so forth). Sources are formatted differently from just about everything else on the planet. I explain all the rules in *Research Papers For Dummies* (Wiley, 2002) and *Punctuation: Simplified and Applied* (Webster's New World, 2005). If you don't want to beautify my royalty statement, feel free to check out any of the many Web sites devoted to source citation, including www.mla.org and www.apa.org.

Part IV

Polishing Without Wax — The Finer Points of Grammar

The 5th Wave   By Rich Tennant

In this part . . .

Think of this part of the book as sandpaper — a set of scratchy, annoying rules that rub the rough edges off of your writing. After you polish a paragraph according to the information in this part, the finished product will have the correct pronouns (Chapter 17), the appropriate verb tense (Chapter 18), and no misplaced descriptions (Chapter 19). All of your comparisons will be logical and complete (Chapter 20), and none of your sentences will be unbalanced (Chapter 21). Plus, the information in this part prepares you for the topics hit heavily by standardized tests — the lovely alphabet soup of SATs and ACTs that you wade through to get to college. For the finer points of grammar, read on.

Chapter 17

Pronouns and Their Cases

Edgar Rice Burroughs' famous character Tarzan is a smart fellow. Not only can he survive in the natural world, but he also teaches himself a fair-sized English vocabulary, saves his beloved Jane from quicksand, and — when he travels to England — learns how to tie his shoelaces. Despite all these accomplishments, one task trips him up. He never seems to grasp pronoun-verb pairs. "Me Tarzan, you Jane," he says over and over. "I am Tarzan" is apparently beyond him.

Millions of suffering grammar students know exactly how Tarzan feels. Choosing the correct pronoun is enough to give even a thirteen-year-old a few gray hairs. (I have a whole section on my head just from the *who/whom* issue, which, by the way, I discuss in Chapter 23.) But there's actually a logic to pronouns, and a few tips go a long way toward making your choices more obvious. In this chapter, I cover the three sets, or *cases*, of pronouns — subject, object, and possessive. So grab a vine and swing into the jungle of pronouns.

Me Like Tarzan: Choosing Subject Pronouns

The subject is the person or thing that is doing the action or being talked about in the sentence. (For more on locating the subject, see Chapter 4.) You can't do much wrong when you have the actual name of a person, place, or thing as the subject — in other words, a noun — but pronouns are another story.

Legal subject pronouns include *I, you, he, she, it, we, they, who,* and *whoever.* If you want to avoid a grammatical felony, stay away from *me, him, her, us, them, whom,* and *whomever* when you're selecting a subject. Also avoid the *–self* pronouns (*myself, himself, herself, ourselves,* and so forth) when you're scouting out a subject, unless you throw one next to another subject for emphasis, as in *I myself will select the proper pronoun.*

Here are some examples of pronouns as the subject of a sentence:

> *I* certainly did tell Lulu not to remove her nose ring in public! (*I* is the subject of the verb *did tell.*)

> Al and *she* will bring their killer bees to the next meeting of the Unusual Pets Association. (*She* is the subject of the verb *will bring.*)

> *Whoever* marries Larry next should negotiate a good prenuptial agreement. (*Whoever* is the subject of the verb *marries.*)

Compounding interest: Pairs of subjects

Most people do okay with one subject, but sentences with two subjects are a different story. For example, I often hear my otherwise grammatically correct students say such things as

> *Robert* and *me* are going to the supermarket for some chips.

> Although *her* and *I* haven't met, we plan to have dinner soon.

See the problem? In the first sample sentence, the verb *are going* expresses the action. To find the subject, ask *who* or *what are going.* The answer right now is *Robert and me are going,* but *me* isn't a subject pronoun. Here's the correct version:

> *Robert* and *I* are going to the supermarket for some carrots and celery. (I couldn't resist correcting the nutritional content, too.)

In the second sample sentence, the action — the verb — is *have met.* (*Not* isn't part of the verb.) *Who* or *what have met?* The answer, as it is now, is *her* and *I. I* is a legal subject pronoun, but *her* is not. The correct version is as follows:

> Although *she* and *I* haven't met, we plan to have dinner soon.

One good way to check your pronouns is to look at each one separately. If you've developed a fairly good ear for proper English (and Chapter 26 tells you how to do so), isolating the pronoun helps you decide whether you've chosen correctly. You may have to adjust the verb a bit when you're speaking about one subject instead of two, but the principle is the same. If the pronoun doesn't sound right as a solo subject, it isn't right as part of a pair either. Here is an example:

ORIGINAL SENTENCE: *Ella* and *her* went to the spitball-shooting contest yesterday.

CHECK 1: *Ella* went to the spitball-shooting contest yesterday. Verdict: sounds okay.

CHECK 2: *Her* went to the spitball-shooting contest yesterday. Verdict: sounds terrible. Substitute *she.*

CHECK 3: *She* went to the spitball-shooting contest yesterday. Verdict: much better.

RECOMBINED, CORRECTED SENTENCE: *Ella* and *she* went to the spitball-throwing contest yesterday.

Which sentence is correct?

A. Bud, you, and me appointed the judges for the spitball-shooting contest, so we have to live with their decisions, however wrong.

B. Bud, you, and I appointed the judges for the spitball-shooting contest, so we have to live with their decisions, however wrong.

Answer: Sentence B is correct. *I* is a subject pronoun, and *me* is not. If you take the parts of the subject separately, you can usually hear the correct answer.

Attracting appositives

Do you want to say the same thing twice? Use an appositive. An *appositive* is a noun or a pronoun that is exactly the same as the noun or pronoun that precedes it in the sentence. Check out these examples:

Raven, the girl whose hair matches her name, is thinking of changing her name to Goldie.

Tee Rex, holder of the coveted Dinosaur of the Year trophy, has signed an endorsement deal with a company that makes extra-large sneakers.

Roger, the Spy of the Month, will hold a press conference tomorrow at 10 a.m.

Lola, a fan of motorcycles, acknowledges that life in the fast lane is sometimes hard on the complexion.

Do you see the pair of matching ideas in each sentence? In the first, *Raven* and *the girl whose hair matches her name* are the same. In the next sentence, *Tee Rex* and *holder of the coveted Dinosaur of the Year trophy* make a pair. In the third, *the Spy of the Month* is the same as *Roger*. In the last sentence, *Lola* and *a fan of motorcycles* are the same. The second half of each pair *(the girl whose hair matches her name, holder of the coveted Dinosaur of the Year trophy, the Spy of the Month,* and *a fan of motorcycles)* is an appositive.

Appositives fall naturally into most people's speech and writing, perhaps because human beings feel a great need to explain themselves. You probably won't make a mistake with an appositive unless a pronoun or a comma is involved. (See Chapter 13 for more information on appositives and commas.)

Pronouns can serve as appositives, and they show up mostly when you have two or more people or things to talk about. Here are some sentences with appositives and pronouns:

> The winners of the raffle — Ali and he — will appear on the *Tonight Show* tomorrow. (Appositive = *Ali* and *he*)

> The judges for the spitball contest, Sally and she, wear plastic raincoats. (Appositive — *Sally* and *she*)

> The dancers who broke their toenails, Lulu and I, will not appear in the closing number. (Appositive = *Lulu* and *I*)

Why are *he, she* and *I* correct? In these sample sentences, the appositives are paired with the subjects of the sentence *(winners, judges, dancers)*. In a sense, the appositives are potential substitutes for the subject. Therefore, you must use a subject pronoun.

The appositive pronoun must always match its partner; if you pair it with a subject, the appositive must be a subject pronoun. If you pair it with an object, it must be an object pronoun.

You can confirm pronoun choice with the same method that I describe in the previous section. Take each part of the pair (or group) separately. Adjust the verb if necessary, and then listen to the sentence. Here's the check for one of the sentences that I used earlier:

> CHECK 1: The judges for the spitball contest wear plastic raincoats. Verdict: sounds okay.

> CHECK 2: Sally wears plastic raincoats. (You have to adjust the verb because *Sally* is singular, not plural, but the pronoun sounds okay.)

> CHECK 3: She wears plastic raincoats. (Again, you have to adjust the verb, but the pronoun sounds okay.)

Bottom line: Isolate the pronoun and listen. If you have spent some time listening to educated speech or reading good books, your "ear" for good English should help you decide whether the pronoun is correct.

Picking pronouns for comparisons

Lazy people that we are, we all tend to take shortcuts, chopping words out of our sentences and racing to the finish. This practice is evident in comparisons. Read the following sample sentences:

> Lulu denied that she had more facial hair than he.

That sentence really means

> Lulu denied that she had more facial hair than he had.

If you say the entire comparison, as in the preceding example, the pronoun choice is a cinch. However, when you drop the verb *(had)*, you may be tempted to use the wrong pronoun, as in this sentence:

> Lulu denied that she had more facial hair than him.

Sounds right, doesn't it? But the sentence is wrong. The words you say must fit with the words you don't say. Obviously you aren't going to accept

> Lulu denied that she had more facial hair than him had.

Him had is just too gross. The technical reason? *Him* is an object pronoun, but you're using it as the subject of *had*.

Whenever you have an implied comparison — a comparison that the sentence suggests but doesn't state completely — finish the sentence in your head. The correct pronoun becomes obvious.

Implied comparisons often contain the word *than* (as in the preceding sample sentences). The words *so* and *as* are also frequently part of an implied comparison:

> The dancers that Michael hired are not as flexible as they.

> Eggworthy gave Larry as much trouble as her.

> Ralph, live in concert on Broadway, is as entertaining as she.

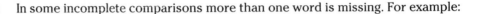
The complete comparisons are as follows:

> The dancers that Michael hired are not as flexible as they are.
>
> Eggworthy gave Larry as much trouble as Eggworthy gave her.
>
> Ralph, live in concert on Broadway, is as entertaining as she is.

In some incomplete comparisons more than one word is missing. For example:

> Grandmother gives my sister more souvenirs than me.

means

> Grandmother gives my sister more souvenirs than Grandmother gives to me, because my sister is a spoiled brat and is always flattering the old bat.

and

> Grandmother gives my sister more souvenirs than I.

means

> Grandmother gives my sister more souvenirs than I do because I have better things to do with my allowance.

Think before you make a decision because the pronoun choice determines the meaning of the sentence.

Which sentence is correct?

A. Tee Rex broke more claws than I during the fight with Godzilla.

B. Tee Rex broke more claws than me during the fight with Godzilla.

Answer: Sentence A is correct. Read the sentence this way: Tee Rex broke more claws than *I did* during the fight with Godzilla. You can't say *me did*.

Last one! Which is correct?

A. Roger told me more atomic secrets than she.

B. Roger told me more atomic secrets than her.

Answer: Both are correct, depending on the situation. Sentence A means that Roger told me more atomic secrets than *she told me*. Sentence B means that Roger told me more atomic secrets than *he told her*.

Connecting pronouns to linking verbs

Think of linking verbs as giant equal signs, equating two halves of the sentence. All forms of the verb *to be* are linking verbs, as well as verbs such as *seem, appear, smell, sound,* and *taste.* The type of pronoun that begins the equation (the subject) must also be the type of pronoun that finishes the equation. (For more information on finding linking verbs and the pronouns that go with them, see Chapter 2.) In this section, I talk about pairs of subject pronouns with linking verbs. Looking at pairs of words is helpful because choosing pronouns for compound subjects is always hard. Check out this sentence:

> The new champions, who spelled "sassafras" correctly for the first and only time, are him and me.

Correct or incorrect? Here's how to check. Think of the equal sign (the linking verb). If the pronouns are correct, you should be able to reverse the sentence. After all, 2 + 2 = 4 and 4 = 2 + 2.

If I reverse the preceding sample sentence, I get

> Him and me are the new champions who spelled "sassafras" correctly for the first and only time.

Uh oh. *Him and me are.* Not a good idea. What would you really say? *He and I are.* So go back to the original sentence. Change the pronouns. Now the sentence reads

> The new champions, who spelled "sassafras" correctly for the first and only time, are he and I.

In conversation, many people ignore the *reversibility rule* and choose an object pronoun. In conversation you can get away with such a choice, but in formal writing the rules are tighter. If you have a linking verb followed by a pronoun, choose from the subject set.

Which sentence is correct?

A. The students voted "Most Likely to Go to Jail Before Graduation" are Liz and I.

B. The students voted "Most Likely to Go to Jail Before Graduation" are Liz and me.

Answer: In formal English, sentence A is correct. Reverse the sentence: *Liz and I are* the students voted "Most Likely to Go to Jail Before Graduation." Verdict: Fine. If you reverse sentence B, you get *Liz and me are.* This phrasing is not a good idea, though it is acceptable in conversational English. (See Chapter 1 for more information on formal and conversational English.)

Using Pronouns as Direct and Indirect Objects

Previously in this chapter, I've concentrated on subject pronouns, but now it's time to turn to the receiver of the sentence's action — the object. Specifically, it's time to turn to *object pronouns.* (For more information on finding the object, see Chapter 6.) Pronouns that may legally function as objects include *me, you, him, her, it, us, them, whom,* and *whomever.* Here are some examples of direct and indirect object pronouns, all in italic:

> Ticktock smashed *him* right on the nose for suggesting that "the mouse ran down the clock." (*smashed* is the verb; *Ticktock* is the subject; *him* is the object)
>
> Archie married *us,* despite our parents' objections, in a quadruple ring ceremony. (*married* is the verb; *Archie* is the subject; *us* is the object)
>
> Olivier, president and chief operating officer of Actors Inc., sent *me* a horrifying *letter.* (*sent* is the verb; *Olivier* is the subject; *letter* and *me* are objects)

Here's some English teacher terminology for you, if you can stand it. (If not, don't worry. You don't need labels to use object pronouns correctly!) A *direct object* receives the action directly from the verb, answering the questions *whom?* or *what?* after the verb. An *indirect object* receives the action indirectly (clever, those grammar terms), answering the questions *to whom?* or *to what?* after the verb. In the previous sample sentence, *letter* is the direct object and *me* is the indirect object. For more information on direct and indirect objects, see Chapter 6.

Which sentence is correct?

A. After a great deal of discussion, the principal punished we, the innocent, for the small herd of cows that disrupted the cafeteria yesterday.

B. After a great deal of discussion, the principal punished us, the innocent, for the small herd of cows that disrupted the cafeteria yesterday.

Answer: Sentence B is correct. *Us* is the object of the verb *punished.*

Choosing objects for prepositions

Prepositions — words that express relationships such as *about, after, among, by, for, behind, since,* and others — may also have objects. (For a more complete list of prepositions, see Chapter 8.) Here are some examples, with both the preposition and the object pronoun italicized:

Max, fearful for his pet tarantula, gave his dog *to us* yesterday.

Belle's dance solo is a problem *for her* because she can't find a suitable costume.

Michael's latest play received a critical review *from them*.

Archie didn't like the window so he simply plastered *over it*.

The object word answers the usual object questions (*whom? what?*), as in these examples:

Max, fearful for his pet tarantula, gave his dog to *whom*? Answer: to *us*.

Belle's dance solo is a problem for *whom*? Answer: for *her*.

Michael's latest play received a critical review from *whom*? Answer: from *them*.

Archie didn't like the window, so he simply plastered over *what*? Answer: over *it*.

Also notice that all the pronouns — *us, him, her, them, it* — come from the set of object pronouns.

Which sentence is correct?

A. The conversation between Al and I always revolves around piano-tuning.

B. The conversation between Al and me always revolves around piano-tuning.

Answer: Sentence B is correct. *Between* is a preposition. *Between* whom? *Between Al and me. Me* is one of the objects of the preposition *between*.

For some reason, the phrase *between you and I* has caught on. However, it's time to unhook it! *Between* is a preposition, so object pronouns follow it. The pronoun *I* is for subjects, and *me* is for objects. So between you and me, *me* is the word you want.

Attaching objects to verbals

Isn't *verbal* a strange word? It sounds like something you keep in a little cage with an exercise wheel. But a *verbal* isn't a furry pet. It's a word derived from a verb (a word that expresses action or state of being) that functions as a noun or as a description (in other words, as an adjective or an adverb). In this section I show you how to select a pronoun for that coveted role, object of a verbal. (Everyone in Hollywood is auditioning for the part.) Later in this chapter, in the section entitled "Dealing with Pronouns and '-Ing' Nouns," I address another way that pronouns interact with verbals.

The English language is the proud owner of three types of verbal. Don't worry about which is which. Their official names aren't important when you're choosing a pronoun. (They're called *gerund*, *participle*, and *infinitive*, if you absolutely have to know. To learn more about verbals, check out Chapter 24.) Take a look at these verbals and their objects, both of which are italicized. Also notice the real verb in each sentence, which I've underlined:

> Melanie <u>loves</u> *dancing the Apostrophe*, but Lulu thinks that dance is strange.

> Lola <u>left</u> the biker convention *to play some dance tunes* for Melanie.

> Oliver, *having watched Melanie*, <u>signed</u> up for polka lessons.

As you see, the verbals look like verbs. However, in the first sentence *dancing* isn't acting as a verb. *Dancing* is a thing that Melanie loves. In other words, it's a noun. In the second example, *to play* provides a reason why Lola left the biker convention. Therefore *to play* describes the verb *left* (*left* why? *to play*). In the third example, *having watched Melanie* gives you more information about *Oliver*, a noun. Anything that describes a noun is functioning as an adjective.

To find the object of a verbal, ask the object questions: *whom? what?* after the verbal.

Fortunately, you don't need to know much about the parentage of any verbals you encounter. Just be sure to attach an object pronoun to any and all verbs. Here's the preceding set of example sentences, this time with pronouns instead of nouns:

> Melanie loves *dancing it*.

> Lola left the biker convention *to play them* for her friend Melanie.

> Oliver, *having watched her*, signed up for polka lessons.

Which sentence is correct?

A. Oliver loves to show Melanie and I his new dance moves.

B. Oliver loves to show Melanie and me his new dance moves.

Answer: Sentence B is correct. *To show* is a verbal. *To show whom? To show Melanie and me. Me* is one of the objects of the verbal *to show*.

Seeing double causes problems

You'll probably choose the correct object pronoun when there's only one in the sentence, but compounds (pairs or larger groups), cause problems. The solution is fairly easy: Check each part of the compound separately. Your ear helps you find the right choice. Here are some examples:

ORIGINAL SENTENCE: Paris, pleading poverty, presented Perry and me with a check for fifteen cents.

CHECK 1: Paris, pleading poverty, presented Perry with a check for fifteen cents. Verdict: The sentence sounds fine.

CHECK 2: Paris, pleading poverty, presented me with a check for fifteen cents. Verdict: The sentence sounds fine. When you isolate the pronoun, *me* is obviously the correct choice. You're unlikely to accept *Paris, pleading poverty, presented I with a check for fifteen cents.*

Try another one.

ORIGINAL SENTENCE: Perry, claiming to be far richer than Donald Trump, presented the government and he with a billion dollars.

CHECK 1: Perry, claiming to be far richer than Donald Trump, presented the government with a check for a billion dollars. Verdict: The sentence is fine.

CHECK 2: Perry, claiming to be far richer than Donald Trump, presented he with a check for a billion dollars. Verdict: *presented he?* Nope. The sentence doesn't work.

CHECK 3: Perry, claiming to be far richer than Donald Trump, presented him with a check for a billion dollars. Verdict: Now the sentence sounds right.

RECOMBINED SENTENCE: Perry, claiming to be far richer than Donald Trump, presented the government and him with a check for a billion dollars.

Pronouns of Possession: No Exorcist Needed

Possessive pronouns show (pause for a drum roll) possession. Not the movie head-twisting-backwards kind of possession, but the kind where somebody owns something. Possessive pronouns include *my, your, his, her, its, our, their, mine, yours, hers, ours, theirs,* and *whose.* Check out the following sample sentences:

Michael took *his* apple out of the refrigerator marked "Open Only in Case of Emergency."

Sure that the computer had beeped *its* last beep, Lola shopped for a new model.

To *our* dismay, Roger and Lulu opened *their* birthday presents two days early.

Vengeance is *mine.*

Lester slapped the dancer *whose* stiletto heels had wounded Lola's big toe.

The possessive pronouns in these examples show that the apple belongs to Michael, the beep belongs to the computer, the dismay belongs to us, and the presents belong to Roger and Lulu. Vengeance belongs to *me.* (*Mine* is the possessive pronoun that refers to something *I* own, something that belongs to *me.*) The last sentence is a little more complicated. The word *whose* refers to the *dancer.* The stiletto heels belong to the dancer. The big toe belongs to Lola, but possession is shown in this example with a possessive noun *(Lola's)* not a possessive pronoun *(her).*

Notice that none of the possessive pronouns have apostrophes. They never do! Ever! Never ever! Putting apostrophes into possessive pronouns is one of the most common errors. *(It's* doesn't mean *belongs to it. It's* means *it is.)*

Which sentence is correct?

A. Smashing the pumpkin on his mother's clean floor, Rocky commented, "I believe this gourd is yours."

B. Smashing the pumpkin on his mother's clean floor, Rocky commented, "I believe this gourd is your's."

Answer: Sentence A is correct. No possessive pronoun has an apostrophe, and *yours* is a possessive pronoun.

Dealing with Pronouns and "-Ing" Nouns

The rule concerning possessive pronouns and "-ing" nouns is broken so often that it may be a losing battle. However, the rule isn't completely useless, like many of the other rules that people break. Moreover, this rule is actually logical. Some nouns that end in *-ing* are created from verbs. (In grammarspeak, they're called *gerunds,* a member of the verbal family I discuss in "Attaching an object to a verbal" earlier in this chapter.)

When you put a pronoun in front of one of these nouns, you must be sure that the pronoun is possessive. Standardized test-makers love to check whether you know this fact. And now you do! Here are some examples:

Just because I once got a speeding ticket, my parents object to *my taking* the car for even short drives. (not *me taking*)

Lola knows that *their* creating a dress code has nothing to do with the fact that she recently pierced her toes. (not *them* creating)

Eggworthy's wife likes *his* singing in the shower. (not *him* singing)

The goldfish accept *our* placing food in the tank so long as we don't try to shake their fins. (not *us placing*)

Why possessive? Here's the reasoning. If you put a possessive pronoun in front of the noun, the noun is the main idea. If you read

Lulu couldn't stop talking about *my*

you don't have all the information you need. You're practically leaning forward, waiting for the next word. Contrast the example above with this one:

Lulu couldn't stop talking about *me.*

Now you can stop. You have all the information you need — except of course what Lulu said about *me.* That's confidential. Back to grammar: The possessive pronoun sends you forward; an object pronoun stops you cold. Therefore:

My parents object to the *taking* of the car. They don't object to *me.*

Lola knows something about the *creating* of a dress code. She may not know anything about *them.*

Eggworthy's wife likes the *singing.* She may not like *him.*

The goldfish accept *placing* food. They don't accept *us.*

 Some *-ing* words weren't created from verbs, and some *-ing* words aren't nouns. Don't worry about distinguishing between one and the other. Just apply this simple test: You need a possessive if the meaning of the sentence changes radically when you drop the *-ing* word. Check out this example:

Roger loves me singing and always invites me to perform at his concerts.

If I drop the *-ing* word, the sentence says

Roger loves me.

Now there's a radical change of meaning. Clearly the sentence is incorrect. The correct version is

Roger loves my singing.

Now the focus is on *singing,* not on *me.*

Which sentence is correct?

A. Stunned by my low batting average, the coach forbade my swinging at every pitch.

B. Stunned by my low batting average, the coach forbade me swinging at every pitch.

Answer: Sentence A is correct. The coach went on and on about *my swinging at every pitch* and never mentioned anything about my personal life. (In sentence B, he's forbidding *me,* all of me.)

Try another. Which sentence is correct?

A. The boss hates you answering the phone with "Whassup, dude?"

B. The boss hates your answering the phone with "Whassup, dude?"

Answer: Sentence B is correct. The boss doesn't know you enough to hate you (the meaning of Sentence A). Of course, if she got to know you better . . . but I won't go there. Sentence B places the emphasis on *answering.* The possessive *your* puts it there. The boss objects to "Whassup, dude?" as a client's introduction to the company. I can't imagine why.

Chapter 18

Fine-Tuning Verbs

Do verbs tie your tongue (well, actually, your pen) in knots? Are you constantly editing yourself to avoid verb problems? In Chapter 3, I cover the basics: choosing the correct verb in easy situations. Here I hit the hard stuff — sentences that puzzle most people. To fine-tune your verb skills, read on.

Giving Voice to Verbs

Verbs can have two voices. No, not soprano and tenor. Verbs can be either active or passive. Take a look at these two examples:

> "The window *was broken* yesterday," reported Eggworthy, carefully hiding his baseball bat under the sofa.

> "I *broke* the window yesterday," reported Eggworthy, regretfully handing his baseball bat to his mother.

How do the two versions differ? Grammatically, Eggworthy's statement in the first sentence focuses on the receiver of the action, the *window,* which received the action of *breaking.* The verb is *passive* because the subject is not the person or thing doing the action but instead the person or thing receiving the action. In sentence two, the verb is in active voice because the subject (*I*) performed the action (*broke*). When the subject is acting or being, the verb is *active.*

To find the subject of a sentence, locate the verb and ask *who?* or *what?* before the verb. For more information on subjects, see Chapter 4.

Here are some active and passive verbs:

> Lulu *gives* a free-tattoo coupon to Lola. (active)
>
> Lola *is convinced* by Lulu to get a tattoo. (passive)
>
> Roger *convinces* Lulu to visit the tattoo parlor too. (active)
>
> Lulu *is tattooed* by Lola. (passive)

Label the verbs in these sentences as active or passive.

> A. The omelet was made with egg whites, but the yolks were discarded.
>
> B. Eggworthy slobbers when he eats eggs.

Answer: Sentence A is passive *(was made, were discarded)*, and sentence B is active *(slobbers, eats)*.

Try one more. Which is active and which is passive?

> A. The nail was hammered into that sign by Roger.
>
> B. Roger is building a tank for his pet piranhas.

Answer: Sentence A is passive *(was hammered)*, and sentence B is active *(is building)*.

Actively Seeking a Better Voice

Unless you're trying to hide something, or unless you truly don't know the facts, you should make your writing as specific as possible. Specifics reside in active voice. Compare these pairs of sentences:

> The president of the Egg-Lovers' Club *was murdered* yesterday. (The cops are still looking for the villain who wielded the hammer and crushed the president's skull like a @el well, like an eggshell.)
>
> Sir Francis Bacon murdered the president of the Egg-Lovers' Club yesterday. (Bacon will soon move into a maximum-security cell.)

> It *is recommended* that the furnace not be cleaned until next year. (Someone wants to save money, but no one is taking responsibility for this action. If the furnace breaks when the thermometer hits 20 below because too much glop is inside, no one's name comes up for blame.)

The superintendent *recommends* that the furnace not be cleaned until next year. (Now the building's residents may threaten the superintendent with the icicles they chip off their noses.)

Do you notice how these active-verb sentences provide extra information? In the first pair of sample sentences, we know the name of the murderer. In the second pair, we know who recommends postponing maintenance of the furnace. Knowing (in life as well as in grammar) is usually better than not knowing, and active voice — which generally provides more facts — is usually better than passive voice.

Active voice is also better than passive because active voice tends to use fewer words to say the same thing. Compare the following sentences:

Lulu was failed by the teacher because the grammar book was torn up by Lulu before it was ever opened. (20 words)

The teacher failed Lulu because Lulu tore up the grammar book before opening it. (14 words)

Okay, six words don't make the difference between a 900-page novel and a 3-page story, but those words do add up. If you're writing a letter or an essay, switching from passive to active voice may save you one-third of your words — and therefore one-third of the reader's energy and patience.

Right about now you may be remembering a past homework assignment: the teacher asked for 500 words on *Hamlet* and you had only one teeny idea about the play. You may have thought that padding was a good idea! Wrong. Your teacher (or boss) can see that you've buried only one teeny idea in those piles of paragraphs. Besides losing points for knowing too little, you're likely to lose points for wasting the reader's time. The solution? Write in active voice and don't pad your writing.

Some questions on the SAT and ACT ask you to "revise" a sentence by choosing the best of five possible versions. Fairly often, the correct answer changes the passive verb of the original to active voice.

Which sentence works better?

A. The omelet was made with whipped egg whites and chopped ham, but the yolks were discarded.

B. Eggworthy made an omelet of whipped egg whites and chopped ham but discarded the yolks.

Answer: Sentence B, which employs active voice (*made, discarded*) is preferable to Sentence A, which has passive verbs (*was made, were discarded*). Not only is Sentence B one word shorter, but it also provides more information (the name of the cook).

Try another: Choose the better sentence.

A. The Omelet Contest was run so poorly that some entries were labeled "dangerous" by the health officer.

B. Sal Monella ran the Omelet Contest so poorly that the health officer labeled some entries "dangerous."

Answer: Sentence B wins! Its active verb (*ran*) creates a stronger sentence than the passive verb (*was run*) of Sentence A. Also, Sentence B supplies the name of the contest official who forgot to refrigerate the cooking supplies.

Adding Meaning with Strong Verbs

Though *English Grammar For Dummies* focuses on grammar, I can't resist throwing in a few hints about style. You can get a lot of mileage out of strong verbs — those that add meaning and detail to your sentence. You can also water down your writing with blah, weak verbs. In this section, I show you how to select verbs that can bench-press with the best.

"There is" a problem with boring verbs

In my writing class, I always ask the students to describe a standard school chair. Inevitably, I read sentences like these:

There is a curved seat.

There are five slats on the back.

There is a school identification mark on the bottom of the chair.

Nothing's wrong with these sentences. They're all grammatically correct, and they're all accurate. But I bet they made you yawn. *There is* and *there are*, as well as their cousins — *there was, there will be, there has been*, and others — are standard (and therefore boring) expressions. How about swapping them for something stronger? Here you go:

The seat curves to fit your bottom.

Five slats support your back.

The school stamps an identification mark on the bottom of each chair.

Don't you think the second set of sentences is more interesting? You get more information, and the verbs — *curves, support*, and *stamps* — catch the reader's eye.

In a writing sample for the SAT or other standardized test, graders watch for sophisticated usage. They want to see that you can manipulate language. *There is/are* sentences aren't very sophisticated, though they can sometimes be useful. When you find yourself constructing a sentence this way, pause. Can you come up with a more interesting verb?

Does your writing "have" a problem?

If they're overused, forms of the verb *to have* can also put your reader to sleep faster than a sedative. (The Grammarians Code obliges me to point out that *to have* is an infinitive — the grandpappy that gives its name to a verb family but never functions as a verb in a sentence. Chapter 17 tells you more than you ever wanted to know about how infinitives *do* function in a sentence.) Now, back to verb choices. Sometimes nothing works better than *to have*, and of course you need some forms of this verb to indicate tense — the time of the action or state of being. ("Putting It in Order: Sequence of Tenses" in this chapter tells you more about verb tense issues, as does Chapter 2.) But too often *has*, *had*, or *have* ends up in a sentence because the writer is too tired to think of something more creative. Try changing

> The chair has a shiny surface.
>
> The slats have rounded edges as big as my finger.

to

> The chair shone under the fluorescent light.
>
> The rounded edges fit my finger perfectly.

Okay, I added some information to the second set, but you see my point. *Shone* and *fit* are more interesting than *has* and *have.* Plus, after you plop in a good verb, other ideas follow, and the whole sentence improves.

Don't just "say" and "walk" away

To say and *to walk* are fine, upstanding members of the verb community, but they don't give you much information. Why *say* when you can *declare, scream, whisper, hint, bellow, assert, remark* or do any one of the zillions of alternatives available to you when you're describing communication? For movement, consider *stroll, saunter, plod, strut, rush, speed, zig-zag,* and — well, you get the point by now. Look for verbs that go beyond the basics, that add shades of meaning to your sentence. Here are some before-and-after sentence sets to illustrate how more specific verbs pep up your sentences:

BEFORE: Heidi said she was tired of climbing mountains.

AFTER: Heidi contended that she was tired of climbing mountains. (Now you know that she's speaking with someone who may not believe her.)

ANOTHER AFTER: Heidi murmured that she was tired of climbing mountains. (Here Heidi's a bit shy or perhaps fearful.)

ONE MORE AFTER: Heidi roared that she was tired of climbing mountains. (In this sentence no one is going to mess with Heidi — not without a struggle!)

BEFORE: Heidi's hiking partner walked away from her.

AFTER: Heidi's hiking partner edged away from her. (The partner knows that Heidi's in one of her moods and trouble is on the way.)

ALSO AFTER: Heidi's hiking partner stomped away from her. (Now the partner is angry!)

THE LAST AFTER: Heidi's hiking partner wandered away from her. (The partner isn't paying attention.)

Your word-processing program probably has a built-in *thesaurus* — a reference work that lists synonyms for most verbs. You can also buy a thesaurus in book form. If you're looking over your writing and need some spicier verbs, a thesaurus can suggest some alternatives. Be cautious: verbs, like all words, may be similar but not exactly the same. The list for *stroll* includes *ramble* and *promenade.* You may *ramble* (or *amble,* another verb on this list) without a fixed destination or purpose. If you *promenade,* you're probably also in recreational mode, but this time you have an audience. Bottom line: don't insert a verb or any other verb into your sentence unless you're sure you know what it means.

Putting It in Order: Sequence of Tenses

All verbs express information about three time periods: the present, the past, and the future. Unfortunately, human beings have a tendency to want more specific information about timing. Enter about a million shades of meaning, closely followed by about a million rules.

For information on the basic tenses of verbs, see Chapter 3. In this chapter, I focus on some special cases — which verbs to use when more than one thing is happening.

To clarify what's happening when, timelines accompany some of the examples in this section. Match the events on the timeline to the verbs in the sentence to see where in time each tense places an action.

Both the SAT and the ACT obsess about verb tense. Expect to see at least a few questions containing the verb-tense issues described in this section.

Case 1: Simultaneous events — main verbs

Look at the italicized verbs in each of these sample sentences:

> Maya *swiped* a handkerchief and daintily *blew* her noise. (*swiped* and *blew* = two events happening at almost the same moment; both verbs are in past tense)

> Maya *will be* in court tomorrow, and the judge *will rule* on her case. (*will be* and *will rule* = two events happening at the same time; both verbs are in future tense)

> Maya *is* extremely sad about the possibility of a criminal record, but she *remains* hopeful. (*is* and *remains* = states of being existing at the same time; both verbs are in present tense)

If two actions take place at the same time (or nearly the same time), use the same tense for each verb.

Case 2: Simultaneous events — verbals

The verb doesn't express all the action in a sentence. Some verb forms don't act as the official verb in the sentence; in fact, they don't act as verbs at all, even though they give you some information about an event. These verb forms are called *verbals*. In the following sentences, check out the italicized verbals. Also keep your eye on the main verb, which is underlined. Notice that the same verbal matches with present, past, and future verbs and places the two actions at the same time or close enough in time to make the difference irrelevant. Also notice that none of the verbals are formed with the words *have* or *had*. (*Have* and *had* help to express actions taking place at different times. See Case 6 later in this section for more information and examples of *have* and *had* in action.)

> *Swiping* a handkerchief, Maya daintily <u>blows</u> her nose. (The *swiping* and the *blowing* take place at nearly the same time — in the present.)

> *Swiping* a handkerchief, Maya daintily <u>blew</u> her nose. (The *swiping* and the *blowing* took place at nearly the same time — in the past.)

> *Swiping* a handkerchief, Maya <u>will</u> daintily <u>blow</u> her nose. (The *swiping* and the *blowing* will take place at nearly the same time — in the future.)

Another variation:

> *To blow her nose daintily,* Maya <u>swipes</u> a handkerchief. (The *blowing* and the *swiping* take place at nearly the same time — in the present.)

> *To blow her nose daintily,* Maya <u>swiped</u> a handkerchief. (The *blowing* and the *swiping* took place at nearly the same time — in the past.)

> *To blow her nose daintily,* Maya <u>will swipe</u> a handkerchief. (The *blowing* and the *swiping* will take place at nearly the same time — in the future.)

No one in the known universe needs this information, so continue reading only if you love grammatical terms. *Participles* are verb forms that may act as adjectives. In the preceding sample sentences, *swiping* is a present participle, and *swiping a handkerchief* is a participial phrase describing *Maya.* The action expressed by the present participle takes place at the same time (or nearly the same time) as the action expressed by the main verb. *To blow* is an infinitive, the basic form of a verb. Infinitives never function as verbs in the sentence. In the previous sample sentences, *to blow her noise daintily* is an infinitive phrase describing *Maya.* For more information on infinitives, see Chapters 2 and 17. For tips on using participles and infinitives creatively, see Chapter 24.

Case 3: Events at two different times in the past

Everything in the past happened at exactly the same moment, right? Oh, if only this statement were true. History tests would be much easier, and so would grammar. Sadly, you often need to talk about events that took place at different times in the past. Verb tenses create an order of events — a timeline — for your reader. Check out the italicized verbs in this sentence:

> Maya *had* already *swiped* the handkerchief when she *discovered* the joys of honesty.

There are two events to think about, one taking place before the other. (Unfortunately for Maya, the joy of honesty came after the theft, for which she's doing ten to twenty in the penitentiary.) Note the timeline:

For two events in the past, write the earlier event with *had* and the more recent event in simple past tense (without *had*). For grammar-lovers only: Verbs written with *had* are in the past perfect tense. (See Chapter 3 for definitions of tenses.)

Scan these examples:

> Because of Lulu's skill with a needle, where a hole in the sock *had gaped,* a perfect heel now *enclosed* her tender foot. (Event 1: the hole in the sock gapes; event 2: the mended sock covers the foot.)

> When Roger *had inserted* the microfilm, he *sewed* the hole in the now illegal teddy bear. (Event 1: Roger inserts the microfilm; event 2: Roger sews the bear.)

> Though she *had lost* her wallet, Ella *kept* a tight grip on her sanity. (Event 1: Ella loses her wallet; Event 2: Ella does not lose her mind.)

> After the song *had* been *played* at least twelve times, Michael *shouted,* "Enough!" (Event 1: The song is played twelve times; event 2: Michael loses it.)

A common error is using *had* for everything. Wrong! Don't use *had* unless you're consciously putting events in order:

> WRONG: Maya had dried her eyes and then she had gone to see the judge.

> RIGHT: After Maya had dried her eyes, she went to see the judge.

Also, sometimes you may want to talk about events in the past without worrying about specific times. You *went* on vacation, *had* a great time, *sent* some postcards, *ate* a lot of junk food, and *came* home. No need for *had* in this description because the order isn't the point. You're just making a general list. Use *had* when the timing matters. Don't overuse it.

Note: You may encounter one other use of *had,* the subjunctive. See Chapter 22 if you have to know absolutely everything about *had* — and believe me, you don't.

Which sentence tells you about events that happened at different times?

A. Slipping the judge a fifty-dollar bill, Maya hoped for mercy.

B. Although she had slipped the judge only one fifty-dollar bill, Maya hoped for mercy.

Answer: Sentence B reports events at different times. Maya tried the bribe at 10 a.m. and spent the rest of the day planning a trip to Rio (cancelled when her ten-to-twenty-year jail term was announced). In sentence A, Maya bribes and hopes at the same time.

One more question. Which sentence reports events happening at two different times?

A. To prepare for her trial, Maya bought a copy of *Be Your Own Lawyer!*

B. Maya had bought a copy of *Be Your Own Lawyer!* when the trial began.

Answer: Sentence B has two events, one earlier than the other. The purchase of the book *(had bought)* happened before the trial *(began)*. In sentence A, the two events *(to prepare, bought)* happen at the same time.

Case 4: More than two past events, all at different times

This rule is similar to the one described in Case 3. Apply this rule when you talk about more than two events in the past:

Maya *had baked* a cake and *had inserted* a sharp file under the icing before she *began* her stay in jail.

Now the timeline is as follows:

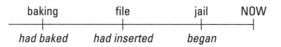

What do you notice? The most recent event *(began her stay in jail)* is written without *had*. In other words, the most recent event is in simple past tense. Everything that happened earlier is written with *had* — that is, in past perfect tense. For more information on tenses, see Chapter 3.

Here are some examples:

Max *had bent* his knees and *had bowed* his head before he *shot* the spitball. (Events 1 and 2: Max tries to look respectful. Event 3: Max shoots the spitball, proving once and for all that he can't act respectfully.)

Michael *had planned* the shower, and Lola *had* even *planned* the wedding by the time Ella *agreed* to marry Larry. (Events 1 and 2: Michael and Lola visit the wedding coordinator. Event 3: Ella makes the biggest mistake of her life.)

Elizabeth *had composed* a sonata, *played* it for royalty, and *signed* a recording contract before she *reached* her tenth birthday. (Events 1, 2, and 3: Elizabeth writes the music, performs it, and makes big bucks. Event 4: Elizabeth's mom puts ten candles on the cake.)

In the last example three verbs — *composed, played,* and *signed* — form a list of the actions that Elizabeth performed before her tenth birthday. They all have the same subject (*Elizabeth*). The word *had* precedes only *composed,* the first verb of the three. You may omit the word *had* in front of *played* and *signed* because they are part of the same list and they all have the same subject. The reader knows that the word *had* applies to all three of the verbs. In other words, the reader understands that *Elizabeth had composed, had played,* and *had signed.*

Identify the events in this sentence and put them in order.

Where patriots had fought and wise founders had written a constitution, a fast-food catfish restaurant stood.

Answer: Events 1 and 2: People with a better idea fight the old government and write a plan for a new government. Event 3: In the free and successful society that results, someone builds a restaurant after suing the landmarks preservation commission for the right to tear down a historic building.

Case 5: Two events in the future

Leaving the past behind, it's time to turn to the future. Read this sentence:

Ratrug *will have completed* all 433 college applications before they are due.

Ratrug's applications will be error-filled — he spelled his name *Ratrig* on at least three — but they will be done before the deadline. *Deadline* is the important word here, at least regarding verb tense. The *have* form of the future, also called *future perfect tense,* involves a deadline. You don't necessarily see two verbs in the sentence, but you do learn about two events:

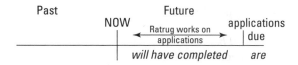

Use the future perfect tense to talk about the earlier of the two events.

Here are a few examples:

> Maya *will have served* all of her sentence before the parole board meets. (The deadline in the sentence is the parole board meeting.)
>
> By nine tonight, Eggworthy *will have* successfully *scrambled* the secret message. (The deadline in the sentence is nine o'clock.)
>
> Anna *will have left* for Lulu's trip up Mount Everest by the time the mountaineering supply company sends her gear. (The deadline in the sentence is the delivery of mountain-climbing supplies.)

Which sentence is correct?

> A. Shakey will have tossed the salad tonight.
>
> B. Shakey will have tossed the salad out the window before anyone has a chance to taste it.

Answer: Sentence B is correct. Future perfect tense involves a deadline, which in this sentence is *before anyone has a chance to taste it.*

Case 6: Different times, different verb forms

Remember those weird verb forms from Case 2, earlier in the chapter? The verbals? When they express different times, a helping verb *(having* or *have)* is involved.

For reasons that I can't begin to imagine, this topic is a favorite of standardized test-makers.

Check out this sentence:

> *Having sealed* the letter containing his job application, Nobrain *remembered* his name.

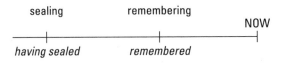

In other words, Nobrain's job application — unless he rips open the envelope — is anonymous because the *sealing* of the letter took place before the *remembering* of his name.

Here are additional examples:

> *Having finished* her homework, Elizabeth *turned* on the television to watch the oatmeal-wrestling tournament. (Event 1: Elizabeth finishes her homework at 2 a.m. Event 2: The tournament begins at 3 a.m. The networks seem reluctant to broadcast the match during prime time. I wonder why.)

> *Having won* all the votes, Lola named herself "Empress-in-Chief." (Event 1: Lola gets 100 percent of the votes. Event 2: Lola goes crown shopping.)

> *Having exhibited* the painting in Mel's new gallery, Elizabeth considered herself an all-around artistic genius. (Event 1: Elizabeth convinces Mel to hang her *Homework Blues* still life. Event 2: Elizabeth adds an art link to her Web page.)

If you have a life, skip this paragraph. If you like grammar, read on to learn the technical terms relevant to Case 6. The *present participle* (*finishing,* for example) combines with present, past, and future verbs to show two events happening at the same time or at nearly the same time. The *present perfect* form of the participle (*having finished*) combines with present, past, and future verbs to show two events happening at different times.

Another one of the verb-forms-that-aren't-verbs, the *infinitive*, may also show events happening at two different times. The *present perfect infinitive* (*to have finished,* for example) is the one that does this job. Don't worry about the name; just look for the *have.* Here's an example:

> It was helpful *to have bought the cookbook* before the dinner party. (Event 1: Pre-party, panicked trip to the bookstore. Event 2: Guests arrive, unaware that they're about to eat Alfalfa-Stringbean Surprise.)

The *have* form (the present perfect form) of the infinitive always places an event *before* another in the past. Don't use the *have* form unless you're putting events in order:

WRONG: I was wrong to have attended the party.

RIGHT: I was wrong to attend the party. The music was terrible and there was nothing to eat but vegetables.

ALSO RIGHT: I was wrong to have attended the party before I got a chance to investigate the menu. Shakey's salad was terrible.

She done him wrong

The word *done* is never a verb all by itself. A true party animal, this verb form insists on being accompanied by helping verbs. In grammar-speak, *done* is a past participle of the verb *to do.* Naked, shivering, totally-alone participles never function as verbs. Here are some examples:

WRONG: He done all he could, but the sky fell anyway.

RIGHT: He had done all he could, but the sky fell anyway.

WRONG: She done him wrong.

RIGHT, BUT A BAD SENTENCE: She has done him wrong.

BETTER SENTENCE: What she has done to him is wrong.

You may blame the fact that so many people create sentences like the first example *(He done all he could)* on one of the many joys of English

grammar. Some past participles —those of regular verbs — look exactly the same as the plain past tense. Consider the verb *to walk:*

PLAIN PAST TENSE: I *walked* twenty miles.

PRESENT PERFECT TENSE: I *have walked* twenty miles.

WHAT THESE TWO SENTENCES HAVE IN COMMON: The word *walked,* which is a verb in the first example and a past participle — part of a verb — in the second example.

WHY ENGLISH DOES THIS: I have no idea.

BOTTOM LINE: You may use *walked* alone or with a helper because the same word may be both a past tense verb and a participle. You may not use *done* by itself as a verb, however, because it's not the past tense of *to do.* The past tense of *to do* is *did.*

Which sentence shows two events happening at the same time, and which shows two events happening at different times?

A. Running up the clock, the mouse chatted with his friends.

B. Having run up the clock, the mouse chatted with his friends.

Answer: Sentence A shows two events happening at the same time. The mouse is running and chatting with his friends. Sentence B shows two events happening at different times. The mouse has arrived at the top of the clock and is now chatting with his friends. (Notice that the word *having* is involved, indicating that different events are occurring at different times.)

Reporting Information: The Verb Tells the Story

Flipping his hair over each of his three shoulders, the alien *told* us about the explosion on his planet. The gas of three rocket tanks *caught* fire and *destroyed* the spaceport terminal, he *said.* He *went* on to explain that almost everyone on the planet *was affected,* including the volleyball team, which *sustained* significant losses. All their courts, he *said, were covered* with rubble, and they *forfeited* the intergalactic tournament.

The alien's story is summarized speech. I'm not quoting him directly. If I were, I'd insert some of his exact words:

"Oh, the humanity!" he cried.

In the previous summarized speech, the verbs are all in past tense. Although rare, it's possible to summarize speech in present tense also. Present tense adds an extra dose of drama:

Flipping his hair over each of his three shoulders, the alien *tells* us about the explosion on his planet. The gas of three rocket tanks *catches* fire and *destroys* the spaceport terminal, he *says.* He *goes* on to explain that almost everyone on the planet *is affected,* including the volleyball team, which *sustains* significant losses. All their courts, he *says, are covered* with rubble, and they *forfeit* the intergalactic tournament.

When reporting information, either present or past tense is acceptable. However, mixing tenses is *not* acceptable. Don't move from one to the other, except for one special case, which I describe in the next section, "Recognizing Eternal Truths: Statements That Are Always in Present Tense."

WRONG: Shakey *said* that he *had tossed* the salad out the window. It *hits* a pedestrian, who *sues* for lettuce-related damages. (The first two verbs are in past tense, and the next two are in present tense.)

RIGHT: Shakey *said* that he *had tossed* the salad out the window. It *hit* a pedestrian, who *sued* for lettuce-related damages. (All verbs are in a form of the past tense.)

Correct the verb tense in this paragraph. The verbs are in italics.

Lola *testified* that she *excavated* at the town dump every Tuesday afternoon before she *attends* choir practice. She often *found* arrow heads, broken pottery, discarded automobile tires, and other items of interest.

> One day she *discovers* a metal coil about two feet long. On one end of the coil *was* a piece of gum. As she thoughtfully *removes* the gum and *starts* to chew, a whistle *blew*. Roger *sprinted* into the dump at top speed. "Get your hands off my gum," he *exclaims*. Roger *smiles*. His anti-gum-theft alarm *had worked* perfectly.

Answer: The story is in two different tenses, past and present. To correct it, choose one of the two. Here is the past tense version, with the changed verbs underlined:

> Lola *testified* that she *excavated* at the town dump every Tuesday afternoon before she *attended* choir practice. She often *found* arrow heads, broken pottery, discarded automobile tires, and other items of interest. One day she *discovered* a metal coil about two feet long. On one end of the coil *was* a piece of gum. As she thoughtfully *removed* the gum and *started* to chew, a whistle *blew*. Roger *sprinted* into the dump at top speed. "Get your hands off my gum," he *exclaimed*. Roger *smiled*. His anti-gum-theft alarm *had worked* perfectly.

Here is the present tense version, with the changed verbs underlined:

> Lola *testifies* that she *excavates* at the town dump every Tuesday afternoon before she *attends* choir practice. She often *finds* arrow heads, broken pottery, discarded automobile tires, and other items of interest. One day she *discovers* a metal coil about two feet long. On one end of the coil *is* a piece of gum. As she thoughtfully *removes* the gum and *starts* to chew, a whistle *blows*. Roger *sprints* into the dump at top speed. "Get your hands off my gum," he *exclaims*. Roger *smiles*. His anti-gum-theft alarm *has worked* perfectly.

One special note: When you're not reporting what someone says, you can make a general statement about something that always happens (someone's custom or habit) using present tense. You can easily combine such a statement with a story that focuses on one particular incident in the past tense. Therefore, the preceding story may begin in present tense and move to past tense in this way:

> Lola *excavates* at the town dump every Tuesday afternoon before she *attends* choir practice. She often *finds* arrow heads, broken pottery, discarded automobile tires, and other items of interest.

Up to here in the story, all the verbs are in present tense because the story tells of Lola's habits. The story isn't reporting what someone said. In the next sentence, the story switches to past tense because it examines one particular day in the past.

One day she *discovered* a metal coil about two feet long. On one end of the coil *was* a piece of gum. As she thoughtfully *removed* the gum and *started* to chew, a whistle *blew.* Roger *sprinted* into the dump at top speed. "Get your hands off my gum," he *exclaimed.* Roger *smiled.* His anti-gum-theft alarm *had worked* perfectly.

When you're revising a paragraph on the writing section of the SAT I or the English portion of the ACT, keep your eye out for verb-tense errors.

Recognizing Eternal Truths: Statements That Are Always in Present Tense

What's wrong with these sentences?

> Anna explained that one plus one *equaled* two.
>
> Ms. Belli said that the earth *was* round.
>
> She added that diamonds *were made* of carbon.

Well, you may be thinking,

> *Equaled* two? What does it equal now? Three?
>
> *Was* round? And now it's a cube?
>
> *Were* made of carbon? Now they make diamonds from pastrami?

In others words, the verb tense is wrong. All of these statements represent eternal truths — statements that will never change. When you write such statements, you must always write in present tense, even if the statement was made in the past:

> Anna explained that one plus one *equals* two.
>
> Ms. Belli told us that the earth *is* round.
>
> She went on to say that diamonds *are made* of carbon.

Which sentence is correct?

A. Michael said that Lulu had a cold.

B. Michael said that Lulu has a cold.

Answer: Sentence A is correct. Lulu's cold is not an eternal truth, though it has lasted three weeks and shows no signs of letting up. Be consistent in verb tense.

Do you have the energy for one more? Find the correct sentence.

   A. Lulu explained that the sun was very hot.

   B. Lulu explained that the sun is very hot.

Answer: Sentence B is correct. The sun can burn you from millions of miles away, as I found out at the beach last week. It's not likely to turn into a snowball anytime soon.

Chapter 19

Saying What You Want to Say: Descriptive Words and Phrases

. . . .

In This Chapter

▶ Placing descriptions so that the sentence says what you mean

▶ Beginning a sentence with a description

▶ Using infinitives as descriptions

▶ Avoiding double meanings for descriptive words

▶ Omitting words without losing meaning

. . . .

*O*nce upon a time, the ancestor of our Modern English, Old English, was the language of the land. Most words had many forms: one to show that the word received an action and one to show that it performed an action. Because the words themselves carried so many aspects of meaning, you could arrange them in many ways and still say the same thing. Word order was less important in Old English than it is in Modern English.

The good news is that speakers of Modern English don't have to learn dozens of forms of words. The bad news is that Modern English speakers have to be careful about word order. Most people do all right with nouns and verbs, but descriptions are another matter. In this chapter, I show you some common mistakes of placement. Specifically, I show you how placing a description in the wrong spot can completely wreck your sentence.

Ruining a Perfectly Good Sentence: Misplaced Descriptions

Can you spot what's wrong with this sentence?

Lulu put a ring in her pierced nose that she had bought last week.

The describing words *that she had bought last week* follow the word *nose*. The way the sentence is now, *that she had bought last week* describes *nose*. The Internet sells plenty of unusual items, but not noses (yet), though I imagine a Web address for plastic surgeons offering discount nose jobs is out there somewhere.

Here's the correction:

> In her pierced nose Lulu put a ring that she had bought last week.

Now *that she had bought last week* follows ring, which Lulu really did buy last week.

If you encounter a misplaced description in your writing (or on a test), be sure that your revision doesn't create another error. Here's an example of a faulty revision, still working from the sentence about Lulu's nose:

> Lulu put a ring that she had bought last week in her pierced nose.

In this version Lulu's shopping took place inside her nose, which *is* rather large, but not spacious enough for a jewelry store. Why? Because *in her pierced nose* tells you where something happened. The sentence has two verbs, *put* and *had bought*. The description describes the nearest action, which, in the faulty revision, is *had bought*. In the true correction, *in her pierced nose* is at the beginning of the sentence, closer to *put* than to *had bought*.

I'm not a big fan of grammar terms, but if you're curious, here's the deal: The description *that she bought last week* is an adjective clause. It describes the noun *ring*. For more information on adjective clauses, see Chapter 24.

Here's another description that wandered too far from home:

> Lulu also bought a genuine, 1950-model, fluorescent pink hula-hoop with a credit card.

According to news reports, toddlers and dogs have received credit card applications, but not plastic toys — at least as far as I know. Yet the sentence says that the hula-hoop comes with a credit card. How to fix it? Move the description:

> With a credit card Lulu also bought a genuine, 1950-model, fluorescent pink hula-hoop.

Granted, most people can figure out the meaning of the faulty sentence, even when the description is in the wrong place. Logic is a powerful force. But chances are your reader or listener will pause a moment to unravel what you've said. The next couple of sentences may be a washout because your audience is distracted.

The rule concerning description placement is simple: Place the description as close as possible to the word that it describes.

Maybe because professors are tired of moving descriptions around in student papers, college entrance tests (the SAT or ACT) question you thoroughly on this topic.

Which sentence is correct?

   A. Roger put the paper into his pocket with atomic secrets written on it.

   B. Roger put the paper with atomic secrets written on it into his pocket.

Answer: Sentence B is correct because the paper has atomic secrets written on it, not the pocket.

Try another. Which sentence is correct?

   A. Anna peddled to the Mathematics Olympics on her ten-speed bicycle with a complete set of differential equations.

   B. Anna peddled on her ten-speed bicycle to the Mathematics Olympics with a complete set of differential equations.

   C. With a complete set of differential equations, Anna peddled on her ten-speed bicycle to the Mathematics Olympics.

Answer: Sentence C is correct. In sentence A, the bicycle has ten speeds, two tires, and a set of equations — not very useful in climbing hills and swerving to avoid taxis! In sentence B, the Mathematics Olympics has a complete set of differential equations. Perhaps so, but the sentence revolves around Anna, so the more likely meaning is that Anna has the equations. Only in sentence C does Anna have the equations. (By the way, she won a silver medal in the little known sport known as Peddle Solving. Contestants do math while riding exercise bikes.)

Continually? continuously? making mistakes

Two description pairs trespass on each other's territory — *continuously/continuous* and *continually/continual*. Which pair should you turn to express your meaning? Read on.

Continual and *continually* refer to events that happen over and over again, but with breaks in between each instance. (*Continual* describes nouns, and *continually* describes verbs.) *Continuous* and *continuously* are for situation without gaps. (As you've probably guessed, *continuous* attaches to nouns, and *continuously* to verbs.) *Continuous* noise is steady, uninterrupted, like the drone of the electric generator in your local power plant. *Continual* noise is what you hear when I go bowling. You hear silence (when I stare at the pins), a little noise (when the ball rolls down the alley), and silence again (when the ball slides into the gutter without hitting anything). After an hour you hear noise (when I finally hit something and begin to cheer). In case you're wondering, I'm a very bad bowler.

Here are a couple of examples of these two descriptions in action:

WRONG: Jim screamed *continually* until Lola stuffed rags in his mouth.

WHY IT'S WRONG: Jim's screams don't come and go. When he's upset, he's really upset, and nothing shuts him up except force.

RIGHT: Jim screamed *continuously* until Lola stuffed rags in his mouth.

WHY IT'S RIGHT: In this version, Jim takes no breaks.

WRONG: Ella's *continuous* attempts to impress Larry were unsuccessful, including the fruit basket she sent him on Monday and the piranha she Fed-Exed on Tuesday.

WHY IT'S WRONG: Ella's attempts stop and start. She does one thing on Monday, rests up, and then does another on Tuesday.

RIGHT: Ella's *continual* attempts to impress Larry were unsuccessful, including the fruit basket she sent him on Monday and the piranha she Fed-Exed on Tuesday.

WHY IT'S RIGHT: Now the sentence talks about a recurring action.

By the way, this pair had a cameo appearance on a recent standardized test. Test-takers, refer to these examples *continually* so they'll remain in your memory *continuously*.

Keeping Your Audience Hanging: Danglers

How can you describe something that isn't there? Descriptions must have something to describe. This idea seems simple, and it *is* simple when the description is one word attached to another. You're not likely to say,

I want to buy a red.

when you're putting together a Santa Claus outfit for a holiday party. Instead you automatically declare,

> I want to buy a red suit.

In the preceding sentence, *red* describes *suit.* However, two types of descriptions tend to cause as many problems as a double-date with your ex: participles and infinitives. These descriptions look like verbs, but they don't function as verbs. In grammarspeak, they're known as *verbals.* (You can find out more about verbals in Chapter 24.)

In this section, I show you common mistakes with participles and infinitives. Don't worry about the names; you don't need them. Just place these descriptions properly.

Dangling participles

Read this sentence:

> Munching a buttered sausage, the cholesterol really builds up.

As you see, the sentence begins with a verb form, *munching,* but *munching* isn't the verb in the sentence. It's a participle — a verb form that describes. (The real verb in the sentence is *builds.*) But participles have to describe something or someone. *Munching* must be tacked onto a muncher. So who is munching? You? Eggworthy? Everyone in the local diet club? In the sentence, no one is munching. Descriptive verb forms that have nothing appropriate to describe are called *danglers* or *dangling modifiers.* To correct the sentence, add a muncher:

> Munching a buttered sausage, Eggworthy smiled and waved to his cardiologist.

In sentences beginning with a descriptive verb form, such as a participle, the subject must perform the action mentioned in the descriptive verb form. In the sample sentence, Eggworthy is the subject of the sentence. The sentence begins with a descriptive verb form, *munching a buttered sausage.* Thus, Eggworthy is the one who is munching. (For more information on identifying the subject of a sentence, see Chapter 4.) If you want the cardiologist to munch, say

> Munching a buttered sausage, the cardiologist returned Eggworthy's wave.

Here's another example:

> Sitting on the park bench, the soaring space shuttle briefly delighted the little boy.

Oh really? The space shuttle is sitting on a bench and soaring at the same time? Defies the laws of physics, don't you think? (Also, park rules clearly state that no intergalactic vehicles are allowed on benches.) Try again:

> Sitting on the park bench, the little boy was briefly delighted by the soaring space shuttle.

Now *little boy* is the subject of the sentence, so the introductory description applies to him, not to the space shuttle. Another correction may be

> The soaring space shuttle briefly delighted the little boy who was sitting on the park bench.

Now the descriptive words *sitting on the park bench* are placed next to little boy, who in fact is the one sitting, being delighted by the soaring space shuttle.

This topic is so popular on the SAT that it deserves another example. Here's a faulty sentence:

> Skidding over the icy pavement, the old oak tree couldn't escape the speeding sports car.

You spotted the problem, right? The *tree* is the subject of the sentence, but a tree can't be the thing *skidding over the icy pavement.* That sort of thing happens only in Harry Potter movies. Now for the better version:

> Skidding over the icy pavement, the speeding sports car slammed into the old oak tree.

Now the *speeding sports car* is skidding. No problem. Well, no grammar problem anyway. The traffic cop sees the situation a little differently.

Which one is correct?

A. Sailing swiftly across the sea, Samantha's boat was surely a beautiful sight.

B. Sailing swiftly across the sea, the sight of the beautiful boat made Samantha sob.

Answer: Sentence A is correct. *Sailing swiftly across the sea* describes Samantha's boat. Samantha's boat is performing that action. Sentence B is wrong because in sentence B *sight,* the subject, is sailing. (And of course, a *sight* can't sail.)

Dangling infinitives

Another common dangler is an infinitive (to + verb) that begins a sentence.

> To sew well, a strong light is necessary.

This sentence may sound correct to you. After all, sewing in the dark is hard. But think about the meaning for a moment. Who is sewing? No one, at least the way the sentence is now written. Moving the infinitive may make the sentence sound better to your ears, but the move doesn't solve the problem:

> A strong light is necessary to sew well.

There's still no one sewing, so the sentence is still incorrect. To fix the problem, you must add a person:

> To sew well, you need a strong light. (*You* are sewing.)

> To sew well, sit near a strong light. (*You* is understood in this command sentence.)

> To sew well, everyone needs a strong light. (*Everyone* is sewing.)

> To sew well, Betsy insists on at least a 75-watt bulb. (*Betsy* is sewing.)

An infinitive at the beginning of a sentence *may* be legal. Check out this sentence:

> To sew well is Betsy's goal.

In the preceding sentence, *to sew well* isn't a description. It's an activity that is Betsy's goal. In other words, *to sew well* is the subject in this sentence. How do you tell the difference between a subject and a description? A subject pairs with a verb (*is* in the example sentence) and answers the questions *who? or what?* (For help finding the subject of a sentence, turn to Chapter 4.) A description is an add-on, contributing more information about something else in the sentence.

Which sentence is correct?

  A. To enjoy a good cup of coffee, a clean coffee pot is essential.

  B. A clean coffeepot is essential to enjoy a good cup of coffee.

Answer. Neither A nor B is correct. (I threw in one of those annoying teacher tricks just to keep you alert.) Neither sentence has a coffee drinker in it. So who's enjoying the coffee? No one. A true correction must add a person:

To enjoy a good cup of coffee, *you* start with a clean coffeepot.

To enjoy a good cup of coffee, caffeine *addicts* start with a clean coffeepot.

To enjoy a good cup of coffee, *Anna* starts with a clean coffeepot.

To enjoy a good cup of coffee, start with a clean coffeepot. (Now *you* [understood in this command sentence] are the coffee drinker.)

One more round: Which sentence is correct?

A. To enjoy his morning coffee was Malachy's greatest pleasure.

B. To enjoy his morning coffee, Malachy got up an hour earlier than his annoying little brother.

Answer. Both A and B are correct. (I couldn't resist another teacher trick. Sorry.) In Sentence A, *To enjoy his morning coffee* is the subject of the verb *was.* (What *was? To enjoy his morning coffee was.*) In Sentence B, the infinitive isn't dangling. *Malachy* is the person who *got up* early.

Avoiding Confusing Descriptions

Location, location, location! That's what real estate agents say matters, and it's also what grammarians declare. In this section, I examine the hot spot located between two actions. A descriptive word there may confuse your reader. Take a look at the following example:

The teacher that Roger annoyed often assigned detention to him.

What does the sentence mean? Did Roger *often annoy* the teacher? (I'm a teacher, and Roger would certainly annoy me. His burps alone . . . but back to grammar.) Perhaps the teacher *often assigned* detention to Roger. (Yup. Sounds like something Roger's teacher would do.)

Do you see the problem with the sample sentence? It has two distinct, possible meanings. Because *often* is between *annoying* and *assigning*, it may be linked to either of those two actions. The sentence violates a basic rule of description: All descriptions must be clear. You should never place a description where it may have two possible meanings.

How do you fix the sentence? You move *often* so that it is closer to one of the verbs, thus showing the reader which of two words *only* describes. Here are two correct versions, each with a different meaning:

The teacher that Roger often annoyed assigned detention to him.

In this sentence *often* is closer to *annoyed*. Thus, *often* describes *annoyed*. The sentence communicates to the reader that after 514 burps, the teacher finally flipped and assigned detention to Roger.

Here's a second possibility:

> The teacher that Roger annoyed assigned detention to him often.

Now *often* is closer to *assigned*. The reader understands that *often* describes *assigned*. The sentence tells the reader that the teacher vowed "not to take anything from that little brat" and assigned detention to Roger every day of the school year, including winter break and Presidents' Day.

Correct or incorrect? You decide.

> The pig chewing on pig chow happily burped and made us all run for gas masks.

Answer: Incorrect. You don't know if the pig is *chewing happily* or *burping happily*. Here's how to correct the sentence:

> The pig chewing happily on pig chow burped and made us all run for gas masks.

or

> The pig chewing on pig chow burped happily and made us all run for gas masks.

One other correction is possible here: the addition of a set of commas. If you set off the description with commas, the reader connects the description to the right verb. Therefore, these two sentences are also okay:

> The pig, chewing on pig chow happily, burped and made us all run for gas masks.
>
> The pig, chewing on pig chow, happily burped and made us all run for gas masks.

I have to warn you about the comma-correction. You can't always throw in a comma and fix a problem. In fact, sometimes you create an addition mistake by adding a comma! Check out Chapter 13 for comma advice, or fix the sentence by moving the description.

You may be tempted to fix a description by tucking it inside an infinitive:

> Betsy's song is strange enough to *intensely* captivate creative musicians.

Technically, you shouldn't split an infinitive (to + verb — *to captivate* in this sentence).

> Right: to captivate intensely

> Wrong: to intensely captivate

This rule is often ignored and probably on the way out of the grammar rule books. But if you're writing for a super-strict reader, be careful of split infinitives.

The most commonly misplaced descriptions are single words: *only, just, almost,* and *even.* See Chapter 7 for a complete explanation of how to place these descriptive words correctly.

Finding the Subject When Words Are Missing from the Sentence

In the never-ending human quest to save time, words are often chopped out of sentences, especially sentences texted while you're sipping a half-caf, nonfat latte and running for a bus. (Bad idea on so many levels, by the way, as I explained to the lady who splashed me with her latte recently.) The assumption is that the sentence is still understandable because the listener or reader supplies the missing piece. Not a bad assumption, as long as you understand what you can chop and what you need to leave alone. Check out these examples:

> While sleeping, Johann dreamed that he was a giant cappuccino.

> Although screaming in rage, Lola managed to keep an eye on the clock.

> If caught, Roger will probably deny everything.

> Lulu snored when dreaming of little sheep.

Do you understand what these sentences mean? Here they are again, with the missing words inserted and italicized:

> While *he was* sleeping, Johann dreamed that he was a giant cappuccino.

> Although *she was* screaming in rage, Lola managed to keep an eye on the clock.

> If *he is* caught, Roger will probably deny everything.

> Lulu snored when *she was* dreaming of little sheep.

As you see, the subject and part of the verb are missing in each of the sample sentences. The reader fills in both.

You need to remember only one rule for these sentences: The missing subject must be the same as the subject that is present. In other words, if your sentence lacks more information, the reader or listener will assume that you're talking about the same person or thing in both parts of the sentence. Here are some examples:

> WRONG: While missing a shovel, the hole in Lulu's backyard was dug by a backhoe.

> UNINTENDED MEANING: While the hole was missing a shovel, the hole in Lulu's backyard was dug by a backhoe.

> CORRECTION: While missing a shovel, Lulu rented a backhoe to dig a hole in her backyard.

> MEANING OF CORRECTED SENTENCE: While she was missing a shovel, Lulu rented a backhoe to dig a hole in her backyard.

> ADDITIONAL UNINTENDED EFFECT: Lulu, not knowing how to drive a backhoe, hit a power line and brought down the entire electrical system of the Northeast.

> WRONG: When showering, Roger's beauty routine requires industrial-strength cleaning products.

> UNINTENDED MEANING: When Roger's beauty routine is showering, the beauty routine requires industrial-strength cleaning products.

> CORRECTION: When showering, Roger requires industrial-strength cleaning products.

> MEANING OF CORRECTED SENTENCE: For each of his twice-yearly showers, Roger has to apply the kind of glop that removes rust from old battleships.

> ADDITIONAL UNINTENDED EFFECT: Roger's bathtub is on the Environmental Protection Agency's list of toxic waste sites.

Which sentence is correct?

A. Since conducting the leak test, Dripless's pipe has been watertight.

B. Since conducting the leak test, Dripless reported that the pipe was watertight.

C. Since he conducted the leak test, Dripless's pipe has been watertight.

Not boring, but often wrong

If you go on trial for breaking a picture window, you want a *disinterested* jury, but not an *uninterested* lawyer. Why? Because *disinterested* means fair, unprejudiced. *Uninterested* means wake me up when it's over because I really don't care. Don't confuse these two descriptions! Here's an example:

WRONG: Lulu tried to catch Roger's attention, but he was *disinterested* in what she had to say.

WHY IT'S WRONG: Roger is never fair, but he is quite self-centered. In this sentence, the writer intends to show that Roger is ignoring Lulu.

RIGHT: Lulu tried to catch Roger's attention, but he was *uninterested* in what she had to say.

WHY IT'S RIGHT: Now Roger is bored, his usual state when he is not looking into the mirror, contemplating his own wonderfulness.

One more round:

WRONG: The *uninterested* executive made a decision based solely on the facts, not because of any special relationship with the seller, who happened to be her mother-in-law.

WHY IT'S WRONG: If the executive is *uninterested*, she won't make a decision at all. She'll be playing golf with all the other executives who can't summon up any curiosity about their own companies.

RIGHT: The *disinterested* executive made a decision based solely on the facts, not because of any special relationship with the seller, who happened to be her mother-in-law.

WHY IT'S RIGHT: Now the executive is fair, deciding the issue on its own merits, not on the fact that her mother-in-law will never speak to her again during Sunday dinner if the sale doesn't go through.

Answer: Sentences B and C are both correct. The missing subject in sentences A and B is *Dripless*. In sentence A, *Dripless's pipe* is the subject of the second part of the sentence, so there is a mismatch between the two parts of the sentence. In sentence B, *Dripless* is the subject of the second part of the sentence. The two halves of the sentence match. In sentence C, a subject *(he)* is supplied, so the two halves of the sentences don't have to have the same subject.

Chapter 20

Good, Better, Best: Comparisons

. . . .

In This Chapter

▶ Adding *-er* and *-est* to descriptions

▶ Using *more/less* and *most/least* correctly

▶ Understanding some irregular comparisons

▶ Identifying words that can't be compared

▶ Avoiding illogical comparisons

▶ Writing double comparisons correctly

. . . .

*I*s your knowledge of comparisons *more better* or *less worse*? If you chose one of those two alternatives, this chapter is for you because *more better* and *less worse* are both incorrect. English has two ways of creating comparisons, but you can't use them together and they're not interchangeable. In this chapter, I show you how to tell the difference between the two types of comparisons, how to use each correctly, and how to avoid some of the common errors of comparisons. I don't, however, tell you which comparisons to avoid altogether, such as *Which stock is a better buy?* and *Am I a better dancer than your last date?* You have to figure out those dilemmas yourself.

Ending It with -Er or Giving It More

Take a close look at the comparisons in these sentences:

Roger's smile is *more evil* than Michael's, but Michael's giggle sounds *cuter*.

Eggworthy searched for the *least efficient* sports utility vehicle, believing that global warming is *less important* than having the *raciest* image in the parking lot.

Betsy's *most recent* symphony was *less successful* than her *earlier* composition.

Anna's *older* sister is an even *greater* mathematician than Anna herself, though Anna has the edge in geometry.

Lulu's *latest* tattoo is *grosser* than her first, but Lulu, not the *shyest* girl in the class, is looking for the *most extreme* design for her next effort.

What did you notice about the comparisons in the preceding sample sentences? Here's the stripped-down list: *more evil, cuter, least efficient, less important, raciest, most recent, less successful, earlier, older, greater, grosser, latest, shyest, most extreme.*

Some of the comparisons were expressed by adding *-er* or *-est,* and some were expressed by adding *more, most, less,* or *least* to the quality that's being compared. How do you know which is appropriate? (Or, to use a comparison, how do you know which is *better?*) The dictionary is the final authority, and you should consult one if you're in doubt about a particular word. However, there are some general guidelines:

- Add *-er* and *-est* to most single-syllable words.

- If the word already ends in the letter *e,* don't double the *e* by adding *-er* or *-est.* Just add *-r* or *-st.*

- *-Er* and *-est* endings are not usually appropriate for words ending in *-ly.*

The dictionary is your friend

You can learn a lot about a word from the dictionary, whether you check an Internet site or lug a ten-pound volume off a shelf. The average dictionary entry tells you

- The part of speech

- The pronunciation

- The definitions of the word, listed in order of importance

- Some common expressions using the word

- Other forms of the word

- Something about the history of the word — its earlier forms or its linguistic ancestors

- A ruling on whether the word is acceptable in formal English

Because dictionaries were a paper-only form for centuries, dictionary publishers favored a set of abbreviations that packed maximum information into minimal space. Most of those abbreviations have migrated to electronic media, even though the Internet allows a little more elbow room. Therefore, reading a dictionary entry may resemble a trip to a foreign country — one where everyone else seems to know the language and customs and is happy to leave you out of the picture.

Let me put you in the picture. Here's a very special dictionary entry, with the parts decoded for the average reader. (By the way, don't look for this word in a real dictionary; I made it up.) Just match the letters in the dictionary entry with the explanations below.

A. chukblok B. (chuck–blahk) **C.** n. **D.** *pl.* chuk-bloks. **E.** 1. The state currency of Larencia. 2. The national bank of Larencia. 3. In economics, a very high protective tariff: a *chukblok* against imported bananas. **F.** 4. *Informal* extremely rich person: he's a walking *chukblok.* **G.** 5. *obs.* A coin made of chewing gum. **H.** – *adj.* 1. rich: She put a *chukblok* icing on that cake. 2. illegal: The *chukblok* plan was bound to backfire. **I.** [<O.L. *chublah*<ML. chubare a coin.] **J. Syn**. n. coins, money, moolah, spending green. *adj.* well-heeled, well-off, illicit. **K.** – **to see chukbloks in the trees** *Slang.* To assume that one is about to get rich. – **to flip one's chukblok** *Informal.* To bet all of one's money on the throw of the dice.

Here are the letter identifications:

A. The word.

B. The pronunciation. The symbols here are a little confusing, but most dictionaries provide a key in the front of the book or somewhere on the web site. The key explains the pronunciation symbols by showing you the same sound in some easily recognizable words.

C. The part of speech.

D. The abbreviation *pl.* means *plural,* and this part of the entry tells you how to form the plural of this word.

E. The definitions. The most commonly used definitions are first.

F. *Informal* tells you that you shouldn't use that particular meaning in formal writing.

If the word isn't labeled, it's acceptable in formal writing.

G. *Obs.* means "obsolete" and tells you that a meaning is no longer used.

H. Another part of speech. The *adj.* abbreviation tells you that you can also use *chukblok* as an adjective, in addition to using it as a noun. The meanings listed after *adj.* explain what the word means when it is used as an adjective. Again, the definitions are in order from the most common meaning to the rarest.

I. These symbols tell you the family tree of the word *chukblok.* The abbreviation *O.L.* refers to *Old Larencian,* a language that I made up. *ML.* is an abbreviation; it refers to *Middle Larencian,* another language that I made up. In the brackets, you learn that you can trace the history of *chukblok* to the Old Larencian word *chublah,* which in turn may be traced to a Middle Larencian word *chubare,* meaning *coin.*

J. Another abbreviation. *Syn.* means *synonym.* Following this symbol are words that mean the same as the noun and adjective versions of *chukblok.*

K. The meaning of common expressions with the word *chukblok.* One is slang and the other informal; neither is acceptable in formal writing.

Table 20-1 is a chart of some common descriptions of Lola, with both the *-er* and *-est* forms. Note: To understand Lola's personality, you need to know to what (or to whom) she's being compared, so I include a few clues.

Table 20-1	Common Descriptions	
Description of Lola	**-ER form**	**-EST form**
able	abler than Lulu	ablest of all the budding scientists in her atom-splitting class
bald	balder than an eagle	baldest of the models
cute	cuter than an elf	cutest of all the assassins
dumb	dumber than a sea slug	dumbest of the congressional candidates
edgy	edgier than caffeine	edgiest of the atom splitters
friendly	friendlier than a grizzly bear	friendliest person on the block
glad	gladder than the loser	gladdest of all the lottery winners
heavy	heavier than a "before" ad for a diet book	heaviest of all the sumo wrestlers
itchy	itchier than she was before she sat in poison ivy	itchiest of all the patients in the skin clinic

Notice that when the last letter is *y*, you must often change the *y* to *i* before you tack on the ending.

Table 20-2 contains even more descriptions of Lola, this time with *more, less, most,* and *least* added:

Table 20-2	Two-word Descriptions	
Description of Lola	**More/Less form**	**Most/Least form**
(Lola runs) jerkily	more jerkily than the old horse	most jerkily of all the racers
knock-kneed	less knock-kneed than an old sailor	least knock-kneed of all the beauty pageant contestants
lily-livered	less lily-livered than the saloon owner in an old movie	least lily-livered of all the florists
magnificent	more magnificent than a work of art	most magnificent of all the ninjas

Description of Lola	**More/Less** *form*	**Most/Least** *form*
notorious	more notorious than a princess	most notorious of the florists
oafish	less oafish than the young prince	least oafish of all the cab drivers
prune-faced	less prune-faced than her teacher	least prune-faced of the grammar students
queenly	more queenly than Queen Elizabeth	most queenly of all the models
rigid	less rigid than a grammarian	least rigid of the traffic cops

These two tables give you a clue about another important comparison characteristic. Did you notice that the second column is always a comparison between Lola and *one other* person or thing? The addition of *-er* or *more* or *less* compares two things. In the last column of each chart, Lola is compared to a group with more than two members. When the group is larger than two, *-est* or *most* or *least* creates the comparison and identifies the extreme.

To sum up the rules:

✔ Use *-er* or *more/less* when comparing only two things.

✔ Use *-est* or *most/least* when singling out the extreme in a group that is larger than two.

✔ Never combine two comparison methods, such as *-er* and *more*.

For the grammar fan: The *-er* or *less/more* form of comparison is called *comparative* and the *-est* or *least/most* form of comparison is called *superlative*.

Which sentence is correct?

A. Lola, fresh from drinking a cup of cream, was the more cheerful of all her friends in the dairy bar.

B. Lola, fresh from drinking a cup of cream, was the most cheerful of all her friends in the dairy bar.

Answer: Sentence B is correct. The sentence singles out Lola as the extreme in a group (Lola's usual position), so you need *most* here, not *more*.

Try another. Which sentence is correct?

A. Eggworthy's design for a new carton is simpler than the one his competitor hatched.

B. Eggworthy's design for a new carton is more simpler than the one his competitor hatched.

Answer: Sentence A is correct. Never combine two forms of comparison. Sentence B hits the penalty box because it combines the *-er* form with the word *more.*

Last one. Which sentence is correct?

   A. Of all the cars in the parking lot, Eggworthy's is the newer.

   B. Of all the cars in the parking lot, Eggworthy's is the newest.

Answer: Sentence B is correct. Eggworthy's car is compared to more than one other car.

Breaking the Rules: Irregular Comparisons

Whenever English grammar gives you a set of rules that make sense, you know it's time for the irregulars to show up. Not surprisingly, then, you have to create a few common comparisons without *-er, -est, more/less,* or *most/ least* — the regular comparisons I explain in the preceding section.

Good, bad, well

I think of these as the "report card" comparisons because they evaluate quality. The first word of each line provides a description. The second word shows you that description when two elements are beings compared. The last word is for comparisons of three or more.

   ✔ Good, better, best

   ✔ Bad, worse, worst

   ✔ Well, better, best

Time to visit *good, bad,* and *well* when they're on the job:

Although Michael's trumpet solo is *good* and Roger's is *better,* Lulu's trumpet solo is the *best* of all.

Lulu's habit of picking at her tattoo is *bad,* but Ralph's constant sneezing is *worse.* Eggworthy's tendency to crack jokes is the *worst* habit of all.

Lola sings *well* in the shower, but Max sings *better* in the bathtub. Ralph croons *best* in the hot tub.

What's the difference between *good* and *well*? *Good* is an adjective and describes nouns (people, places, things, ideas). *Well* is an adverb and describes verbs (actions or states of being), except when you're talking about health. For more information on *good* and *well*, check out Chapter 7.

Answer this question in correct English (and then correct the question itself).

> Who's the baddest kid in the playground?

Answer: The *worst* (not *baddest*) kid in the playground is Roger, unless Lola is in one of her moods. The correct question is *Who's the worst kid in the playground?*

Here's another:

> Who plays more better blues?

Answer: No one. Use *more* or *better,* but not both, to make the comparison. Other ways to word the question include:

> Who plays better blues — Michael or Lulu?
>
> Who plays the best blues?
>
> Who plays the blues best?
>
> Of the two saxophonists, who plays better blues?

Last one. Which sentence is correct?

> A. Michael says that he is feeling worse today than yesterday, but his statement must be considered in light of the fact that today is the algebra final.
>
> B. Michael says that he is feeling more bad today than yesterday, but his statement must be considered in light of the fact that today is the algebra final.

Answer: Sentence A is correct. *More bad* is incorrect; use *worse.*

Little, many, much

These are the measuring comparisons, words that tell you about quantity. The first word on each line is the description, the second creates comparisons between two elements, and the last word applies to comparisons of three-plus elements.

- Little, less, least
- Many, more, most
- Much, more, most

Check out these words in action (actually, in sentences, but you know what I mean):

Lulu likes a *little* grape jelly on her pizza, but Eggworthy prefers *less* exotic toppings. Of all his creations, Lulu likes chocolate pizza *least*.

Roger spies on *many* occasions, but he seldom uncovers *more* secrets than his brother Al. Lola is the *most* successful spy of all.

Anna has *much* interest in mathematics, though she's *more* devoted to her trumpet lessons. Of all the musical mathematicians I know, Anna is the *most* likely to succeed in both careers.

Many or *much*? How do you decide which word is needed? Easy. *Many* precedes plurals of countable elements (*many crickets or shoes*, for example) and *much* precedes words that express qualities that may not be counted, though these qualities may sometimes be measured (*much noise or sugar*, for instance).

Which sentence is correct?

A. Anna and Michael studied together for the algebra final, but Michael is the least prepared.

B. Anna and Michael studied together for the algebra final, but Michael is less prepared.

Answer: Sentence B is correct. *Less* is the word you want when comparing two elements. Because you're comparing only Anna and Michael, *less* triumphs over *least*, which is a good word when you're comparing Anna, Michael, Lola, and the rest of the study group — in other words, three or more elements.

Never More Perfect: Using Words That You Can't Compare

Is this chapter more unique than the previous chapter? No, definitely not. Why? Because nothing is *more unique*. The word *unique* means "one of a kind." Either something is one of a kind, or it's not. Yes or no, true or false, one or zero (when you're speaking in computer code). No halfway point, no degrees of uniqueness, no . . . well, you get the idea. You can't compare something that's unique to anything but itself. Check out the following examples:

WRONG: The vase that Eggworthy cracked was more unique than the Grecian urn.

ALSO WRONG: The vase that Eggworthy cracked was fairly unique.

ALSO WRONG: The vase that Eggworthy cracked was almost unique.

WRONG AGAIN: The vase that Eggworthy cracked was very unique.

RIGHT: The vase that Eggworthy cracked was unique.

ALSO RIGHT: The vase that Eggworthy cracked was unique, as was the Grecian urn.

RIGHT AGAIN: The vase that Eggworthy cracked was more unusual than the Grecian urn.

WHY IT'S RIGHT: *Unusual* is not an absolute term, so you can use it in comparisons.

The word *unique* is not unique. Several other words share its absolute quality. One is *perfect.* Something is perfect or not perfect; nothing is *very perfect* or *unbelievably perfect* or *somewhat perfect.* (I am bound, as a patriotic American, to point out one exception: The United States Constitution contains a statement of purpose citing the need to create "a more perfect union.") Another absolute word is *round.* Your shape is *round* or *not round.* Your shape isn't *a bit round, rounder,* or *roundest.* Here are some examples:

WRONG: "Lola is *extremely perfect* when it comes to grammar, as I am," said Lulu.

WHY IT'S WRONG: *Perfect* is absolute. There are no degrees of perfection.

RIGHT: "Lola is *nearly perfect* when it comes to grammar, as I am," said Lulu.

WHY IT'S RIGHT: You can approach an absolute quality, comparing how close someone or something comes to the quality. Lola and Lulu approach perfection, but neither achieves it.

ALSO RIGHT: "Lola is *perfect* when it comes to grammar, as I am," said Lulu.

WHY THEY'RE RIGHT: You may approach *perfect,* as in *nearly perfect.* You may also be *perfect,* without any qualifiers.

WRONG: Of the two circles drawn on the chalkboard, mine is rounder.

WHY IT'S WRONG: The shape is round or it's not round. It can't be *rounder.* Also, by definition circles are *round.*

RIGHT: Of the two *shapes* drawn on the chalkboard, mine is *more nearly round.*

RIGHT AGAIN: Neither of the two shapes drawn on the chalkboard is *round,* but mine approaches *roundness.*

As some of the "RIGHT" sentences in the preceding examples illustrate, you can't compare absolute qualities, but you can compare how close people or things come to having those qualities. Look at these examples:

> Lola thinks that her latest nose ring is an *almost perfect* accessory.

> Ralph's new hooked rug is *more nearly circular* than his previous effort.

> Lulu's style of relaxation *approaches uniqueness*.

One more word causes all sorts of trouble in comparisons: *equally*. You hear the expression *equally as* quite frequently. You don't need the *as* because the word *equally* contains the idea of comparison. For example:

> WRONG: Roger got a lighter sentence than Lulu, but he is *equally as* guilty because he stole as many doughnuts as she did.

> RIGHT: Roger got a lighter sentence than Lulu, but he is *equally* guilty because he stole as many doughnuts as she did.

> ALSO RIGHT: Roger got a lighter sentence than Lulu, but he is as guilty as she is because he stole the same number of doughnuts.

Find the correct sentence(s).

A. Michael's recent drama is even more unique than his last play.

B. Michael's recent drama is even more unusual than his last play.

C. Michael's recent drama is unique, as was his last play.

Answer: Sentences B and C are correct. Sentence A incorrectly compares an absolute *(unique)*. In sentence B *more unusual* expresses a correct comparison. Sentence C tells you that Michael's recent drama is unique and that his last play was also unique. The absolute is not being compared but simply applied to two different things.

Which is correct?

A. Anna's last chess move, when compared to the grandmaster's, is equally mistaken.

B. Anna's last chess move, when compared to the grandmaster's, is equally as mistaken.

Answer: Sentence A is correct. Do not say *equally as* because the word *equally* expresses the concept of comparison.

Leaving Your Audience in Suspense: Incomplete Comparisons

What's wrong with this sentence?

> Octavia screamed more chillingly.

Maybe these hints will help:

> Octavia screamed more chillingly. Uh oh, thought Max, yesterday I thought she would burst my eardrum. If she screamed more chillingly today, I'd better get my earplugs out before it's time for tomorrow's lungfest.

or

> Octavia screamed more chillingly. Max, rushing to aid Carmen, whose scream of terror had turned his blood to ice, stopped dead. Octavia sounds even worse, he thought. I'd better go to her first.

or

> Octavia screamed more chillingly. "Please," said the director, "I know that you have just completed take 99 of this extremely taxing verbal exercise, but if you are going to star in my horror movie, you'll have to put a little more into it. Try again!"

Now the problem is clear. The comparison in the examples is incomplete. Octavia screamed more chillingly than … than what? Until you finish the sentence, your readers are left with as many possibilities as they can imagine. Bottom line: Don't stop explaining your comparison until you get your point across. Look at the following example:

WRONG: Octavia screamed more chillingly.

RIGHT: Octavia screamed more chillingly than I did the day Lulu drove a truck over my toe.

ALSO RIGHT: Octavia screamed more chillingly than she ever had before, and Max resolved to come to her aid as soon as he had finished all five courses of his lunch.

RIGHT AGAIN: Octavia screamed more chillingly than she had in the previous takes, but the director still decided to hire a different actress.

Here's another comparison with a fatal error. Can you spot the problem?

> Lulu loved sky-diving more than Lola.

Need another hint? Read on:

> Lulu loved sky-diving more than Lola. Lola sobbed uncontrollably as she realized that Lulu, whom she had always considered her best friend, was on the way to the airport instead of on the way to Lola's party. What a disappointment!

or

> Lulu loved sky-diving more than Lola. Lola was fine for the first 409 jumps, but then her enthusiasm began to flag. Lulu, on the other hand, was climbing into the airplane eagerly, as if it were her first jump of the day and as if the rattle snake had not crawled into her parachute on the last landing.

See the problem? *Lulu loved sky-diving more than Lola* is incomplete. Your reader can understand the comparison in two different ways, as the two stories illustrate. The rule here is simple: Don't omit words that are necessary to the meaning of the comparison.

> WRONG: Lulu loved sky-diving more than Lola.

> RIGHT: Lulu loved sky-diving more than she loved Lola.

> ALSO RIGHT: Lulu loved sky-diving more than Lola did.

One more time. What's the problem now?

> "My life is the best," explained Ralph.

This one is so easy that you don't need stories. *Best* how? In money, fame, love, health, lack of body odor, winning lottery tickets, access to boy-band concerts? Ralph's friends may understand his statement, but no one else will.

Remember: In making a comparison, be clear and complete.

Are you *so* tired of comparisons *that* you're ready to send this chapter to the shredder? Well, hang on a little longer as I explain the word *so*. Technically, *so* should be part of a pair — a comparison created with *so* and *that*. Lots of people use *so* alone as an expression of intensity:

> Lulu's last sky dive was so spectacular.

The preceding sentence is fine in conversational English. In formal English, however, *so* shouldn't be alone. Finish the comparison, as in this sentence:

> Lulu's last sky dive was so spectacular that the pilot begged her to fly away with him.

Which sentence is correct?

A. My cat Agatha slapped her tail more quickly.

B. My cat Agatha slapped her tail more quickly than Dorothy.

Answer: Both are wrong. (Sorry! Trick question.) The meaning is unclear in both A and B. In sentence A, the reader is left asking *more quickly than what?* In sentence B, the sentence may mean *my cat Agatha slapped her tail more quickly than she slapped Dorothy* or *my cat Agatha slapped her tail more quickly than Dorothy slapped the cat's tail.* Neither comparison is complete.

Try another. Which sentence is correct?

A. Betsy played that piano concerto as emotionally as Michael did, but with fewer mistakes.

B. Betsy played that piano concerto just as emotionally, despite the fact that she has no real feeling for "The Homework Blues #3."

Answer: Sentence A is correct. In sentence B, the reader wonders about the basis of comparison for the emotions of Betsy's playing. Did she play the concerto *as emotionally as the other works on her program, such as "The Falling Piano Concerto"?* Or did she play the concerto *as emotionally as Roger, who has less technical skill but a deep-seated hatred of homework.* Sentence A expresses the basis of comparison.

Joe DiMaggio Played Better Than Any Baseball Player: Illogical Comparisons

Before I start, here's an explanation of the heading for those of you who (gasp of pity here) don't like baseball. Joe DiMaggio was a baseball player. Actually, a great baseball player — one of the best, and a New York Yankee. So what's wrong with the title sentence? It takes (gasp of astonishment) Joltin' Joe out of the group of baseball players. It makes him (swoon of sorrow) a *non*-baseball player. To keep Joltin' Joe in the sport, add *other:*

WRONG: Joe DiMaggio played better than any baseball player.

RIGHT: Joe DiMaggio played better than any other baseball player.

ALSO RIGHT: The Yankees rule! (Sorry, can't help myself. I'm a fan.)

The rule for comparisons here is very simple: Use the word *other* or *else* when comparing someone or something to other members of the same group. Check out the following examples:

WRONG: The star soprano of the Santa Lola Opera, Sarah Screema, sings louder than anyone in the cast.

WHY IT'S WRONG: The sentence makes it clear that Sarah is in the cast, but the comparison implies that she's not in the cast. Illogical!

RIGHT: The star soprano of the Santa Lola Opera, Sarah Screema, sings louder than anyone *else* in the cast.

WRONG: That robot short-circuits more frequently than any mechanical device.

WHY IT'S WRONG: A robot is, by definition, a mechanical device, but the comparison takes the robot out of the group of mechanical devices.

RIGHT: That robot short-circuits more frequently than any *other* mechanical device.

Here's another problem. Can you find it?

Max's nose is longer than Michael.

Okay, before you say anything, I should mention that Michael is tall — not skyscraper tall, but at least six-two. Now do you see what's wrong with the sentence? Max's nose, a real tourist attraction for its length *and* width (not including the pimple at the end) is about four inches long. It is *not* longer than Michael. It is longer than Michael's *nose*.

WRONG: Max's nose is longer than Michael.

RIGHT: Max's nose is longer than Michael's nose.

ALSO RIGHT: Max's nose is longer than Michael's.

One more example:

Al's toe ring is as wide as Denny.

I don't think so. Denny is a fairly trim fellow, but even so his waist measures 33 inches. If Al wore a toe ring that wide, no shoes would fit and walking would be a real adventure. Thus

WRONG: Al's toe ring is as wide as Denny.

RIGHT: Al's toe ring is as wide as Denny's toe ring.

ALSO RIGHT: Al's toe ring is as wide as Denny's.

Here's the bottom line:

✔ Make sure your comparisons are logical.

✔ Check to see that you have compared what you want to compare — two things that are at least remotely related.

✔ If the first part of the comparison involves a possessive noun or pronoun (showing ownership), the second part of the comparison probably needs a possessive also. For more information on possessive nouns, see Chapter 11. For more information on possessive pronouns, see Chapter 17.

TEST ALERT

Which is more difficult, the SAT Writing section or the ACT English section? I don't know. I do know that both test you on the material covered in this section.

Which sentence is correct?

A. The pug is cuter than any breed of dog.

B. The pug is cuter than any other breed of dog.

Answer: Sentence B is correct, at least in terms of grammar. (Please feel free to cross out "pug" and substitute your favorite dog breed.) By definition, a pug is a dog, and sentence A implies that pugs aren't. The word *other* in sentence B returns pugs to dogdom.

Getting Two for the Price of One: Double Comparisons

No one will misunderstand you if you break this rule, but grammarians everywhere will hunt you down and tsk-tsk you into outer space: When you're making two comparisons at the same time, finish the first one before you begin the second. In other words, don't say,

Dimwit is as dumb, if not dumber than Elvin.

In the previous sentence, you're really trying to say two different things:

1. Dimwit is as dumb as Elvin.

2. Dimwit may be dumber than Elvin.

First of all, and completely apart from grammar, you ought to make a decision. As dumb as? Dumber than? Don't leave your reader in suspense. Take the plunge and express your real opinion. Grammatically, you may sit on the fence, but only if you finish the first comparison before going on to number two. Here's how you finish:

Dimwit is as dumb as Elvin, if not dumber.

What a difference an *as* makes! Now the sentence is complete after the word *Elvin,* so the *if* statement is an add-on, as it should be. In the incorrect version, you're missing an *as.* (I did warn you that only grammarians would care, remember?)

Which sentence is correct?

A. The winner of this year's "Prettiest Dog Contest" is as pretty as, if not prettier than, last year's champion.

B. The winner of this year's "Prettiest Dog Contest" is as pretty, or even prettier, than last year's champion.

Answer: Sentence A is correct. Sentence B has an incomplete comparison, *as pretty.* The complete comparison is *as pretty as,* which you find in sentence A.

Chapter 21

Parallels Without the Lines

. . . .

In This Chapter

▶ Constructing parallel sentences

▶ Being consistent in form, tense, and voice

▶ Using pairs of conjunctions correctly

▶ Keeping comparisons parallel

. . . .

In art class, you draw parallels. In math class, you plot them on a graph. In grammar, you create parallel constructions. When I say parallel constructions, I'm not talking about lines that look like train tracks. I'm talking about the need for balance in speech and writing, the need to create sentences that aren't lopsided. I'm talking about the reason Hamlet says, "To be or not to be" instead of "Being or not to be." In this chapter, I show you how to avoid several everyday errors of parallelism, or what the hard-hatted grammarian calls *faulty construction.*

If you're of test-taking age, be aware that parallelism plays a starring role in the SAT, but is less important on the ACT. Why? I have no idea. Maybe one of the SAT-writers was mugged by an unparallel sentence during childhood.

Constructing Balanced Sentences

Can you spot the problem in this sentence?

> Larry wanted with all his heart to find a bride who was smart, beautiful, and had millions of chukbloks, the currency of his native land.

Not counting Larry's matrimonial ideas, the sentence has another problem: It's not parallel. Concentrate on the part of the sentence following the word *was.* Larry's dream bride needed these characteristics:

✔ Smart

✔ Beautiful

✔ Had millions of chukbloks

Do you see that these three descriptions don't match? The first two are adjectives. The third consists of a verb *(had)* and an object *(millions of chukbloks).* (For more information on adjectives, see Chapter 7. For more information on verbs and objects, see Chapters 2 and 6.) But all three descriptions are doing the same job in the sentence — describing Larry's dream bride. Because they're doing the same job, they should match, at least in the grammatical sense. Here's one revised list:

✔ Smart

✔ Beautiful

✔ Rich in chukbloks

✔ Nearsighted (I added this one because I've actually seen Larry.)

And here's another:

✔ Intelligence

✔ Beauty

✔ Millions of chukbloks

✔ Bad eyesight

Both lists are fine. In the first set, all the characteristics of Larry's bride are adjectives. In the second set, all the characteristics are nouns. You can use either list. Just don't take some elements from one and some from another. Here are the revised sentences:

> Larry wanted with all his heart to find a bride who was smart, beautiful, nearsighted, and rich in chukbloks, the currency of his native land.

> Larry wanted with all his heart to find a bride with intelligence, beauty, bad eyesight, and millions of chukbloks, the currency of his native land.

Parallelism is especially important when you're making a presentation or a bulleted list. If one item is a complete sentence, all the items should be. If you're listing nouns, make sure every item is a noun. For more on bulleted lists, see Chapter 16. Check out this presentation slide. See if you can spot the error.

This year's goals for employees of Kubla Khan, Inc. include the following:

✔ To visit the stately dome

✔ Rafting the sacred river Alph

✔ Locating a competent dulcimer-player

Uh oh. One item doesn't match: *To visit the stately dome.* In case you care, here's how the list appears to a grammarian: *to visit* is an infinitive, but the next two items in the list, *rafting* and *locating*, are gerunds. Though gerunds and infinitives are both *verbals* — forms of a verb that don't function as verbs in the sentence — you can't mix and match them freely. Here are three possible corrections for the list:

- ✔ Visiting the stately dome
- ✔ Rafting the sacred river Alph
- ✔ Locating a competent dulcimer-player

or

- ✔ To visit the stately dome
- ✔ To go rafting on the sacred river Alph
- ✔ To locate a competent dulcimer-player

or

- ✔ Full-time workers must visit the stately dome.
- ✔ Executives are expected to go rafting on the sacred river Alph.
- ✔ The first employee to locate a competent dulcimer-player will receive a bonus.

Whenever you're writing a presentation slide or a sentence with more than one subject, object, or verb, make a list and check it twice, whether or not you believe in Santa Claus. Everything doing the same job must match grammatically.

Check out these additional examples:

> NOT PARALLEL: Anna said that whenever anything went wrong, whenever someone let us down, or in case of disaster, she would "feel our pain."

> WHAT'S WRONG: The three things that Anna said are not parallel. Two have subject–verb combinations *(anything went, someone let),* and one *(in case of disaster)* does not.

> PARALLEL: Anna said that whenever anything went wrong, whenever someone let us down, or whenever disaster struck, she would "feel our pain."

> WHY IT'S PARALLEL: Now the three things that Anna said are all subject–verb combinations.

ALSO PARALLEL: Anna said that in the event of mistakes, disloyalty, or disaster, she would "feel our pain."

WHY IT'S PARALLEL: Now the things that Anna said are all expressed as nouns: *mistakes, disloyalty, disaster.*

Another set for you to read:

NOT PARALLEL: Eggworthy, a gourmet cook and renowned for his no-cholesterol omelets, thinks that French cooking is "overrated."

WHAT'S WRONG: The *and* joins two descriptions of Eggworthy. One is a noun (*cook*) and one is a descriptive verb form (*renowned for his no-cholesterol omelets*).

PARALLEL: Eggworthy, a gourmet cook renowned for his no-cholesterol omelets, thinks that French cooking is "overrated."

WHY IT'S PARALLEL: When you remove the *and*, the problem is solved. Now the descriptive verb form (*renowned*) describes the noun (*cook*).

Identify the correct sentence(s).

A. Larry found the honeymoon suite restful, exotic, tasteful, and in the less-populated section of his kingdom.

B. Larry found the honeymoon suite restful, exotic, and tasteful. It was located in the less-populated section of his kingdom.

C. Larry found the honeymoon suite restful, exotic, tasteful, and remote.

Answer: Sentences B and C are correct. If you list the qualities of Larry's honeymoon suite as expressed in sentence A, you have

✔ Restful

✔ Exotic

✔ Tasteful

✔ In the less-populated section of his kingdom

The first three are adjectives, but the last is a prepositional phrase. (For more information about prepositional phrases, see Chapter 8.) Because they don't match, the sentence is not parallel. In sentence B, the three adjectives are alone in one sentence. The prepositional phrase is in its very own sentence. Sentence C expresses all the characteristics of Larry's honeymoon suite as adjectives.

To avoid parallelism errors, you don't have to know the correct grammatical terms. Just use your common sense and listen. A parallel sentence has balance. A non-parallel sentence doesn't.

Shifting Grammar into Gear: Avoiding Stalled Sentences

If you've ever ridden in a car with a stick shift, you know that smooth transitions are rare (at least when I'm driving). If something is just a little off, the car bucks like a mule. The same thing is true in sentences. You can, at times, shift tense, voice, or person, but even the slightest mistake stalls your sentence. In this section, I explain how to avoid unnecessary shifts and how to check your sentence for consistency.

Steering clear of a tense situation

Check out this sentence with multiple verbs:

> Larry begs Ella to marry him, offers her a crown and a private room, and finally won her hand.

Now make a list of the verbs in the sentence:

- ✔ Begs
- ✔ Offers
- ✔ Won

The first two verbs are in present tense, but the third shifts into past for no valid reason. Stall! If the verbs in this sentence were gears in a stick shift, your car would conk out. All three verbs should be in present tense or all three should be in past tense. Here are the corrected versions of the sentence:

> Larry begs Ella to marry him, offers her a crown and a private room, and finally wins her hand. (All three verbs are in present tense.)

or

> Larry begged Ella to marry him, offered her a crown and a private room, and finally won her hand. (All three verbs are in past tense.)

Sometimes in telling a story, you must shift tense because the action of the story requires a change in time. For example:

> Betsy always *practices* for at least ten hours a day, unless she *is giving* a concert. Last week she *flew* to Antarctica for a recital. When she *arrived*, the piano *was frozen*. Nevertheless, the show *went* on. Next week Betsy *will practice* twelve hours a day to make up for the time she *lost* last week.

Betsy's story has present *(practices)*, present progressive *(is giving)*, past *(flew, arrived, was frozen, went, lost)*, and future tenses *(will practice)*. Each change of tense is justified by the information in the story. (For more information on verb tense, see Chapters 3 and 18.) Here are some additional examples of justified and unjustified shifts in verb tense:

> WRONG: Max *slips* on the ice, and after obsessively checking every inch of his skull in the mirror, *decided* that he *had hurt* his head.

> WHY IT'S WRONG: The first verb is in present tense. The sentence shifts to past tense for no reason.

> RIGHT: Max *slipped* on the ice, and after obsessively checking every inch of his skull in the mirror, *decided* that he *had hurt* his head.

> SENTENCE THAT LOOKS WRONG BUT ISN'T: Ralph *needs* a loan because he *bet* his entire paycheck on a horse that *came* in first in the eighth race. (Unfortunately, the horse was running in the seventh race.)

> WHY IT LOOKS WRONG: The first verb is in present tense, and the next two are in past tense.

> WHY IT'S RIGHT: Both tenses are justified. The first part talks about Ralph now, explaining his present condition with a reference to the past. The shift is acceptable because the meaning of the sentence makes the shift necessary.

Which sentence is correct?

A. Eggworthy scrambled to the finish line a nano-second before the next fastest racer and then raised his arms in victory.

B. Eggworthy scrambles to the finish line a nano-second before the next fastest racer and then raises his arms in victory.

Answer: Both sentences are correct. (Don't you hate trick questions?) In sentence A, both *scrambled* and *raised* are in past tense. No shift, no problem. In sentence B, both *scrambles* and *raises* are in present tense. Again no shift, again no problem.

Don't change tenses in a bulleted list (assuming you've got verbs there). If the bullet points mark off your summer achievements, don't mix *learned grammar* and *have more confidence*. Go for *learned grammar* and *gained confidence* or *know grammar* and *have more confidence*.

Keeping your voice steady

The voice of a verb — not baritone or soprano — is either *active* or *passive*. (For more information on voice, see Chapter 18.) Like tense, the voice of the verbs in a sentence should be consistent unless there's a good reason for a shift. I should point out that a shift in voice is not a grammar felony; think misdemeanor or maybe even parking ticket. Nevertheless, avoid unnecessary shifts if you can do so without writing yourself into a corner. Here's a sentence with an unjustified shift in voice:

> Larry *polished* the diamond engagement ring, *rechecked* the certificate of authenticity, and *was* completely *demolished* when his intended bride *said* no.

Do you see the problem? A checklist makes it obvious:

- ✔ Polished
- ✔ Rechecked
- ✔ Was demolished
- ✔ Said

The first two verbs and the last one are in active voice, but the third is in passive voice.

A number of changes can take care of the problem:

> Larry *polished* the diamond engagement ring, *rechecked* the certificate of authenticity, and *cried* like a baby when his intended bride *said* no.

or

> Larry *polished* the diamond engagement ring and *rechecked* the certificate of authenticity. His intended bride completely demolished him with her refusal.

Notice that the list of verbs in the corrected sentences are all in active voice: *polished, rechecked, cried* and *polished, rechecked, demolished*. In general, active voice is better than passive. Listen to this clunker:

The diamond engagement ring was polished and the certificate of authenticity was rechecked by Larry, and Larry was completely demolished when "no" was said to him by his intended bride.

Nope. I don't think so. The passive verbs create an awkward, wordy mess.

Bulleted lists containing verbs also need consistent voice. Don't switch from active to passive unnecessarily.

Which sentence is correct?

A. Lulu popped the cork from the champagne, reached for the chilled glasses, and was shocked to learn that the caviar had been confiscated by customs officials.

B. Lulu popped the cork from the champagne, reached for the chilled glasses, and was shocked to learn that customs officials had confiscated the caviar.

C. Lulu popped the cork from the champagne, reached for the chilled glasses, and staggered in shock when she heard that customs officials had confiscated the caviar.

Answer: Sentence C is best because all of the verbs *(popped, reached, staggered, heard,* and *had confiscated)* are in active voice.

Knowing the right person

Ah, loyalty. One of the most celebrated virtues, in life as well as in grammar! Loyalty in grammar relates to what grammarians call *person.* In *first person,* the subject narrates the story: In other words, *I* or *we* acts as the subject of the sentence. In *second person,* the subject is being spoken to, and *you* (either singular or plural) is the subject. In *third person,* the subject is being spoken about, using *he, she, it, they,* or any other word that talks *about* someone or something.

To be grammatically loyal, don't start out talking from the point of view of one person and then switch to another point of view in a sentence, unless you have a valid reason for doing so. Here's an example of an unnecessary shift in person:

To celebrate his marriage, Larry promised amnesty to all the bigamists currently in his jails because you need to do something spectacular on such important occasions.

The first part of the sentence talks about *Larry*, so it's in third person. The second part of the sentence, which begins with the word *because*, shifts to *you* (second person). Making the correction is simple:

> To celebrate his marriage, *Larry* promised amnesty to all the bigamists currently in his jails because *he* needs to do something spectacular on such an important occasion.

or

> To celebrate his marriage, *Larry* promised amnesty to all the bigamists currently in his jails because *everyone* needs to do something spectacular on such important occasions.

or

> To celebrate his marriage, *Larry* promised amnesty to all the bigamists currently in his jails because a *ruler* needs to do something spectacular on such important occasions.

All three of the preceding sentences are correct. Why? In the first, *Larry* is the subject of the first part of the sentence, and *he* is the subject of the second part. No problem. In the second correction, Larry (third person) is matched with *everyone* (a third person pronoun). In the third correction example, third-person Larry is followed by *ruler*, another third-person noun.

Time for another round:

> WRONG: *I* am planning to pick up some of those coins; *you* can't pass up a chance for free money!

> WHY IT IS WRONG: The first part of the sentence is in first person (*I*) and the second part of the sentence shifts to *you*, the second person form. Why shift?

> RIGHT: *I* am planning to pick up some of those coins; *I* can't pass up a chance for free money!

Make sure your sentences are consistent in person. Unless there's a logical reason to shift, follow these guidelines:

- ✔ If you begin with first person (*I* or *me*), stay in first person.

- ✔ If you begin with second person *(you)*, stay in second person.

- ✔ If you begin with third person, talking *about* someone or something, make sure that you continue to talk *about* someone or something.

Which sentence is correct?

A. Whenever a person breaks a grammar rule, you get into trouble.

B. Whenever a person breaks a grammar rule, he or she gets into trouble.

C. Whenever a person breaks a grammar rule, they get into trouble.

Answer: Sentence B is correct. *A person* matches *he or she* because both talk about someone. In sentence A, *a person* does not match *you*. Sentence A shifts from third to second person for no logical reason. Sentence C stays in third person, talking about someone, but *a person* is singular and *they* is plural — a mismatch. (For more information on singular and plural pronouns, see Chapter 9.)

Try one more. Which is correct?

A. Everybody loves somebody sometime because all you need is love.

B. Everybody loves somebody sometime because all anybody needs is love.

Answer: Sentence B is correct. Sentence A shifts from third person *(everybody)* to second *(you)* with no reason other than a pathetic attempt to quote song lyrics. Sentence B stays in third person *(everybody, anybody).*

Seeing Double: Conjunction Pairs

Most joining words fly solo. Single words — *and, but, nor, or, because, although, since,* and so on — join sentences or parts of sentences. Some joining words, however, come in pairs. (In grammarspeak, joining words are called *conjunctions.* Double conjunctions are called *correlatives.* Forget these facts immediately! Just remember how to use joining words properly.) Here are some of the most frequently used pairs:

- ✔ Not only/but also
- ✔ Either/or
- ✔ Neither/nor
- ✔ Whether/or
- ✔ Both/and

Some of these words show up in sentences without their partners. No problem! Just make sure that when they do act as conjunction pairs, they behave properly. Here's the rule: Whatever fills in the blanks after these pairs of conjunctions must have the same grammatical identity. The logic here is that conjunctions have partners, and so do the things they join. You may join two nouns, two sentences, two prepositional phrases — two whatevers! Just make sure the things that you join match. Check out this example:

Not only Larry but also his bride yearned for a day at the beach. (The conjunction pair joins two nouns, *Larry* and *his bride*.)

Either you or I must break the news about the sardine to Larry. (The conjunction pair joins two pronouns, *you* and *I*.)

Nouns and pronouns are equals when it comes to parallelism. Because pronouns take the place of nouns, you may mix them without ill effect:

Neither Ralph nor he has brought a proper present to Larry's wedding. (The conjunction pair joins a noun, *Ralph*, and a pronoun, *he*.)

Here's another example:

Both *because he stole the garter* and *because he lost the ring*, Roger is no longer welcome as best man. (This conjunction pair joins two subject–verb combinations.)

To help you spot parallelism errors in sentences with conjunction pairs, here are a few mismatches, along with their corrections:

NOT PARALLEL: Either *Lulu will go with Larry to the bachelor party* or *to the shower*, but she will not attend both.

WHY IT'S NOT PARALLEL: The first italicized section is a subject–verb combination. The second italicized section is a prepositional phrase.

PARALLEL: Lulu will go with Larry either *to the bachelor party* or *to the shower*, but she will not attend both. (Now you've got two prepositional phrases.)

NOT PARALLEL: Both *her lateness* and *that she was dressed in white leather* insulted the royal couple.

WHY IT'S NOT PARALLEL: First italicized section is a noun, but the second is a subject–verb combination.

PARALLEL BUT A LITTLE REPETITIVE: Both *the fact that she was late* and *the fact that she was dressed in white leather* insulted the royal couple. (Now the italicized sections are both subject–verb combinations.)

PARALLEL: Both *her lateness* and *her white leather clothing* insulted the royal couple. (Now the italicized sections are both nouns (with a couple of descriptions attached) — a more concise solution.)

Which sentence is correct?

A. Lulu neither needled Larry nor his bride about the fact that the bride's mother has a slight but noticeable moustache.

B. Lulu needled neither Larry nor his bride about the fact that the bride's mother has a slight but noticeable moustache.

Answer: Sentence B is correct. In sentence A, *neither* precedes a verb *(needled)* but *nor* precedes a noun *(his bride)*. In sentence B, *neither* precedes a noun *(Larry)* and so does *nor (his bride)*.

Try another. Which sentence is best?

A. Both the way she danced and the way she sang convinced Michael to award Lola a starring role in Michael's new musical, *The Homework Blues.*

B. Both the way she danced and her superb singing convinced Michael to award Lola a starring role in Michael's new musical, *The Homework Blues.*

C. Both her graceful dancing and superb singing convinced Michael to award Lola a starring role in Michael's new musical, *The Homework Blues.*

Answer: Sentence C is best. Two nouns, *dancing* and *singing*, are linked by the conjunctions. True, sentence A is grammatically correct because a noun–subject–verb combination *(the way she danced, the way she sang)* follows both parts of the conjunction pair. However, sentence A is a little wordy; *the way* appears twice. In sentence B, the first half of the conjunction pair *(both)* is followed by a noun *(way)* and then a subject–verb combination *(she danced)*. The second part of the conjunction pair *(and)* is followed only by a noun *(singing)*.

Avoiding Improper Comparisons

The grammar police will arrive, warrant in hand, if your comparisons aren't parallel. Comparisons to watch out for include the following:

- More/than
- But not
- As well as

Comparisons with these words are tricky but not impossible. Just be sure that the elements you are comparing match grammatically. Check out these examples:

Lulu was more *conservative* than *daring* in her choice of clothes for Larry's wedding.

Even so, Larry liked *the way Lulu moved* but not *the way she looked.*

Lulu enjoyed the ceremonial *garter-toss* as well as the ritual *bouquet-bonfire.*

The italicized words in each sentence pair off nicely. In the first sample sentence, *conservative* and *daring* are both descriptions. In the second sample sentence, *the way Lulu moved* and *the way she looked* are similar constructions — nouns described by adjective clauses, if you absolutely must know. In the third sample sentence, *garter-toss* and *bouquet-bonfire* are both nouns.

To illustrate parallel comparisons further, here are some incorrect and corrected pairs:

> WRONG: Lola sang more forcefully than with the correct notes.
>
> WHY IT'S WRONG: *forcefully* and *with the correct notes* don't match.
>
> RIGHT: *Lola sang* more *forcefully* than *correctly.*
>
> WHY IT'S RIGHT: The sentence compares two adverbs.

Here's another example:

> WRONG: Ella assumed *that she would live in a separate castle* but not *spending every hour with Larry.*
>
> WHY IT'S WRONG: The words *but not* join a subject–verb combination and verb form.
>
> RIGHT: Ella assumed *that she would live in a separate castle* but not *that she would spend every hour with Larry.*
>
> WHY IT'S RIGHT: The sentence compares two subject–verb combinations.

A question may have occurred to you: How do you know how many words of the sentence are being joined? In other words, in the preceding sample sentences, how did I figure out how much to italicize? The decision comes from the meaning of the sentence. Forget grammar for a moment and put yourself into reading comprehension mode. Decide what you're comparing based on the ideas in the sentence. Now check the two ideas being compared and go back into grammar mode. Do the ideas match grammatically? If so, you're fine. If not, reword your sentence.

Which sentence is correct?

A. Michael told Max that the ceremony was canceled but not that the couple planned to elope.

B. Michael told Max that the ceremony was canceled but not about the planned elopement.

Answer: Sentence A is correct. *That the ceremony was canceled* matches *that the couple planned to elope.* In sentence B, *that the ceremony was canceled* has a subject–verb pair, but *about the elopement* is a prepositional phrase with no subject–verb pair.

Summon up your energy and try again. Which sentence is correct?

A. Lulu's assumption that the snake was more showy than dangerous proved fatally wrong.

B. Lulu's assumption that the snake was more putting on a show than it was dangerous proved fatally wrong.

Answer: Sentence A is correct. *Showy* matches *dangerous*; both are descriptions. In sentence B, *putting on a show* has a verb form but not a subject. Its partner, *it was dangerous*, has both a subject and a verb.

Part V
Rules Even Your Great-Aunt's Grammar Teacher Didn't Know

The 5th Wave   By Rich Tennant

"I hate the synonyms part of this test.
I always get stumped, stymied,
and puzzled."

In this part . . .

Learned philosophers in the Middle Ages used to argue about the number of angels that could fit on the head of a pin. That debate was only a little less complicated than the grammar rules in this part. Chapter 22 explains the moods of verbs (yes, they have moods). Chapter 23 shows you how to choose the proper pronoun for all sorts of weird sentences. The next chapter deals with the inner workings of the sentence and helps you spruce up your writing style. Bottom line: If you want to learn some of the pickiest grammar rules ever devised, this part's for you.

Chapter 22

The Last Word on Verbs

Daniel stomps in, slams the door, and grabs the remote. As he raises the volume on the wrestling match to supersonic level, Lola asks politely, "Is anything wrong?" In reply, Daniel lowers his eyebrows to the tip of his nose and glares silently. Lola shrugs and goes out to spread the word: Daniel is in one of his Moods. Beware.

*V*erbs have moods too, but they're a lot more polite about showing them than Daniel. A little change of form, and presto, the verb is in a different mood.

Verbs in modern English have three moods: *indicative*, *imperative*, and *subjunctive*. Indicative is the most common; the two other moods — imperative and subjunctive — enter speech and writing less frequently. In this chapter, I give you the lowdown on these three verb types so you're sure to know the mood of any verb without consulting a mind reader. I also tell you how to avoid a common mistake — double negatives.

Getting a Feel for Everyday Verbs: The Indicative Mood

Almost all verbs are in indicative mood. *Indicative* is the everyday, this-is-what-I'm-saying mood, good for questions and statements. All the lessons about verbs in this book — aside from those later in this chapter — discuss verbs in the indicative mood. (This fact, by the way, is totally useless. Forget it immediately.)

Think of indicative verbs as the permanent cast of a TV show. They are always around and are familiar to everyone.

The indicative verbs are italicized in the following sentences:

Betsy *displayed* her musical range when she *played* a Bach concerto and a heavy-metal hit in the same concert.

Larry *will be* the principal tenant of the honeymoon hotel as soon as Ella *agrees* to marry him.

Eggworthy often *dreams* about bacon.

Commanding Your Verbs: The Imperative Mood

Don't worry about imperatives; they're fairly simple. *Imperative verbs* give commands. Most imperative verbs don't have a written (or spoken) subject. Instead, the subject in an imperative (command) sentence is *you-understood.* The word *you* usually does not appear before the imperative verb. The reader or listener simply understands that *you* is implied.

Here's a command. Read these examples of imperative verbs, italicized in the following sentences:

Eat a balanced diet.

Climb every mountain.

Calculate the odds.

No matter what happens, *hit* the road.

Fake a sincere smile and you've got it made.

Think of imperative verbs as recurring guest stars on a sitcom, the characters who show up every three or four episodes just to add a little flavor to the mix.

There's almost nothing you can do wrong in creating an imperative sentence, so this topic is a free pass. *Go* fishing, or if you're in the mood to torture yourself, *move* on to the subjunctive.

DEMONS

Rising to the occasion and sitting pretty

Two pairs of confusing verbs — *rise* and *raise* and *sit* and *set* — may have added a wrinkle or two to your forehead. Never fear: here's some wrinkle-remover.

Rise means "to stand," "to get out of bed," or "to move to a higher rank" under one's own power. *Raise* means "to lift something or someone else up" or "to bring up children or animals." Check out these verbs in action:

Eggworthy *rises* when a poultry expert enters the room.

Eggworthy is currently an apprentice, but he hopes to *rise* to the rank of master poultry-breeder some day.

He *raises* roosters on his farm, delighting the neighbors every morning at sunrise.

When a nest is too low, Eggworthy *raises* it to a higher shelf.

Sit is the verb you use when you're creating a lap by moving your rear into a seat or onto the floor. *Set* means "to place something else on a surface." These verbs are irregular in form. The past tense of *sit* is *sat*; the past tense of *set* is, surprisingly, *set*. (Very economical. One word for two tenses!) Take a peek at these sentences:

Sheila *sits* on the porch, monitoring the neighbors' activities.

Roger catches Sheila's attention when he carefully *sets* his briefcase next to the fire extinguisher.

Mike smiled as he *set* the "Wet Paint" sign under the bench.

Max *sat* on the freshly painted park bench, wondering why Mike looked so cheerful.

By the way, in conversational English (see Chapter 1), *to set a spell* is a charming way to express a short period of relaxation, which takes place sitting down. Just be careful when you're speaking or writing formal English to distinguish between *sit* and *set*.

Here's another way to think about these two pairs: *Rise* and *sit* are self-contained actions. The subject acts upon him- or herself. *Raise* and *set* are actions that begin with one person (or thing) and move to another person or thing. You *rise* or *sit* by yourself; you *raise* or *set* something else.

Discovering the Possibilities: The Subjunctive Mood

Headache time! The subjunctive mood is rare, but it draws errors like a magnet. Master this topic and you'll qualify for the title "Grammarian of the Year." Subjunctive verbs show up when you state something that is contrary to fact. They may also express indirect commands, requests, and wishes. I tackle each of these situations in the following sections.

Subjunctive verbs make only a few cameo appearances. Like a pampered superstar, a subjunctive shows up only when the situation is exactly right.

Using subjunctives with "were"

Tevye, the main character in the musical *Fiddler on the Roof,* sings "If I Were a Rich Man" with the sadness of a man who knows that he'll never be anything but poor. Tevye's song is about a *condition contrary to fact* — something that is not true. Take note of the verb in the title: *were.* Normally (that is to say, in an indicative sentence) the subject–verb pair would be *I was.* But Tevye sings *If I were* because he isn't a rich man. The verb *were* is in subjunctive mood.

Unless someone is going to quiz you on it, don't worry about the terminology. Just know that if you're expressing a condition contrary to fact, you need the verb *were* for present and future ideas. (Past tense is different. See the next section, "Creating subjunctives with 'had.'") Here are some examples of present and future tense:

> SUBJUNCTIVE: If Roger *were* an honorable spy, he would not reveal the atomic secret hidden in the bean burrito.
>
> WHY IT'S SUBJUNCTIVE: Roger is not an honorable spy, and he's going to blab the secret.
>
> WHAT THE NORMAL SUBJECT–VERB PAIR WOULD BE: Roger was.

> SUBJUNCTIVE: If Anna *were* less talented in mathematics, she would have taken fewer algebra courses.
>
> WHY IT'S SUBJUNCTIVE: Anna's a math genius, the kind of student who always says that the test was "totally hard" and then wrecks the curve with a 96.
>
> WHAT THE NORMAL SUBJECT–VERB PAIR WOULD BE: Anna was.

To sum up, in subjunctive sentences, *were* is usually all you need (unlike in the Beatles' song, when love is all you need). Here are a few details about subjunctive for present or future statements of conditions contrary to fact:

✔ Use *were* for all subjects in the part of the sentence that expresses what is not true. (If she *were* entranced by Max's explanation.)

✔ For the other part of the sentence, use the helping verb *would.* (Lola *would stare* at him in silence.)

✔ Never use the helping verb *would* in the untrue part of the sentence. For example:

> WRONG: If I would have been president, I would ask the Martian colony to secede.

RIGHT: If I were president, I would ask the Martian colony to secede.

WRONG: Daniel acted as though he would have been grammarian-in-chief.

RIGHT: Daniel acted as though he were grammarian-in-chief.

Which sentence is correct?

   A. Ella would be happier if she would have been in the Marines.

   B. Ella would be happier if she were in the Marines.

Answer: Sentence B is correct. The *if* part of the sentence contains a subjunctive verb *(were)* because it expresses something that is not true. The *if* part of the sentence should never contain the helping verb *would*.

As *though* may sometimes sub for *if* in a condition-contrary-to-fact sentence. Check out the following:

SUBJUNCTIVE: Eggworthy hurtled through the air *as though* a giant metal device were intent on scrambling him.

WHY IT'S SUBJUNCTIVE: Eggworthy is not being pursued by giant eggbeaters. He is actually hurtling through the air because he is on a skateboard with one bad wheel.

WHAT THE NORMAL SUBJECT–VERB PAIR WOULD BE: Giant metal device was.

Creating subjunctives with "had"

Subjunctives also pop up from time to time with the helping verb *had*. For past tense sentences, the *had* belongs in the part of the sentence that is contrary to fact. The contrary-to-fact (that is, the lie) part of the sentence may begin with *if,* or the *if* may be understood.

Just for comparison: in non-subjunctive sentences — the past tense is expressed by a single-word, past tense verb. The *had* form, in a non-subjunctive sentence, is used only to show one action happening before another. (See Chapter 18 for more information.) Here are a few examples of the past subjunctive:

SUBJUNCTIVE WITH THE WORD *IF*: If Lola *had known* about the atomic secret, she would not have eaten that burrito.

SUBJUNCTIVE WITHOUT THE WORD *IF: Had* Lola *known* about the atomic secret, she would not have eaten that burrito.

WHY IT'S SUBJUNCTIVE: Lola knew nothing about the atomic secret; Roger told her that the crunch in the burrito came from an undercooked bean.

WHAT THE NORMAL SUBJECT–VERB PAIR WOULD BE: Lola knew.

SUBJUNCTIVE WITH THE WORD *IF:* If Larry *had married* less often, he would have enjoyed this ceremony more.

SUBJUNCTIVE WITHOUT THE WORD *IF:* Had Larry *married* less often, he would have enjoyed this ceremony more.

WHY IT'S SUBJUNCTIVE: Larry has been married more times than he can count.

WHAT THE NORMAL SUBJECT–VERB PAIR WOULD BE: Larry married.

Which sentence is correct?

A. If Betsy would have played the tuba, the gang would have listened to her CD more often.

B. If Betsy had played the tuba, the gang would have listened to her CD more often.

Answer: Sentence B is correct. Betsy played the piano, not the tuba, so subjunctive is appropriate. The word *would* is never part of an *if* statement.

Using subjunctives with commands, wishes, and requests

Larry loves to exercise his royal power, so he needs many subjunctive verbs. I've italicized those verbs in these sentences:

His Majesty decrees that all his subjects *be* counted and then beheaded.

His Majesty asks that the governor of each province *climb* the nearest Alp and *jump* off the top.

His Majesty further insists that his favorite wedding planner *remain* in the palace.

The italicized verbs are all subjunctive. These sentences need subjunctives because they express wishes, requests, or indirect commands. (Commands that are given directly to the person who is supposed to follow them are in imperative mood. See " Commanding Your Verbs: The Imperative Mood," earlier in this chapter.)

Now I lie me down to sleep . . .

Whoever invented the verbs *lie* and *lay* had an evil sense of humor. Besides meaning "not to tell the truth," *lie* also means "to rest or to plop yourself down, ready for a snooze" or "to remain." *Lay* means "to put something down, to place something." Here are some examples:

Sheila likes to *lie* down for an hour after lunch. Before she hits the couch, she *lays* a soft sheet over the upholstery.

Roger *lies* in wait behind those bushes. When unsuspecting tourists *lay* down their picnic blankets, he swoops in and steals their lunches.

So far, this topic isn't too complicated. The problem — and the truly devilish part — comes in the past tense. The past tense of *lie* (to rest, to recline, to remain) is *lay*. The past tense of *lay* (to put or place) is *laid*. Check out these examples:

Sheila *lay* down yesterday, but a car alarm disturbed her rest. She immediately went to the street and *laid* a carpet of nails in front of the offending vehicle.

Yesterday, while Roger *lay* in wait, a police officer *laid* a hand on Roger's shoulder. "You are under arrest," intoned the cop.

One more complication: When you add *has, had,* or *have* to the verb *lie* (to rest, to recline, to remain), you say *has lain, had lain, have lain.* When you add *has, had,* or *have* to the verb *lay* (to put or place), you say *has laid, had laid, have laid.* In other words:

Sheila *has lain* in the hammock all morning, and her brothers *have laid* a basket of red ants on the ground beneath her. When Sheila gets up, she'll be surprised!

Roger *has lain* in the lumpy bunk all night, but no one *has laid* a blanket over him.

In the previous sample sentences, the normal subject–verb pairs (the indicative pairs) would be *subjects are, governor climbs, wedding planner remains.* In these subjunctive sentences, all subjects take the same form of the verb — the infinitive minus the *to.* (For more information on infinitives, see Chapter 2.) Thus you have

to sleep: subjunctive = sleep

to slobber: subjunctive = slobber

to sneak: subjunctive = sneak

and so forth.

In everyday communication, many speakers of perfectly good English avoid the subjunctive and use an infinitive or the helping verb *should* instead. Here are Larry's requests, with infinitives or *should* instead of subjunctive verbs:

His Majesty wants his subjects *to be counted* and then *beheaded.*

His Majesty says that the governor of each province *should climb* the nearest Alp and *jump* off the top.

His Majesty wants his favorite wedding planner *to remain* in the palace.

Which sentence is correct?

A. Larry requests that his honeymoon attendants are paid by the hour.

B. Larry requests that his honeymoon attendants be paid by the hour.

Answer: Sentence B is correct. The subjunctive verb *(be)* expresses the request. (The infinitive *to be* minus the *to* equals subjunctive.)

When "If" Isn't Subjunctive

As you're reading about the subjunctive *if,* you may think that all sentences with the word *if* need a subjunctive verb. Nope. Some *if* sentences don't express a condition contrary to fact; they express a possibility, something that may happen. The *if* sentences that express a possibility take a plain old, normal, indicative verb. Here are some examples:

NON-SUBJUNCTIVE *IF* SENTENCE: If I am elected, I promise to cut taxes.

WHY IT'S NOT SUBJUNCTIVE: Everyone who says this truly believes that victory is possible.

NON-SUBJUNCTIVE *IF* SENTENCE: If Roger goes to prison, he will take a burrito cookbook with him.

WHY IT'S NOT SUBJUNCTIVE: Prison is a possibility.

NON-SUBJUNCTIVE *IF* SENTENCE: If Larry divorces, he'll remarry soon.

WHY IT'S NOT SUBJUNCTIVE: Divorce is a possibility. In fact, Larry is already looking around.

To sum up: in an *if* sentence, use a normal, everyday, indicative verb for something that's possible. If something is untrue, use a subjunctive verb.

Which sentence is correct?

A. If the weather is as bad as the forecaster predicts, Lola will leave her motorcycle in the garage.

B. If the weather were as bad as the forecaster predicts, Lola will leave her motorcycle in the garage.

DEMONS

Try and figure these out: Verbs and infinitives

Now that you've read this heading, do you see what's wrong with it? *Try and* means that you're going to do two different things: *try* (first task) and *figure out* (second task). But you don't have two tasks in mind, do you? *Try and* is a common expression, but not a correct one. Here's what you really mean: *try to figure this one out. Try to* follows the normal English pattern of a verb and an infinitive. *Try to remember* the verb-infinitive rule and *try to forget* about *try and*.

Answer: Sentence A is correct. A storm is a real possibility; in fact, the sentence tells you that the forecaster predicts bad weather (although I have to say that my grandmother's knee was more accurate in predicting storms than any technology I've seen). Back to grammar: sentence A contains the normal verb, *is.* Sentence B expresses a condition contrary to fact. Lola hasn't left yet, so there's no way to know the weather. Thus the subjunctive verb *were* is wrong.

Do you have the strength for one more round? Identify the correct sentence.

    A. Lola studied Roger's new tattoo. If Lulu was the designer, Lola concluded, the tattoo would be more artistic.

    B. Lola studied Roger's new tattoo. If Lulu were the designer, Lola concluded, the tattoo would be more artistic.

Answer: Sentence B is correct. The intent of the sentence is to express Lola's judgment, which is that Lulu didn't design Roger's tattoo. The *if* statement therefore tells you about something that isn't true, so you need the subjunctive verb, *were.*

Deleting Double Negatives

In some lucky languages, the more negatives the better. In English, however, two negatives are a no-no. (By the way, no-no is *not* a double negative! It's just slang for something that's prohibited.) I explain the basic double-negative errors in Chapter 8. Here I tell you about some of the less obvious forms of double trouble.

I cannot help but think this rule is dumb

One of the most common double negatives doesn't look like one: *cannot help but.* How many times have you heard someone say something like

> Eggworthy *cannot help but* act in that dramatic style because he was trained by a real ham.

Unfortunately, this sentence is wrong because it contains a double negative. The *not* (inside the word *cannot*) and the *but* both express negative ideas. Use one or the other. Don't use both. Here is the correct version:

> Eggworthy *cannot help acting* in that dramatic style because he was trained by a real ham.

If you think this is one in a long list of useless grammar rules, think again. A double-negative mistake can completely wreck your sentence because in English, two negatives make a positive. So when you say *cannot help but,* you actually convey the opposite of what you imagine you're saying (or writing). For example:

> Max told his boss, "I cannot help but ask for a raise."
>
> WHAT HE THINKS HE SAID: I have to ask for a raise.
>
> WHAT HE REALLY SAID: I can't ask for a raise.

> The boss told Max, "I cannot help but say no."
>
> WHAT THE BOSS THINKS SHE SAID: No.
>
> WHAT THE BOSS ACTUALLY SAID: Yes.

Which sentence is correct?

> A. I cannot help but think that this double negative rule is ridiculous.
>
> B. I cannot help thinking that this double negative rule is ridiculous.

Answer: Sentence B is correct. As for the content, I'll let you decide!

I can't hardly understand this rule

No matter what you do, avoid saying or writing *can't hardly* when you're using formal English. *Can't* is short for *cannot,* which contains the negative *not. Hardly* is another negative word. If you combine them, by the logic of grammar, you've said the opposite of what you intended — the positive instead of the negative. Here are a few examples:

Roger commented, "Lulu can't hardly count her tattoos."

WHAT ROGER THINKS HE SAID: Lulu can't count her tattoos.

WHAT ROGER ACTUALLY SAID: Lulu can count her tattoos.

According to Lola, Ella can't hardly wait until her divorce becomes final.

WHAT THE WRITER THINKS THE SENTENCE MEANS: Ella is eager for her divorce to become final.

WHAT THE SENTENCE ACTUALLY MEANS: Ella can wait. (The palace is comfy and Larry isn't around very much.)

A variation of this double negative is *can't scarcely, aren't scarcely,* or *isn't scarcely.* Once again, *can't* is short for *cannot,* clearly a negative. *Aren't* and *isn't* are the negative forms of *are* and *is. Scarcely* is also negative. Use them together and you end up with a positive, not a super-negative.

1 hadn't but one rule on double-negatives

Here's another double negative, in a couple of forms: *hadn't only, haven't only, hasn't only, hadn't but, haven't but,* and *hasn't but.* All express positive ideas because the *not (n't)* part of the verb and the *only* or *but* are both negatives:

WRONG: Al *hadn't but* ten seconds to defuse the bomb before civilization as we know it ended.

WHY IT'S WRONG: As it reads now, the sentence says that Al had more than ten seconds to defuse the bomb, but the little red numbers on the trigger were at seven and decreasing rapidly.

RIGHT: Al *had but* ten seconds to defuse the bomb before civilization as we know it ended.

ALSO RIGHT: Al *had* only ten seconds to defuse the bomb before civilization as we know it ended.

WRONG: Roger *hasn't only* ten nuclear secrets.

WHY IT'S WRONG: The sentence now says that Roger has more than ten secrets, but he just counted them and there are ten.

RIGHT: Roger *has only* ten nuclear secrets.

Which sentence is correct?

A. Ella can't hardly understand those pesky grammar rules.

B. Ella can't help but be confused by those pesky grammar rules.

Answer: Both are wrong. (The official teacher manual orders teachers to play annoying tricks with quizzes.) In sentence A, *can't hardly* is a double negative. In sentence B, *cannot help but* is a double negative.

Now look at these sentences. Which is correct?

A. Ella can scarcely understand those pesky grammar rules.

B. Ella can't help being confused by those pesky grammar rules.

Answer: Sentences A and B are both correct. Ella is serving five to ten in the penitentiary for breaking grammar rules. In sentence A, she has only a little understanding of grammar. In sentence B, she is confused.

It takes two to make a mistake

In English you find three "to's," all sounding exactly alike but spelled differently. (Words that sound alike but are spelled differently are known as *homonyms*). And no, they don't add up to six. *To* may be part of an infinitive *(to speak, to dream)* or it may show movement towards someone or something *(to the store, to me)*. *Two* is the number *(two eyes, two ears)*. *Too* means also *(Are you going too?)* or more than enough *(too expensive, too wide)*. In other words:

> If you *two* want *to* skip school and go *to* the ball game, today's a good day because the teacher will be *too* busy *to* check.

The *two* basketballs that hit Larry in the head yesterday were *too* soft *to* do much damage, but Larry is suing anyway.

Two things you should always remember before you decide *to* break a grammar rule: it is never *too* late *to* learn proper English, and you are never *too* old *to* get in trouble with your teacher.

Chapter 23

The Last Word on Pronouns

*Y*ou've come to it at last: the dreaded chapter where you find out the intricate details of *who/whom* and the like. Be warned: In three nanoseconds, you can easily find something to do that is more interesting than these concepts — training fleas for circus duty, for example, or picking lint out of your belly button.

You're still reading, aren't you? Okay, you asked for it. Here is the last word on pronouns, including who/whom sentences and a host of other really picky pronoun points.

Knowing the Difference Between Who and Whom

The rule for knowing when to use *who* and *whom* is simple; applying the rule is not. First, the rule:

✔ *Who* and *whoever* are for subjects.

  Who and *whoever* also follow and complete the meaning of linking verbs. (In grammarspeak, *who* and *whoever* serve as linking verb complements.)

✔ *Whom* and *whomever* are for objects — all kinds of objects (direct, indirect, of prepositions, of infinitives, and so on).

For more information on subjects, see Chapter 4. For more information on objects and linking verb complements, see Chapter 6.

Before applying the rule concerning *who/whoever* and *whom/whomever*, check out these sample sentences:

> *Whoever* needs help from Roger is going to wait a long time. (*Whoever* is the subject of the verb *needs*.)

> *Who* is calling Lulu at this time of night? (*Who* is the subject of the verb *is calling*.)

> "I don't care *whom* you ask to the prom," exclaimed Michael unconvincingly. (*Whom* is the direct object of the verb *ask*.)

> The mustard-yellow belt is for *whomever* she designates as the hot dog eating champion. (*Whomever* is the direct object of the verb *designates*.)

> For *whom* are you bellowing? (*Whom* is the object of the preposition *for*.)

Now that you know the rule and have seen the words in action, here are two tricks for deciding between *who/whoever* and *whom/whomever*. If one trick seems to work, use it and ignore the other. Here goes . . .

Trick #1: Horse and carriage

According to an old song, "love and marriage go together like a horse and carriage." Grammarians might sing that song with slightly different lyrics: "A subject and verb go together like a horse and carriage." (What do you think? Grammy material?) To use Trick #1, follow these steps:

1. Find all the verbs in the sentence.

2. Don't separate the helping verbs from the main verb. Count the main verb and its helpers as a single verb.

3. Now pair each of the verbs with a subject.

4. If you have a verb flapping around with no subject, chances are *who* or *whoever* is the subject you're missing.

5. If all the verbs have subjects, check them one more time. Do you have any linking verbs without complements? (For more information on complements, see Chapter 6.) If you have a lonely linking verb with no complement in sight, you need *who* or *whoever*.

6. If all subjects are accounted for and you don't need a linking verb complement, you've reached a final answer: *whom* or *whomever* is the only possibility.

Here are two sample sentences, analyzed via Trick #1:

SENTENCE ONE: *Who/Whom* shall I say is calling?

The verbs = *shall say, is calling.*

The subject of *shall say* = *I.*

The subject of *is calling* = Okay, here you go. You need a subject for *is calling* but you're out of words. You have only one choice: *who.*

CORRECT SENTENCE: *Who* shall I say is calling?

SENTENCE TWO: Derek is the ballplayer *who/whom* everyone thinks plays best.

The verbs = *is, thinks, plays.*

The subject of *is* = *Derek.*

The subject of *thinks* = *everyone*

The subject of *plays* = Um. . . m. Once again, a subject shortage occurs. Therefore, you need *who.*

CORRECT SENTENCE: Derek is the ballplayer *who* everyone thinks plays best.

Now you try. Which word is correct?

Agnes buys detergent in one-ton boxes for Roger, *who/whom* she adores in spite of his odor problem.

Answer: *Whom,* because it's the direct object of *adores. Agnes buys, she adores* = subject-verb pairs. Both are action verbs, so no subject complement is needed. Therefore, you need an objective pronoun, *whom.*

Play it again, Sam. Which word is correct?

Anna solves math problems for *whoever/whomever* heads the Olympic Math Team.

Answer: *Whoever.* Surprised? The preposition *for* needs an object, so you might have assumed that *whomever* fills that spot. But use the horse-and-carriage method, and you'll see why *whoever* is best. The sentence has two verbs, *solves* and *heads. Anna* is the subject of *solves.* What's the subject of *heads*? It has to be *whoever.* The real object of the preposition *for* is the entire subject-verb statement: *whoever heads the Olympic Math Team.*

Trick #2: Getting rhythm

This trick relies on your ear for grammar. Most English sentences follow one pattern: Subject-Verb-Object or Subject Complement. Trick #2 is to say the parts of the sentence in this order, even if you have to rearrange the words a little. Here are the steps to follow:

1. Identify the verb in the sentence that seems connected to the *who/ whom* choice. Usually it's the verb nearest *who/whom*. It's also the verb logically connected by meaning — that is, in the same thought as *who/ whom*.

2. Say (aloud, if you don't mind scaring your classmates or co-workers, or silently, if you plan to keep a reputation for sanity) the three parts of the sentence.

   Anything before the verb is *who* or *whoever*.

   If you're working with an action verb, anything after the verb is probably *whom* or *whomever*.

   If you're working with a linking verb, anything after the verb is probably *who* or *whoever*.

Here are two sample sentences analyzed with Trick #2:

SENTENCE ONE: *Who/Whom* will Roger choose for the vacancy in his nuclear spy ring?

The verb is *will choose*.

Will choose is an action verb, so forget about linking-verb complements.

Say aloud: Roger will choose *who/whom*.

Choice = *whom* because the word is after the verb.

Whom = direct object of *will choose*.

CORRECT SENTENCE: *Whom* will Roger choose for the vacancy in his nuclear spy ring?

SENTENCE TWO: Michael will dance the tango with *whoever/whomever* wins the lottery.

This one's more complicated because you've got two verbs, and two separate ideas in the sentence. Fortunately, all you have to do is concentrate on the part of the sentence containing the *whoever/whomever* issue. In other words, the part of the sentence you're examining is *whoever/ whomever wins the lottery*.

The verb is *wins*.

Wins is an action verb, so forget about linking-verb complements.

Say aloud: *whoever/whomever wins the lottery.*

Choice = *whoever* because the word is before the verb.

Whoever = subject of *wins.*

CORRECT SENTENCE: Michael will dance the tango with *whoever* wins the lottery.

Which word is correct?

> *Who/Whom* do you like better, Roger or Michael?

Answer: *Whom* is correct. Change the order of the words to *you do like whom.* Choose *whom* after an action verb. In this sentence, *whom* is the direct object. (By the way, the answer is Michael, no contest. He's much nicer than Roger.)

Once more for old time's sake: which word is correct?

> The ballerina *who/whom* asked Michael to dance has two left feet.

Answer: *Who* is correct. This sentence expresses two ideas — *the ballerina has two left feet* and *who/whom asked Michael to dance.* All you have to do is concentrate on the portion of the sentence containing the *who/whom* problem. Say *who/whom asked Michael.* Choose *who* before the verb. *Who,* of course, is the subject of the verb *asked.*

People have led perfectly pleasant (though grammatically incorrect) lives without knowing the stuff in this section. However, the standardized test-makers consider these topics fair game — and big game, judging from the number of questions they ask about pronoun issues, especially *who* and *whom.*

Replacing Improper Antecedents

The *antecedent* of a pronoun is the word that the pronoun replaces. The antecedent and the pronoun should be completely interchangeable. In other words, you should be able to replace the pronoun with its antecedent (or the antecedent with the pronoun) without changing the meaning of the sentence. To follow this rule, you must make sure that the pronoun has an antecedent to replace. If the pronoun has no antecedent, the pronoun is stranded on a desert island, without a television crew and an immunity challenge. A stranded pronoun is an unhappy pronoun. Furthermore, the pronoun is a picky little part of speech. It refuses to replace any old word. If an antecedent is almost but not quite right, every self-respecting pronoun turns up its nose at the antecedent and calls the grammar police. (For more information on pronouns and their antecedents, see Chapter 9.)

Sometimes the best way to avoid a pronoun error is to write a sentence that doesn't need one. Keep that solution in mind if you begin writing a sentence and stumble over a pronoun issue.

Okay, time for the pronoun police to go to work:

> WRONG: Lola's a lawyer, and I want to study it.

What does *it* replace? *Law,* I suppose. But the word *law* is not in the sentence; *lawyer* is. *Law* and *lawyer* are close, but not close enough.

> RIGHT: Lola's a lawyer, and I want to be one also.
>
> WHY IT'S RIGHT: *One* refers to *lawyer.*
>
> ALSO RIGHT: I'd like to study law, as Lola did.
>
> WHY IT'S ALSO RIGHT: There's no pronoun in the sentence.
>
> ALSO RIGHT: I want to make a lot of money, so I'm going to law school.

Another (trickier) example is:

> WRONG: In Max's poetry, he frequently uses cow imagery.

Who's *he?* Max, I imagine. But *Max* isn't in the sentence. *Max's* — the possessive noun — is in the sentence. You can replace *Max's* by *his* (because *his* is a possessive pronoun), but not by *he.*

> RIGHT: Max frequently writes poetry with cow imagery.
>
> WHY IT'S RIGHT: There's no pronoun in the sentence.
>
> ALSO RIGHT: Stay away from Max's poetry readings unless you are really, really, really fond of cows.

Which sentence is correct?

A. Lola has always been interested in archaeology because she thinks they spend a lot of time in the dirt.

B. Lola has always been interested in archaeology because she thinks archaeologists spend a lot of time in the dirt.

Answer: Sentence B is correct. In sentence A, no proper antecedent exists for *they.* Sentence B replaces *they* with the noun *archaeologists.*

If you're still awake, go for it! Find the correct sentence.

A. In Lulu's sonnets, she compares love to an unopened can of sardines.

B. In Lulu's sonnets, the poet compares love to an unopened can of sardines.

Answer: Sentence B is correct. In sentence A, *she* has no antecedent. Because sentence B doesn't use a pronoun, there's no pronoun error.

Matching Verbs to Pronouns in Complicated Sentences

Singular pronouns must be paired with singular verbs, and plural pronouns must be paired with plural verbs. Easy rule, right? *He says. They say.* No problem. But not all pronouns are as simple as *he* and *they.* Some pronouns — *who, which,* and *that* — are chameleons. They always look the same, but they may be either singular or plural depending upon their antecedents. You have to decode the sentence to decide whether the antecedent is singular or plural. Then you must match the verb to the antecedent. In some sentences with simple structure, the choice is fairly obvious. For example:

> *English Grammar for Dummies* is the book that you're reading. (*that* = book = singular)

> The tax guides that fell off the shelf cost me a million dollars. (*that* = *tax guides* = plural)

In complicated sentences, those singling out something or someone from a group, the choice is not so obvious. To pair the pronoun with the correct verb, use your reading comprehension skills to figure out the meaning of the pronoun. After you know the meaning of the pronoun, the choice between a singular and plural verb is clear. Check out the following examples:

> SENTENCE ONE: Lulu is one of the few choir members who *has/have* more than 11 tattoos.

> The *who* statement is about having more than 11 tattoos.

> According to the sentence, how many choir members are in that category? One or more than one? More than one.

> The *who* refers to *choir members.*

> Choose the plural verb *(have).*

> CORRECT SENTENCE: Lulu is one of the few choir members who *have* more than 11 tattoos.

> SENTENCE TWO: Lulu is the only one of the choir members who *has/have* a tattoo of a motorcycle on her arm.

> The *who* statement is about having a tattoo of a motorcycle.

> The sentence makes it clear that Lulu is the only one with that tattoo.

> *Who* is singular, referring to Lulu.

Choose the singular verb *(has)*.

CORRECT SENTENCE: Lulu is the only one of the choir members who *has* a tattoo of a motorcycle on her arm.

SENTENCE THREE: I love the Grammar Channel, which is one of the many channels that *broadcast/broadcasts* a hit show about pronouns.

The *which* statement is about broadcasting a hit show about pronouns.

According to the sentence, many channels broadcast such shows.

Which is plural, referring to *many channels*.

Choose the plural verb *broadcast*.

CORRECT SENTENCE: I love the Grammar Channel, which is one of the many channels that *broadcast* a hit show about pronouns.

Which word is correct?

Ned claims he is one of the many men who *has/have* been unfairly rejected by Lola.

Answer: *Have.* Lola has rejected more than one man, according to the sentence, so the pronoun *who* and the verb paired with *who* must be plural.

Once more, for old time's sake: Which word is correct?

Ned is the only one of the motorcyclists who still *tries/try* to date Lola.

Answer: *Tries.* The sentence explains that no one else is stupid enough to ask Lola for a date after she's said no once. (I hope Ned was wearing earplugs.) Therefore *who* is singular, as is the verb *tries.*

This, That, and the Other: Clarifying Vague Pronoun References

One pronoun may refer to one noun. A plural pronoun may refer to more than one noun. But no pronoun may refer to a whole sentence or a whole paragraph. Consider the following scenario:

Lulu likes to arrive at school around 11 each day because she thinks that getting up at any hour earlier than 10 is barbaric. The principal, not surprisingly, thinks that arriving two hours late each day is not a good idea. *This* is a problem.

This certainly is a problem, and not because of Lulu's sleeping habits or the principal's beliefs. *This* is a problem because the antecedent of the word *this* is unclear. What does *this* mean? The fact that Lulu arrives around 11? That Lulu thinks getting up before 10 is out of the question? Or that the principal and Lulu are not, to put it mildly, in sync? Or all of the above?

The writer probably intends *this* to refer to *all of the above,* a perfectly good answer on those horrible multiple choice tests you have to take far too often these days. Unfortunately, *all of the above* is not a good answer to the question, "What does the pronoun mean?"

Thus

> WRONG: The new orange dye Lola's hairdresser selected looks horrible, and the cut looks as though it were done by a kindergartener. *This* persuaded Lola to attend the dance wearing her purple wig.

> WHY IT'S WRONG: *This* is referring to the 21 words of the preceding sentence, not to one noun.

> RIGHT: Because the new orange dye Lola's hairdresser selected looks horrible and the cut looks as thought it were done by a kindergartener, Lola decided to attend the dance wearing her purple wig.

> ALSO RIGHT: The fact that the new orange dye her hairdresser selected looks horrible and the cut looks as though it were done by a kindergartener persuaded Lola to attend the dance wearing her purple wig.

> WHY THEY'RE RIGHT: Eliminating *this* eliminates the problem.

As you see in the preceding example, sometimes the only way to avoid this sort of pronoun error is to write a sentence that needs no pronoun at all.

In ordinary speech (conversational English) you may use *this, which,* or *that* to refer to more than one word, as long as your meaning is clear. For example:

> Roger refused to defuse the explosive postage stamp, which angered all the postal workers.

The pronoun *which* in the preceding example refers to the fact that Roger refused to defuse the explosive stamp. Your audience grasps the meaning easily. However, grammatically, the sentence is incorrect because *which* should replace only one noun. Bottom line: In formal writing you should follow the rule and reject the sentence. In informal situations, go ahead and use it.

In both conversational and formal English, avoid vagueness. Never use a pronoun that may refer to two or more ideas; don't leave your reader or listener wondering what you mean. For example:

> Lulu's history research paper was ten days late and ten pages short. That earned Lulu an F on the assignment.

What convinced the teacher to fail Lulu? The lateness or the fact that she wrote exactly 34 words on "The French Revolution: Its Causes and Effects in Relation to the Concept of Democracy"? One of these factors? If so, which one? Or both? Inquiring minds want to know, and the pronoun *that* doesn't tell. Possible corrections include the following:

> Because Lulu's history research paper was ten days late and ten pages short, the teacher failed Lulu. (Now you know that both factors influenced the grade.)

> Lulu's history research paper was ten days late, so the teacher failed Lulu. Even if it had arrived on time, the fact that it was ten pages short would have earned her a low grade on the assignment anyway. (The lateness is primary, but the length mattered also.)

> Lulu's teacher was willing to overlook the fact that Lulu handed in her history research paper ten days late. However, the teacher failed Lulu for writing only 34 words instead of ten pages. (The teacher doesn't care about lateness but objects to the length.)

> Lulu's teacher didn't mind the shortness of Lulu's history research paper, but the teacher failed Lulu anyway because the paper was ten days late. (In this version promptness matters and length doesn't.)

Which correction is best? I can't say, because the original isn't clear. See my point? Vague pronouns lead to multiple interpretations and loss of meaning.

To sum up this simple rule: Be clear when using pronouns.

Which sentence is correct?

> A. The roof leaked and the floor creaked, which kept Ned up all night.

> B. The leaky roof and the creaky floor kept Ned up all night.

Answer: Sentence B, lacking a pronoun, has no pronoun error. Sentence A is incorrect because *which* refers to two ideas, not to one noun.

Need a do-over? Find the correct sentence.

> A. Anna carved a pumpkin and made a pie from the leftovers, which is her favorite Halloween tradition.

> B. Anna carved a pumpkin and made a pie from the leftovers. That's her favorite Halloween tradition.

Answer: Neither is correct. (How irritating am I?) In sentence A, *which* refers to the carving and the pie-making, not to a single noun. In sentence B, *that* (which is part of the contraction *that's*) also refers to more than one noun. Both sentences are out of bounds in formal English. In conversational English, you're fine with both sentences.

In the paper it says . . .

Are you writing about literature or even trashy tabloid journalism? If so, beware of *it* and *they*. Some common errors follow those pronouns. Check out these examples:

> In *Hamlet,* it says that Claudius is a murderer.

Oh really? What does *it* mean? The play can't speak, and the author of the play (Shakespeare) is a *who*. Actually, in *Hamlet,* the ghost says that Claudius is a murderer, but even the ghost is a *he*. In other words, *it* has no antecedent. Reword the sentence:

> In *Hamlet* Claudius is a murderer.

> In *Hamlet* the ghost declares that Claudius is a murderer.

> My teacher says that in *Hamlet* Claudius is a murderer, but I'm not sure because I never understand Shakespeare's plays anyway. Why couldn't he write in plain English? What's up with that?

Here's another example:

> In today's paper *they* say that more and more schools are dropping Shakespeare's plays from the curriculum because of incomprehensible language.

(I should probably say, before I get back to the grammar, that I actually *like* Shakespeare's plays, and not just because I'm an English teacher. Now, back to pronouns.) Who is *they*? Perhaps the authors of an article, but the sentence doesn't make that fact clear. More likely the author of the sentence thinks that *they* is a good, all-purpose pronoun for talking about anonymous or nameless authors. In other words, the antecedent of *they* is "I don't know and I really don't care." Wrong! The antecedent of *they* must be a real, identifiable group of people. Some possible corrections include:

> Today's paper reports that more and more schools are dropping Shakespeare's plays from the curriculum because of incomprehensible language.

> In today's paper, education critic I. M. Ignorentz explains that more and more schools are dropping Shakespeare's plays from the curriculum because of incomprehensible language.

Its or Their? Selecting Pronouns for Collective Nouns

Collective nouns present a problem when it comes to choosing the right pronouns. They're no picnic when you're pairing collective nouns with verbs, either. Never fear. In this section, I help you with both tasks.

Collective nouns (*committee, team, squad, army, class,* and the like) refer to groups. When the group is acting as a unit — doing the same thing at the same time — the noun is singular and the pronouns that refer to it are also singular. In this situation, the collective noun is paired with a singular verb also (if the collective noun is a subject). Here's an example:

> The squad *is* on the move; *it* should be here in plenty of time for the battle.

The collective noun is *squad.* Because the whole squad is moving as a unit, *squad* pairs with the singular verb *is* and the singular pronoun *it.* Similarly, you need a singular possessive pronoun when the collective noun is acting as a unit, as in this sentence:

> The cast will hold *its* annual Thank-God-Michael's-Latest-Play-Is-Over Party tomorrow.

The whole cast is responsible for the party (although Lola is always complaining about doing all the work), so the singular possessive *its* works here. For more information on possessive pronouns, turn to Chapter 9.

Right about now you're probably wondering what happens when the group isn't acting as one unit. Simple. Just break the group down into its component parts and go for plural verbs and pronouns, as in this sentence:

> Some members of the squad *are* eating pizza while others are oiling *their* rocket launchers.

Now you have a plural subject (*members*) partnering a plural verb (*are*) and a plural pronoun (*their*).

Sadly, I have to tell you about a couple of complications in the collective noun situation. Read this sentence:

> The audience rises and is ready to leave after a stirring performance of Michael's new play. (Actually, the audience was ready to leave after the first act, but Lulu had locked the doors.)

In the preceding example sentence, I paired the subject, *audience,* with singular verbs — *rises, is,* and *was.* Those verbs are correct because the audience acts together, a collection of people molded into one unit. So far, so good. But if the audience is a unit, should the audience clap *its* hands or *their* hands? At first glance *its* seems appropriate, because *its* is singular, and *audience* is paired with singular verbs. However, the audience doesn't own a big, collective hand. Every person in the audience has two individual hands (every person except for Ella, who has three, but I won't go into that because she's very sensitive about her body image). Body parts, no matter how unified the group, must belong to separate people. Therefore, you have to dump the collective noun and substitute *members of the audience.* Now you have this sentence:

> The members of the audience rise to *their* feet and clap *their* hands.

Members is the subject. Because *members* is plural, so are the verbs and pronouns (*rise, their*) associated with it.

Here's another sentence to figure out:

> As the orchestra raises *its/their* instruments, Roger searches for the sheet music.

Orchestra is another collective noun. The verb is singular because the orchestra acts in unison, but *its instruments* sounds strange. Okay, maybe the *orchestra* owns all the tubas, violins, and other instruments of destruction. (You should hear them play.) So if the sentence were talking about ownership, *its* would fit:

> The orchestra insures *its* instruments with Lloyds of Topeka.

However, the orchestra can't raise a collectively-owned instrument. Each musician raises his or her own. So *their* and *musicians* make more sense:

> The musicians in the orchestra raise *their* instruments and prepare to demolish Beethoven.

To sum up the general rules on pronouns that refer to groups:

✔ Collective nouns performing one action as a unit take singular verbs and pair with singular pronouns.

✔ Possessive pronouns referring to collective nouns are singular if the item possessed belongs to the entire group.

✔ If the members of the group are acting as individuals, drop the collective noun. Possessive pronouns referring to the members of the group are plural.

✔ Body parts always belong to individuals, not to groups.

Which sentence is correct?

A. The class will hold its annual picnic during the monsoon season because of poor planning by the administration.

B. The class will hold their annual picnic during the monsoon season because of poor planning by the administration.

Answer: Sentence A is correct. The picnic belongs to everyone as a group.

Hit it again. Which sentence is correct?

A. The jury ate its sandwiches during the defense attorney's final argument.

B. The jurors ate their sandwiches during the defense attorney's final argument.

Answer: Sentence B is correct. Although the court system ordered a lovely platter of sandwiches for the *jury* (a collective noun), people eat separately. My tuna-on-rye can't be swallowed by a group. Hence sentence B, which breaks the collective noun into its component parts (*jurors*) is best. *Jurors* is plural, so *their* is the pronoun you want.

A historic or historical occasion

If something is *historical,* it happened and is now history. If something is *historic,* it happened and was important. In one way or another, a *historic* event influenced the course of history as you now understand it. Consider the following:

The little-known American labor leader, Junius P. Michael, shaved at least three times a day because of accusations that he had sabotaged the disposable razor industry by promoting the five-o'clock-shadow look.

This information is *historical;* you can look it up in Michael's autobiography, *My Life in the Fast Lane with No Turn Signal.* Other *historical* events in Michael's tumultuous life include his trip by jet ski through the Erie Canal and his week-long visit to the White House, where he was not invited to sleep in the Lincoln bedroom.

Despite his long life in public service, Junius P. Michael was not involved in any *historic* events whatsoever. Nothing he did merits a moment's consideration by serious historians. (Even when he attended important ceremonies or congressional debates, he had a knack for disappearing into the men's room at the crucial moment, possibly because of his habit of drinking large quantities of iced tea.)

Thus, Junius P. Michael was a *historical,* not imaginary, figure who did not participate in any *historic* events.

Chapter 24

The Last Word on Sentence Structure

- -

In This Chapter

▶ Distinguishing between independent and subordinate clauses

▶ Untangling one clause from another

▶ Using subordinate clauses to make your writing more fluid

▶ Adding variety to your writing with verbals

▶ Avoiding wordy and monotonous sentences

- -

Say I give you a new car. What do you do? Open the hood and check the engine, or hop in and drive it away? The engine-checkers and the drive-awayers are sub-groups of car owners. The engine-checkers have to know what's going on inside the machine. The other group doesn't care about fuel injection and spark plugs. They just want the car to run.

You can also divide speakers of English into two groups. Some people want to understand what's going on inside the sentence, but most just want to communicate. In this chapter, I provide some information for each — the lift-up-the-hood-of-the-sentence group and the drive-English-around-the-block clan. The first part of this chapter digs into the structure of the sentence, defining clauses and verbals. Then I show you how to make your writing more interesting by varying sentence patterns. This chapter also helps you trim your sentences so that they get the point across concisely — a plus in business and academic writing.

Here's a bonus for anyone contemplating higher education: The SAT and the ACT assess the maturity of your writing style, including your ability to vary sentence length and pattern and to avoid repetition. This chapter provides help with these skills.

Understanding the Basics of Clause and Effect

No matter what food you put between two pieces of bread, you've got a sandwich. That's the definition of *sandwich:* bread plus filling. Clauses have a simple definition, too: subject plus verb. Any subject-verb combination creates a clause. The reverse is also true: no subject or no verb = no clause. You can throw in some extras (descriptions, joining words, lettuce, tomato . . . whatever), but the basic subject-verb combination is key. Some sentences have one clause, in which case the whole sentence is the clause, and some have more than one.

Be sure to check your sentences for completeness. Each sentence should contain at least one complete thought, expressed in a way that can stand alone. In grammarspeak, each sentence must contain at least one independent clause (check out "Getting the goods on subordinate and independent clauses," later in this chapter). For more information on complete sentences, see Chapter 5.

Here are a few examples of one-clause sentences:

> Has Eggworthy cracked the Case of the Missing Chicken? (subject = *Eggworthy,* verb = *has cracked*)

> Lulu crossed the Alps in the dead of winter without help from a single elephant. (subject = *Lulu,* verb = *crossed*)

> Cedric and his enemies have reached an agreement about the number of words in a "super-tweet." (subjects = *Cedric and his enemies,* verb = *have reached*)

> Al swam for 15 minutes and rowed for an hour before nightfall. (subject = *Al,* verbs = *swam, rowed*)

Notice that some of the clauses have two subjects and some have two verbs, but each expresses one main idea. Here are a few examples of sentences with more than one clause:

> SENTENCE: Michael struggled out from under the blankets and then he dashed after the enemy agent.

> CLAUSE 1: Michael struggled out from under the blankets (subject = *Michael,* verb = *struggled*)

> CLAUSE 2: then he dashed after the enemy agent (subject = *he,* verb = *dashed*)

> SENTENCE: After Cedric had developed the secret microfilm, Eggworthy sent it to whatever federal agency catches spies.

CLAUSE 1: After Cedric had developed the secret microfilm (subject = *Cedric,* verb = *had developed*)

CLAUSE 2: Eggworthy sent it to whatever federal agency catches spies (subject = *Eggworthy,* verb = *sent*)

CLAUSE 3: whatever federal agency catches spies (subject = *agency,* verb = *catches*)

With your sharp eyes, I'm sure you noticed something odd about the last example. Clause #3 is actually part of clause #2. It's not a misprint. Sometimes one clause is entangled in another. (This topic is deep in the pathless forests of grammar! Get out now, while you still can!)

Here's one more example that's really complicated:

SENTENCE: Whoever ate the secret microfilm is in big trouble.

CLAUSE #1: Whoever ate the secret microfilm (subject = *whoever,* verb = *ate*)

CLAUSE #2: Whoever ate the secret microfilm is in big trouble. (subject = *whoever ate the secret microfilm,* verb = *is*)

Yes, one clause is the subject of another clause. Good grief! What a system. For those who truly love grammar: The subject clause is a noun clause. See "Knowing the three legal jobs for subordinate clauses" later in this chapter for more information.

How many clauses can you find in this sentence?

The microfilm reader that Eggworthy normally uses broke when Eggworthy accidentally dropped his omelet into the motor.

Answer: Three clauses are tucked into this sentence. Did you find them all? Clause #1 = The microfilm reader broke. Clause #2 = that Eggworthy normally uses. Clause #3 = when Eggworthy accidentally dropped his omelet into the motor.

Getting the goods on subordinate and independent clauses

Some clauses are like mature grown-ups. They have their own apartment, pay their own rent, and wash the dishes frequently enough to ward off a visit from the health inspector. These clauses have made a success of life; they're *independent.*

Other clauses are like the brother-in-law character in a million jokes. They still live at home, or they crash on someone's couch. They're always mooching a free meal, and they never visit a Parental Unit without a bag of dirty laundry. These clauses are not mature; they can't support themselves. They're *dependent*. These clauses may be called *dependent clauses* or *subordinate clauses*. (The terms are interchangeable.)

Following are two sets of clauses. Both have subject-verb pairs, but the first set makes sense alone and the second doesn't. The first set consists of independent clauses, and the second of subordinate clauses.

Independent clauses:

> Cedric blasted Bobby with a radar gun.
>
> Bobby was going 50 m.p.h.
>
> The cougar could not keep up.
>
> Did Bobby award the trophy?

Subordinate clauses:

> After Cedric had complained to the race officials
>
> Because Bobby had installed an illegal motor on his skateboard
>
> Which Eggworthy bought from an overcrowded zoo
>
> Whoever ran the fastest

Independent clauses are okay by themselves, but writing too many in a row makes your paragraph choppy and monotonous. Subordinate clauses, however, are not okay by themselves because they don't make complete sentence. To become complete, they have to tack themselves onto independent clauses. Subordinate clauses add life and interest to the sentence (just as the guy crashing on your couch adds a little zip to the household). But don't leave them alone, because disaster will strike. A subordinate clause all by itself is a grammatical felony — a sentence fragment.

Standardized test-makers are hooked on complete sentences. Steer clear of fragments and run-ons (see Chapter 5 for more information) when you're holding a #2 pencil and an answer booklet.

The best sentences combine different elements in all sorts of patterns. In the following example, I join the independent clauses and subordinate clauses to create longer, more interesting sentences:

> After Cedric had complained to the race officials, he blasted Bobby with a radar gun.
>
> Because Bobby had installed an illegal motor on his skateboard, he was going 50 m.p.h.

The cougar, which Eggworthy bought from an overcrowded zoo, could not keep up.

Did Bobby award the trophy to whoever ran the fastest?

Combine the ideas in each of these sets into one sentence.

Set A:

Betsy screamed at the piano mover.

The mover dropped the piano on the delicate foot of the vivacious violinist.

Set B:

Anna solved a quadratic equation.

The equation had been troubling the math major.

Set C:

Michael gave special trophies.

Some people wanted those trophies.

Those people got the trophies.

Answer: Several combinations are possible. Here are three:

A. Betsy screamed at the piano mover who dropped the piano on the delicate foot of the vivacious violinist.

B. Anna solved a quadratic equation that had been troubling the math major.

C. Michael gave special trophies to whoever wanted them.

Knowing the three legal jobs for subordinate clauses

Okay, subordinate clauses can't stand alone. What can they do? They have three main purposes in life, as you see in the following sections.

Describing nouns and pronouns

Yup, subordinate clauses can describe nouns and pronouns. That is, the subordinate clause may give your listener or reader more information about a noun or pronoun in the sentence. Here are some examples, with the subordinate clause in italic:

The book *that Michael wrote* is on the best seller list. *(that Michael wrote* describes the noun *book)*

Anyone *who knows Michael well* will read the book. *(who knows Michael well* describes the pronoun *anyone)*

The book includes some information *that will prove embarrassing to Michael's friends. (that will prove embarrassing to Michael's friends* describes the noun *information)*

You don't need to know this fact, so skip to the next paragraph. Still here? Okay then. Subordinate clauses that describe nouns or pronouns are called *adjectival clauses* or *adjective clauses.* Happy now?

Describing verbs, adjectives, or adverbs

Subordinate clauses can also describe verbs, adjectives, or adverbs. The subordinate clauses tell you *how, when, where,* or *why.* Some examples, with the subordinate clause in italic, are as follows:

Because Michael censored himself, the book contains nothing about the exploding doughnut. *(Because Michael censored himself* describes the verb *contains)*

We will probably find out more *when the movie version is released. (when the movie version is released* describes the verb *will find)*

The government may prohibit sales of the book *wherever international tensions make it dangerous. (wherever international tensions make it dangerous* describes the verb *may prohibit)*

Michael is so stubborn *that he may sue the government. (that he may sue the government* describes the adverb *so)*

More grammar terminology, in case you're having a very dull day: Subordinate clauses that describe verbs are called *adverbial clauses* or *adverb clauses.* Subordinate clauses that describe adjectives or adverbs (mostly in comparisons) are also *adverbial clauses.* Adverbial clauses do the same job as single-word adverbs. They describe verbs, adjectives, or other adverbs.

Acting as subjects or objects inside another clause

This one is a bit more complicated: Subordinate clauses may do any job that a noun does in a sentence. Subordinate clauses sometimes act as subjects or objects inside another clause. Here are some examples, with the subordinate clause in italics:

When the book was written is a real mystery. *(When the book was written* is the subject of the verb *is)*

No one knows *whom Michael hired to write his book. (whom Michael hired to write his book* is the object of the verb *knows)*

Michael signed copies for *whoever bought at least five books. (whoever bought at least five books* is the object of the preposition *for)*

Stop now or risk learning more useless grammar terms. Noun *clauses* are subordinate clauses that perform the same functions as nouns — subjects, objects, appositives, and so on.

Check out the italicized clause in each sentence. Subordinate or independent? You decide.

A. *Even though Michael hit a home run,* our team lost by more than 50 runs.

B. *Eggworthy danced for a while,* but then he said that his head was splitting and sat down.

Answer: In sentence A, the italicized clause is subordinate. In sentence B, the italicized clause is independent.

Untangling subordinate and independent clauses

You have to untangle one clause from another only occasionally — when deciding which pronoun or verb you need or whether commas are appropriate. (See the next section, "Deciding when to untangle clauses," for more information.) When you do have to untangle them, follow these simple steps:

1. Find the subject-verb pairs.

2. Use your reading comprehension skills to determine whether the subject-verb pairs belong to the same thought or to different thoughts.

3. If the pairs belong to different thoughts, they're probably in different clauses.

4. If the pairs belong to the same thought, they're probably in the same clause.

Another method also relies on reading comprehension skills. Think about the ideas in the sentence and untangle the thoughts. By doing so, you've probably also untangled the clauses.

Check out these examples:

SENTENCE: The acting award that Lola received comes with a hefty check.

SUBJECT–VERB PAIRS: *award comes, Lola received*

UNTANGLED IDEAS: 1.) The award comes with a hefty check 2.) Lola received the award.

CLAUSES: 1.) *The acting award comes with a hefty check.* (Independent clause) 2.) *that Lola received* (subordinate clause)

SENTENCE: When Lulu tattoos someone, they stay tattooed.

SUBJECT–VERB PAIRS: *Lulu tattoos, they stay*

UNTANGLED IDEAS: 1.) Lulu tattoos someone 2.) they stay tattooed

CLAUSES: 1.) *When Lulu tattoos someone* (subordinate clause) 2.) *they stay tattooed* (independent clause)

Untangle this sentence into separate clauses.

Lola's last motorcycle, which she bought second-hand, was once owned by Elvis.

Answer: Clause #1 is *Lola's last motorcycle was once owned by Elvis.* Clause #2 is *which she bought second-hand.*

Try another. Untangle the following sentence.

No one knows when Anna sleeps.

Answer: Clause #1 is *no one knows.* Clause #2 is *when Anna sleeps.*

Deciding when to untangle clauses

Why would you want to untangle clauses? Not just because you have nothing better to do. (If you have that much free time, please stop by to clean out my closets.) You should untangle clauses when you're choosing pronouns, verbs, and punctuation. Read on for the whole story.

When you're picking a pronoun

When you're deciding whether you need a subject or an object pronoun, check the clause that contains the word. Don't worry about what the entire clause is doing in the sentence. Untangle the clause and ignore everything else. Then decide which pronoun you need for that particular clause.

Many of the decisions about pronouns concern *who* and *whom.* (For tricks to help you make the *who/whom* choice, see Chapter 23. For a general discussion of pronoun usage, turn to Chapters 9 and 17.)

Here's one untangling example, with the pronoun problem in parentheses:

> SENTENCE: Ella wasn't sure (who/whom) would want a used engagement ring.
>
> UNTANGLED INTO CLAUSES: Clause #1: *Ella wasn't sure.* Clause #2: *(who/whom) would want a used engagement ring.*
>
> RELEVANT CLAUSE: *(who/whom) would want a used engagement ring.*
>
> CORRECT PRONOUN: *who* (subject of *would want*)

When you're deciding on the correct verb

When you're deciding subject-verb agreement in one clause, the other clauses are distractions. (By agreement, I mean matching singular subjects with singular verbs and plural subjects with plural verbs.) If you're writing (not speaking), I recommend that you cross out or cover the other clauses with your finger. Check the clause that worries you. Decide the subject-verb agreement issue, and then erase the crossing-out line or remove your hand. (For more information on subject-verb agreement, see Chapter 10.)

Here are two untangling examples, with the verb choices in parentheses:

> SENTENCE: Larry, whose brides are always thrilled to marry into the royal family, (needs/need) no introduction.
>
> UNTANGLED INTO CLAUSES: Clause #1= *Larry (needs/need) no introduction.* Clause #2= *whose brides are always thrilled to marry into the royal family.*
>
> RELEVANT CLAUSE: *Larry (needs/need) no introduction.*
>
> CORRECT VERB: *needs* (Larry = singular, *needs* = singular)

> SENTENCE: That ring, which Larry recovers after each divorce and reuses for each new engagement, *has/have* received a recycling award.
>
> UNTANGLED INTO CLAUSES: Clause #1 = *That ring has/have received a recycling award.* Clause #2 = *which Larry recovers after each divorce and reuses for each new engagement.*
>
> RELEVANT CLAUSE: *The ring has/have received a recycling award.*
>
> CORRECT VERB: *has* (*ring* = singular, *has* = singular)

When you're figuring out where to put commas

Sometimes you have to untangle clauses in order to decide whether or not you need commas. Go through the same untangling steps that I discuss earlier in the chapter (see "Untangling subordinate and independent clauses") and then flip to Chapter 13 to see how to use commas correctly.

Putting your subordinate clauses in the right place

Finding the correct place to put your subordinate clauses is simple. Clauses acting as subjects or objects nearly always fall in the proper place automatically. Don't worry about them!

Put the subordinate clause that describes a noun or pronoun near the word that it describes. Here are a few examples of proper placement of clauses that describe nouns and pronouns:

> Larry's wedding coordinator, *who planned his last eight ceremonies,* is hiring more staff. (The italicized clause describes the noun *coordinator.*)

> The coordinator took care of every detail; he even baked the cakes *that Larry's guests enjoyed.* (The italicized clause describes the noun *cakes.*)

> Anyone *who is on a diet* should stay away from Larry's weddings. (The italicized clause describes the pronoun *who.*)

If the subordinate clause describes the verb, it may land at the front of the sentence or at the rear. On rare occasions, the clause settles down in the middle of the sentence. Here are some examples:

> *Although Anna understood the equation,* she chose to put a question mark on her answer sheet. (The italicized clause describes the verb *chose.*)

> She wrote the question mark *because she wanted to make a statement about the mysteries of life.* (The italicized clause describes the verb *wrote.*)

> Anna failed the test; but *until her mother found out about the question mark,* Anna was not distressed. (The italicized clause describes the verb *was.*)

For lots more detail on placing all sorts of descriptions in their proper places, see Chapters 7 and 19.

An unbelievably obscure punctuation rule that no normal people follow calls for a semicolon in front of a conjunction — a word that joins — when a comma appears elsewhere in the sentence. (For more information on conjunctions, see Chapter 5.) As someone who's never going to be anything but a nerd, I followed that rule in the preceding sample sentence. Because of the comma after *mark,* I placed a semicolon in front of the conjunction *but.* You should know that if you follow this rule, most of your readers will think that you've made an error. However, a few die-hard grammarians will break into tears of gratitude because someone else knows how to use a semicolon correctly. (Excuse me for a moment while I wipe my eyes.)

Choosing content for your subordinate clauses

What to put in a clause depends upon the writer's purpose. Generally, the most important idea belongs in the independent clause. Subordinate clauses are for less crucial information. Check out these examples:

> IMPORTANT IDEA: Godzilla ate my mother.
>
> LESS IMPORTANT IDEA: My mother was wearing a green dress.
>
> GOOD SENTENCE: Godzilla ate my mother, who was wearing a green dress.
>
> NOT-SO-GOOD SENTENCE: My mother was wearing a green dress when Godzilla ate her.

> IMPORTANT IDEA: Agwamp just won a trillion dollars
>
> LESS IMPORTANT IDEA: His name means "ancient bettor" in an obscure language.
>
> GOOD SENTENCE: Agwamp, whose name means "ancient bettor" in an obscure language, just won a trillion dollars.
>
> NOT-SO-GOOD SENTENCE: Agwamp, who just won a trillion dollars, says that his name means "ancient bettor" in an obscure language.

Of course, some writers stray from this pattern to make a comic point or to emphasize a character trait. Suppose you're writing about someone who, to put it mildly, tends to be self-absorbed. A sentence like the following one emphasizes that trait:

> While the stock price tanked and sales plummeted, the CEO examined his photo on the company Web site.

The wreck of the company isn't a big deal for this negligent CEO, and its placement in the subordinate clause reinforces that fact.

Regardless of what you place in a subordinate clause, be sure to connect it to the sentence properly. For more discussion on joining independent and subordinate clauses, see Chapter 5.

Combine these ideas into a single sentence containing at least one independent and one subordinate clause.

> IDEA #1: an archaeologist made a major discovery
>
> IDEA #2: she was listening to classic rock on the radio
>
> IDEA #3: the ancient betting parlor was filled with discarded lottery tickets

Answer: Several combinations are possible. Here are two:

> While listening to classic rock on the radio, the archaeologist made a major discovery, an ancient betting parlor filled with discarded lottery tickets.

In this version, the subordinate clause is *While listening to classic rock on the radio.* The independent clause is *the archaeologist made a major discovery, an ancient betting parlor filled with discarded lottery tickets.* This version emphasizes the discovery. The *classic rock* information is interesting but not particularly important.

> As she made a major discovery, an ancient betting parlor filled with discarded lottery tickets, the archaeologist listened to classic rock.

Now the subordinate clause is *As she made a major discovery, an ancient betting parlor filled with discarded lottery tickets.* The independent clause is *the archaeologist listened to classic rock.* Placing the musical information in the independent clauses raises its importance. This version might appear in an essay about the role of music in the workplace, archaeologists' daily routines, or the musical tastes of this particular archaeologist.

Getting Verbal

Ah, diversity. Wouldn't the world be boring if everyone and everything were the same? Ah, harmony. Isn't it wonderful when different backgrounds join forces to create a new, improved blend?

In grammar, the new, improved blend of two parts of speech is a *verbal.* Verbals are extremely useful hybrids. In this section, I tell you what's what, and then I show you how to use verbals.

Appreciating gerunds

The noun and the verb get married, move into a little house on the prairie, and pretty soon the patter of little syllables hits the airwaves. The children of this happy marriage are *gerunds.* Gerunds inherit some characteristics from their mother, the verb:

- ✔ They end in -ing and look like verbs — *swimming, dripping, being, bopping, bribing,* and so on.
- ✔ They may be described by words or phrases that usually describe verbs — swimming *swiftly,* dripping *noisily,* being *in the moment,* bopping *to the rhythm of a great new song,* bribing *yesterday,* and so on.

- ✔ The type of clause that usually describes verbs may also describe gerunds — swimming *after the race ends,* dripping *when the cap is not tightened,* being *wherever you should be,* bopping *although you are tired,* bribing *whenever you want something.*

- ✔ They may have objects or subject complements — swimming *laps,* dripping *drops of gooey glop,* being *president,* bopping *Roger on the nose,* bribing *public officials and umpires,* and so on.

From their father, the noun, gerunds inherit only two characteristics, but one is a biggie:

- ✔ BIGGIE: They act as nouns in the sentence. Therefore, gerunds may be subjects, objects, and anything else that a noun can be.

- ✔ NON-BIGGIE: Words that usually describe nouns or pronouns — adjectives — may also describe gerunds — *my* swimming, *noisy* dripping, *illegal* bribing, and so on. (Is there any legal bribing?)

In these examples, I italicized the gerund and all the words associated with it (the *gerund phrase,* in grammarspeak):

Swimming the Atlantic Ocean was not exactly what Ella had in mind when she married Larry. *(swimming the Atlantic Ocean* = subject of the verb *was)*

Anna, a neat person in every possible way, hates *my dripping ice cream on the rug. (my dripping ice cream on the rug* = direct object of the verb *hates)*

The importance of *being earnest in one's playwriting* cannot be over-emphasized. *(being earnest in one's playwriting* = object of the preposition *of)*

After *bopping Roger on the nose,* Michael took off at about 100 m.p.h. *(bopping Roger on the nose* = object of the preposition *after)*

Betsy gave *bribing the umpire* serious consideration when her team lost its 450th game in a row. *(bribing the umpire* = indirect object of the verb *gave)*

Working with infinitives

The *infinitive* is another happy child of two different parts of speech. (See Chapter 2 for more information on infinitives.) The infinitives' mother is the verb, and from her, infinitives inherit several important characteristics:

- ✔ Infinitives look like verbs, with the word *to* tacked on in front — *to dance, to dream, to be, to dally, to prosecute,* and so on.

- ✔ Words or phrases that usually describe verbs may also describe infinitives — to dance *divinely,* to dream *daily,* to be *in the kitchen,* to dally *for hours,* to prosecute *ferociously,* and so on.

✔ Similarly, the type of clause that usually describes verbs may also describe infinitives — to dance *until the cows come home,* to dream *when your heart is breaking,* to be *wherever you want to be,* to dally *even though homework awaits,* to prosecute *because justice demands action,* and so on.

✔ Infinitives may have objects or subject complements — to dance *a jig,* to dream *an impossible dream,* to be *silly,* to prosecute *Roger* for high crimes and misdemeanors, and so on.

The infinitive inherits its job in the sentence from the father. Who, you may ask, is the father of the infinitive? Well, the infinitive's mom gets around, and the father may actually be any one of three parts of speech (shocking, isn't it?):

✔ Most infinitives act as subjects, objects, or subject complements. (Dad is a noun.)

✔ A few infinitives describe nouns. (Dad is an adjective.)

✔ A few infinitives describe verbs. (Dad is an adverb.)

Read these examples of infinitives in their natural habitat, the sentence. I italicized the infinitive and the words associated with it (the *infinitive phrase,* in technical terms):

To dance on Broadway is Lola's lifelong dream. *(to dance on Broadway =* subject of the verb *is)*

During cabinet meetings, Larry likes *to dream with his eyes open. (to dream with his eyes open =* object of the verb *likes)*

Lulu's lifelong goal is *to be silly* when everyone else is serious. *(to be silly =* subject complement of the verb *is)*

The case *to prosecute* is the one about the exploding doughnut. *(to prosecute* describes the noun *case)*

Ella went to that nightclub just *to dally. (to dally* describes the verb *went)*

Participating with a participle

Last but not least of the verbals (a word that is a blend of two different parts of speech) is the participle. *Participles* are actually parts of verbs (hence the amazingly original name). In some sentences participles act as part of the verb, but in those situations, they're not called verbals. I ignore the acting-as-verb participles here, but if you want more information about them, see Chapter 3. When participles are verbals, they, like the other two verbals, inherit some important traits from their mom the verb:

✔ Participles look like verb parts, though they may have several different forms. Some end with *-ing,* some with *-ed,* and some with other letters.

Also, they may have helping verbs. *Driven, coping, elevated, having crossed,* and *gone* are a few examples of participles.

✔ Words or phrases that usually describe verbs may also describe participles — driven *home,* coping *bravely,* elevated *to the position of Emperor,* having crossed *illegally,* gone *with the wind,* and so on).

✔ Similarly, the type of clause that usually describes verbs may also describe participles — driven *although he has two perfectly good feet,* coping *bravely when tragedy strikes,* elevated *because he bribed three officials,* having crossed *where no man has crossed before,* gone *after the sun sets,* and so on.

✔ Participles may have objects or subject complements — elevated *Ella to the position of Empress,* having crossed *the road,* and so on.

From their father, the adjective, participles take one characteristic: They describe nouns and pronouns.

Participles may appear in several different spots in the sentence:

✔ They may precede the noun or pronoun that they describe: *tired* feet (the participle *tired* describes the noun *feet*), *sneezing* dwarves (the participle *sneezing* describes the noun *dwarves*), *burped* baby (the participle *burped* describes the noun *baby*).

✔ They may follow a linking verb, in which case they describe the subject. (A linking verb is a form of the verb *to be* or a sensory verb. See Chapter 2 for more information.)

> Ella is *exhausted.* (The participle *exhausted* follows the linking verb *is* and describes *Ella.*)

> Betsy's concerto sounds *enchanting.* (The participle *enchanting* follows the linking verb *sounds* and describes *concerto.*)

✔ They may follow the noun or pronoun that they describe. In this position, participles often include descriptive words or objects. The participles and the words associated with them — the *participial phrases* — are italicized here:

> Someone, *having angered the herd of cattle,* is running for the fence at the speed of light. *(Having angered the herd of cattle* describes *someone.)*

> I want to repeal the new anti-bubble gum law *passed by the senate. (Passed by the senate* describes *law.)*

✔ Participles may begin the sentence, in which case they must describe the subject of the sentence:

> *Poked in the tummy,* the doll immediately said, "Watch it, Buster!" *(Poked in the tummy* describes *doll.)*

Having been smashed against the picture window, Lola's nose looked sore. *(Having been smashed against the picture window describes* nose.*)*

Spicing Up Boring Sentences with Clauses and Verbals

Which paragraph sounds better?

Michael purchased a new spy camera. The camera was smaller than a grain of rice. Michael gave the camera to Lola. Lola is rather forgetful. She is especially forgetful now. Lola is planning a trip to Antarctica. Lola accidentally mixed the camera into her rice casserole along with bean sprouts and orange marmalade. The camera baked for 45 minutes. The camera became quite tender. Michael unknowingly ate the camera.

Michael purchased a new spy camera that was smaller than a grain of rice. Michael gave the camera to Lola, who is rather forgetful, especially now that she is planning a trip to Antarctica. Accidentally mixed into Lola's rice casserole along with bean sprouts and orange marmalade, the camera baked for 45 minutes. Michael unknowingly ate the camera, which was quite tender.

I'm going to take a guess; you said that the second paragraph was better, didn't you? It's a bit shorter (62 words instead of 69), but length isn't the issue. The first paragraph is composed of short, choppy sentences. The second one flows. Grammatically, the difference between the two is simple. The second paragraph has more subordinate clauses and verbals than the first.

You don't need to know how to find or label clauses or verbals. However, you should read your writing aloud from time to time to check how it sounds. The old saying, variety is the spice of life, applies to writing. Use this checklist to see whether your writing could use a little hot pepper:

- Do all your sentences follow the same basic pattern, subject-verb or subject-verb-complement?

- Have you strung a lot of short sentences together with *and* or a similar joining word?

- Are all your sentences more or less the same length?

If you answered yes to one or more of the preceding questions, a trip to the spice rack is in order. In this section, with a minimum of grammatical labels, I suggest some ways to add flavor to blah sentences.

The clause that refreshes

Have you ever seen those diet ads on late-night television? The before picture shows someone who has apparently eaten a rainforest, and the after picture displays a toothpick-thin body. In this section I provide some before-and-after sentences. No diets — just a change from boring to interesting. My insertions are subordinate clauses, which are italicized. (For more information on subordinate clauses, see "Getting the goods on subordinate and independent clauses" earlier in this chapter.)

> BORING BEFORE VERSION: Max sat on a tuffet. Max did not know that he was sitting on a tuffet. Max had never seen a tuffet before. He was quite comfortable. Then Ms. Muffet came in and caused trouble.

> EXCITING AFTER VERSION: Max, *who was sitting on a tuffet,* did not know *what a tuffet was because he had never seen one before. Until Ms. Muffet came in and caused trouble,* Max was quite comfortable.

Doesn't the "after" paragraph sound better? It's two words shorter (33 instead of 35 words), but more important than length is the number of sentences. The before paragraph has five, and the after paragraph has two. Tucking more than one idea into a sentence saves words and makes your writing less choppy.

Verbally speaking

Verbals pull a lot of information into a little package. After all, they represent a blend of two parts of speech, so they provide two different perspectives in just one word. Look at this sentence, taken from the gerund section, earlier in this chapter:

> Betsy gave *bribing the umpire* serious consideration when her team lost its 450th game in a row.

Without the gerund, you use more words to say the same thing:

> Betsy's team lost its 450th game in a row. Betsy thought about whether she should bribe the umpire. Betsy thought seriously about that possibility.

Okay, the gerund saved you seven words. Big deal! Well, it is a big deal over the course of a paragraph or a whole paper. But more important than word count is sentence structure. Verbals are just one more color in your crayon box when you're creating a picture. Who wants the same old eight colors? Isn't it fun to try something different? Gerunds, infinitives, and participles help you vary the pattern of your sentences. Here's a before-and-after example:

BORING BEFORE VERSION: Lulu smacked Larry. Larry had stolen the sacred toe hoop from Lulu's parrot. The sacred toe hoop was discovered 100 years ago. Lulu's parrot likes to sharpen his beak on it.

EXCITING AFTER VERSION: *Smacking Larry* is Lulu's way of telling Larry that he should not have stolen the sacred toe hoop from her parrot. *Discovered 100 years ago,* the toe hoop serves *to sharpen the parrot's beak.*

LABELS FOR THOSE WHO CARE: *Smacking Lulu* = gerund, *discovered 100 years ago* = participle, *to sharpen the parrot's beak* = infinitive.

Combine these ideas into one or more sentences.

Larry bakes infrequently. He bakes with enthusiasm. His best recipe is for king cake. King-cake batter must be stirred for three hours. Larry orders his cook to stir the batter. The cook stirs, and Larry adds the raisins. Sometimes Larry throws in a spoonful of tuna fish.

Answer: Many combinations are possible, including the following:

Larry's *baking* is infrequent but enthusiastic. His best recipe, king cake, requires three hours of *stirring,* which Larry orders his cook to do. *Adding* raisins and the occasional spoonful of tuna fish is Larry's job. (The italicized words are gerunds.)

Larry, who bakes infrequently but enthusiastically, excels at cooking king cake, which requires three hours of stirring. Ordering his cook to stir, Larry adds raisins and the occasional spoonful of tuna fish. (*who bakes infrequently but enthusiastically* = subordinate clause, *cooking king cake* = gerund, *which requires three hours of stirring* = subordinate clause, *ordering his cook* = participle, *to stir* = infinitive)

You're hanged, but a picture is hung

In Michael's new movie, Lulu stars as the righteous rebel leader *hanged* by the opposition. After the stirring execution scene, the rebels rally, inspired by a picture of Lulu that someone *hung* on the wall of their headquarters.

To hang is a verb meaning *to suspend.* In the present tense the same verb does double duty.

You *hang* a picture and you also *hang* a murderer, at least in countries with that form of capital punishment. Past tense is different; in general, people are *hanged* and objects are *hung.*

Extra! Extra! Deleting All That's Extra From Your Sentences

I live in Manhattan, an island surrounded by water. My 17-story apartment building is tall. It was built many years ago in 1929. I work as a teacher in a school. I write *For Dummies* books about grammar, which explain grammar to readers. I will also consider jumping from the roof of my tall apartment building if I have to write any more boring, repetitive, say-the-same-thing-at-least-twice sentences like these.

Okay, I believe I made my point. Sentences stuffed with filler sound silly and condescend to the reader. I mean, really. *An island surrounded by water* — that's clever. What surrounds other islands? Bagels? My *For Dummies books about grammar explain grammar to readers*. There's a shock. I'm sure you thought my grammar books explained Tai Chi or llama-raising. And once I wrote *repetitive*, I didn't have to tack on *say-the-same-thing-at-least-twice*. One word said it all.

Should you care about wordy, repetitive sentences? For several reasons, you should care very much:

- ✔ If you say the same thing over and over again, your readers or listeners tune you out. Why would they pay close attention? If they miss something because they're, say, calculating the square root of 547 or deciding which body part to pierce, they assume you'll pick up the slack by going over the same ground again. Do you really want an audience that fades in and out? I don't think so.

- ✔ Repetition wastes time, one of the most valuable commodities on earth. As one of my *For Dummies* editors once remarked, "Say it and move on. Our readers are busy!" She was right.

- ✔ If you're writing under pressure — a school assignment or a work project, perhaps — you need fewer minutes to accomplish your task if you don't repeat yourself.

- ✔ Concise writing sounds strong and confident. Take a look at this sentence:

  > In my opinion, I think that homework should possibly be considered for banning, perhaps.

Compare that clunker with this sentence:

  > Homework should be banned.

Do I have to ask which version sounds more forceful? Version 1 fumbles around, hat in hand. Version 2 hits you right on the nose.

A frequent flyer on the SAT Writing and the ACT English tests is repetition. The test-gnomes want to know that you can pare down your prose to its leanest state without sacrificing meaning. I assume they like this topic because professors do NOT like grading papers. Speaking as an English teacher, I'm happier with a 300-word essay than with a 500-word essay that says the same thing.

Take out your pruning shears and give this paragraph a trim. Your answer should include all the information of the original, expressed with fewer words.

> When my elderly grandmother reached the age of 90, she found that her glasses, which helped her eyesight, didn't work as well as they had in previous years. She proceeded to travel to the optometrist, where her eyes were tested and measured as to how much she could see. Grandma tried on several pairs of fashionable frames of the latest style. She chose a gold metal frame by the famous designer, Sebastian Icare, who artistically decides how the frames should look. (81 words)

Answer: Many answers are possible. Here's one:

> When my grandmother was 90, her glasses didn't work as well as they once had. The optometrist tested her eyes. Grandma tried on several fashionable pairs and chose a gold frame by the famous designer, Sebastian Icare. (37 words)

Here's what I cut and why

1. If she's 90, the reader knows she's *elderly*.

2. *Glasses help eyesight.* There's a fact you couldn't figure out by yourself!

3. The verb *had* tells you that the action you're discussing (how well the glasses worked for Grandma) is prior to time when Grandma discovered the problem. So *in previous years* isn't needed.

4. It's not likely that the optometrist made a house call (not in this century — actually, not in this universe!). You don't have to explain that *she proceeded to travel to the optometrist*.

5. *Tested* and *measured* are the same in this context.

6. *Fashionable* and *of the latest style* are the same.

7. *Gold* is a *metal*. Don't state the obvious.

8. Icare is a designer, so his job is to decide *how the frames should look*.

Part VI
The Part of Tens

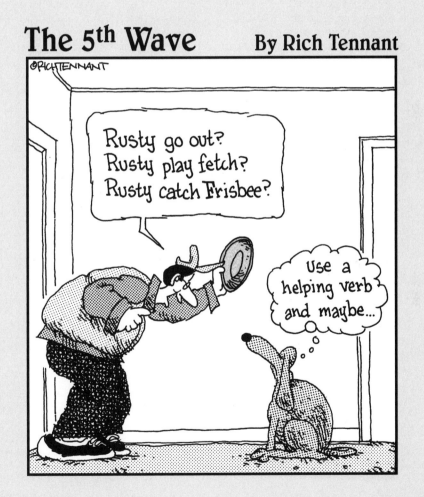

In this part . . .

This section opens the door to a grammatical life beyond *English Grammar For Dummies.* After you've absorbed the rules of grammar, you've still got to apply them. Chapter 26 provides ten strategies to improve your proofreading. (After reading this chapter, you'll never sign a letter "Yurs turly" again.) Chapter 27 lists ten ways to train your ear for good English, a process that inevitably improves your speech and writing. You may not follow all the suggestions that I give you, but you'll find at least some appealing.

Chapter 25

Ten Ways ~~Two~~ to Improve Your Proofreading

· ·

In This Chapter

▶ Checking your work with the help of a computer

▶ Proofreading more effectively

· ·

You read it 50 times and finally clicked the "Send" button. Then you sat there, heart pounding. Was the message good enough? Had you explained yourself well? How would the recipient react? Unable to calm your fears, you sat down to read the text for the 51st time. And that's when you finally saw it — an error. Not a little error, but a big one. An embarrassing one. The grammatical equivalent of a pimple on the tip of your nose.

Sound familiar? A situation like the one above has happened to all of us. In this chapter, I give you ten tricks to improve that all-important final check.

Read Backward

Okay, I know that reading backward sounds crazy, but successful proofreading is about breaking habits. If you read something over and over, after a while you're on automatic pilot. Your eye jumps at exactly the same spot simply because that's where it jumped before. So if you missed the error the first time, you'll miss it again. You've got to do something different to break the monotony of reviewing your work. If you read backward (word by word, not the letters that make up a word), you're in a good frame of mind to catch spelling errors because reading in the wrong direction means that you must check each word separately. If you read backward, you can't swing through a sentence by hopping to every fifth or sixth word.

Wait a While

Your work is done, you've read it, and you've made the corrections. Now what do you do? Save the draft and then put it away and do something else. Go water-skiing, run for president, or clean the closet. Then come back to the writing — refreshed and with a new point of view. You'll see your work with new eyes — and find mistakes.

Of course, this method works only if you've left some time before the deadline. If you finish your report three nano-seconds before your boss or teacher wants to see it, you'll have to forgo this method of proofreading.

Read It Aloud

I know, I know. You don't want to sound like a dork. But reading aloud helps you *hear* your writing in a different way. So blast some music and lock yourself in the bathroom. Read your writing in a normal speaking voice. Did you stumble anywhere? If so, you may have come across an error. Stop, circle the spot, and continue. Later, check all the circles. Chances are you'll find something that should be different.

Delete Half the Commas

During the last two weeks of the grading period, students visit me with their rough drafts in hand for a quick check before the final, graded copy is due. Privately I think of that time as *Comma Season.* I spend most of the day deleting hundreds of punctuation marks. (I also add a handful or two.) If you're like most people, your writing has commas where none are needed. Go back and check each one. Is there a reason for that comma? If you can't identify a reason, take the comma out.

Swap with a Friend

The best proofreading comes from a fresh pair of eyes. After you've written your essay, report, parole petition, or whatever, swap with a friend. You'll see possible errors in your friend's writing, and he or she will see some in yours. Each of you should underline the potential errors before returning the paper. Make sure you check those sections with special care.

Let the Computer Program Help

Not foolproof, by any means, computer grammar- and spell-checks are nevertheless helpful. After you've finished writing, go back and check the red and green lines (or whatever signal your computer supplies). Don't trust the computer to make the corrections for you; the machine makes too many mistakes. The computer identifies only *possible* mistakes and misses many errors (homonyms, for example). Let your own knowledge of grammar and a good dictionary help you decide whether you need to change something.

Check the Verbs

Traps sprinkled in every sentence — that's the way you should look at verbs. Give your work an extra verb check before you declare it finished. Consider *number:* should the verb be singular or plural? Consider *tense:* have you chosen the correct one? Do you have any sentences without verbs? If so, take care of the problem.

Check the Pronouns

Pronouns present potential pitfalls and are also worthy of their own special moment. Give your work an extra once over, this time checking all the pronouns. Singular or plural — did you select the appropriate number? Does each pronoun refer to a specific noun? Did you avoid sexist pronoun usage? Did you give a subject pronoun a job suited to an object pronoun, or vice versa?

Know Your Typing Style

I have a tendency to hold the Shift key down a little too long, so many of my words have two capital letters: THe, KNow, and so on. Do you have a mistake that results from your typing style? Notice when you have to backspace as you type and then check for similar errors when you finish typing.

The Usual Suspects

Look at your earlier writing, preferably something that was corrected by a teacher or someone else in a position to point out your mistakes. Where is the red ink concentrated? Those red-ink areas are the usual suspects that you should identify in future writing. For instance, if you have a number of run-on sentences in an old paper, chances are you'll put a few in a new paper. Put "run-on" on your personal list of common errors. Don't let any piece of writing leave your desk until you've searched specifically for those errors.

Chapter 26

Ten Ways to Learn Better Grammar

This book helps you learn grammar, as does my other Dummies grammar title, *English Grammar Workbook For Dummies.* (Yes, this is a shameless bit of self-promotion. Sorry.) Yet I must admit that these books aren't the only way to improve your communication skills. A few other resources may also help you in your quest for perfect language. In this chapter, I suggest ten ways to learn better grammar.

Read Good Books

You probably won't get far with *Biker Babes and Their Turn-ons* or *You're a Butthead: The Sequel to Snot-Nose.* But good books usually contain good writing, and if you read some, pretty soon your own speech and writing will improve. How do you know whether a particular volume contains good writing? Check the reviews, ask the bookstore clerk, or read the blurb (the comments on the book's jacket). Classics are always a choice, but you may also find modern texts, both fiction and non-fiction, written according to the best grammar rules.

The point is to expose your mind to proper English. When you read, you hear the author's voice. You become accustomed to proper language. After a while correct grammar sounds natural to you, and you detect non-standard English more easily.

Watch Good TV Shows

When I say to watch good TV shows, I'm not talking about programs with audio tracks that are mostly grunts, such as wrestling. I'm referring to shows in which people actually converse. Programs on the nerd networks are a good bet. You know the shows I mean; the producers assume that the audience wants to learn something. The screen has a lot of talking heads (images of commentators, not the rock band) with subtitles explaining why each is an expert. Watch them in secret if you're afraid of ruining your reputation, and pay attention to the words. Don't expect to pick up the finer points of grammar on TV, but you can get some pointers on the basics.

Peruse the News

News broadcasts on radio, television, and the Internet are fine sources of literate (okay, semi-literate on some networks) role models. You can train your ear for grammar at the same time that you learn a lot about current events. Just think of the advantage when you need a pick-up line. Instead of "Come here often?" or "What's your sign?" you can mention our diplomatic stance on Iran. (On second thought, maybe you should stick to astrology.)

Read the Newspaper

Well, read some newspapers. Years ago I started to "pay" my students one point for each grammar error that they found in print. I eventually had to rule out a couple of publications because it was just too easy to gather material. Avoid publications that report Elvis sightings and have headlines like "Man with Four Arms Tests Deodorant for a Living." (I actually saw that headline in a supermarket tabloid!) Read with a grammarian's eye, absorbing *how* the writer expresses an idea.

Flip through Magazines

If all the words in a magazine are in little bubbles above brightly colored drawings, you may not find complete sentences and proper pronoun usage. However, most published writers have at least the fundamentals of good grammar, and you can learn a lot from reading publications aimed at an educated audience. How do you know whether a publication is aimed at an educated audience? Check the articles. If they seem to address issues that you associate with thoughtful readers, you're okay. Even if they address issues that aren't associated with thoughtful readers, you may still be okay. Reading well-written magazine articles will give you some models of reasonably correct grammar. And as a side effect, you'll learn something.

Download Podcasts

Though the Internet has been blamed for the death of language by (in my opinion) hysterical anti-technology types, you can find terrific material online, some of which actually contains proper English. Download audio or video podcasts on your favorite subjects (tennis, anyone? how about ancient Egyptian poetry?) and pay close attention to the language — what people are saying and *how* they're saying it. Your ear for good grammar will sharpen over time. By the way, I'm not advocating that you download *only* material that reflects proper English. You've got to have fun, too. A podcast declaring, "The defense creamed us last night" can be valuable to your mental health, not to mention your social life. Just include *some* nerd-friendly stuff.

Check Out Strunk and White

The best book ever written on writing is *The Elements of Style* (Allyn and Bacon). This book is so tiny that it fits into your shirt pocket. Authors William Strunk, Jr. and E.B. White (yes, the fellow who wrote *Charlotte's Web* and *Stuart Little*) tackle a few grammar issues and make important points about style. You'll spend an hour reading it and a lifetime absorbing its lessons.

Listening to Authorities

Listen! Your teacher or boss probably says that word often, and you should (pause to arrange a dutiful expression) always do what your personal Authority Figure says. Apart from all the other reasons, you should listen in order to learn better grammar. By speaking properly, he or she is probably giving you English lessons along with descriptions of the Smoot-Whatever Tariff Act, the projected sales figures, and so forth.

Reviewing Manuals of Style

No, manuals of style won't tell you whether *eggplant* is one of this year's approved colors or what kind of nose ring Hollywood favors. In way more detail than I can go into in *English Grammar For Dummies,* manuals of style tell you in exhaustive (and exhausting) detail, where to put every punctuation mark ever invented, what to capitalize, how to address an ambassador, and lots of other things that you never really wanted to know. Some universities and a few groups of recognized rule-creators publish manuals of style, in print, and, in some cases, online. If you're writing a term paper or a business report, ask your teacher or boss which manual of style he or she favors. Use the recommended book or Web site as a reference for the picky little things and as a guide to the important issues of writing.

Surfing the Internet

I can't leave this one out, though the Internet contains as many traps as it does guiding lights. Type *grammar* in a search engine and press enter. Sit back and prepare yourself for a flood of sites explaining the rules of grammar. Some sites are very good; some are horrible. University- or school-sponsored URLs (Web addresses), are a safe bet. You can also read some good grammar commentary on the Dummies Web site, *www.dummies.com*.

Index